This Too Was America

ALSO BY TOM MELVILLE
AND FROM MCFARLAND

*Early Baseball and the Rise
of the National League* (2001)

This Too Was America
Philadelphia's Era of Cricket

TOM MELVILLE

McFarland & Company, Inc., Publishers
Jefferson, North Carolina

LIBRARY OF CONGRESS CATALOGUING-IN-PUBLICATION DATA

Names: Melville, Tom, author.
Title: This too was America : Philadelphia's era of cricket / Tom Melville.
Description: Jefferson, North Carolina : McFarland & Company, Inc., Publishers, 2023 | Includes bibliographical references and index.
Identifiers: LCCN 2022058685 | ISBN 9781476691282 (paperback : acid free paper) ∞
    ISBN 9781476648842 (eBook)
Subjects: LCSH: Cricket—Pennsylvania—Philadelphia—History. | Cricket—United States—History. | BISAC: SPORTS & RECREATION / Cricket
Classification: LCC GV928.P46 M45 2023 | DDC 796.35809748/11—dc23/eng/20230112
LC record available at https://lccn.loc.gov/2022058685

BRITISH LIBRARY CATALOGUING DATA ARE AVAILABLE

ISBN (print) 978-1-4766-9128-2
ISBN (ebook) 978-1-4766-4884-2

© 2023 Tom Melville. All rights reserved

No part of this book may be reproduced or transmitted in any form or by any means, electronic or mechanical, including photocopying or recording, or by any information storage and retrieval system, without permission in writing from the publisher.

On the cover: The William Penn Charter school cricket team, Interacademic League cricket champions in 1909. (Penn Charter Class Record); *background* The 19th-century Germantown Cricket Club in Philadelphia, Pennsylvania (© powerofforever/Shutterstock)

Printed in the United States of America

McFarland & Company, Inc., Publishers
    Box 611, Jefferson, North Carolina 28640
        www.mcfarlandpub.com

To the memory of my brothers Mark and Jamie.

atque in perpetuum, frater, ave atque vale
—Catullus

But why put a limit to cricket's appeal?
Why deny her infinite variety?
—Neville Cardus

Table of Contents

Prologue   1

A Note on Technical Cricket Terms   6

ONE. New York/Philadelphia Cricket and the Ball-Playing Spring of the 1840s   7

TWO. The Rise of Philadelphia Cricket and the Uncertainty of a Sporting Identity   17

THREE. Post–Civil War Cricket and Baseball and the Divergence of a Sporting Culture   33

FOUR. Guardian of a Sporting Alternative   45

FIVE. Young America, the Hargreaves Family, and the Assertion of Nativism   58

SIX. Intern to Internationalism   71

SEVEN. Clubs, Players, and the Flowering of Late 19th-Century Philadelphia Cricket   83

EIGHT. Ambivalence of Destiny   104

NINE. "A Civilization of Its Own": The World of Late 19th-Century Philadelphia Cricket   118

TEN. Visions of Viability: The England Tour of 1903 — 140

ELEVEN. Twilight of Internationalism and the Drift from Nativism — 148

TWELVE. Decline, Denial, and Dreams: The Passing of Philadelphia Cricket — 168

Epilogue — 189
Appendix: Casual Olympian — 193
Chapter Notes — 199
Bibliographic Essay — 231
Index — 235

Prologue

The history of cricket in America is the story of the emergence, rise, and final maturity of a national sporting culture. A unique and unusual history insofar as the sport that would usher in the era of "modern" team sports in America, the sport that would provide the impetus, precedent, and inspiration for the elevation of a hereto undeveloped American bat-and-ball playing tradition into a dominant national bat-and-ball form of play and, for years after, "served as a model by which baseball measured its own growth and maturity" was destined to have no place in this sporting culture.[1]

Largely for that reason, scholarly attention has been overwhelmingly preoccupied with cricket's role in the development of modern American sports during the formative antebellum period. As a cultural presence, cricket had reached a more advanced state of development in England decades earlier in its organization, technique, formal rules, and social standing than any American team sport. Introduced in this "modern" form by English immigrants to the United States in the late 1830s, cricket, in this state, has been analyzed and explained as the catalyst, inspiration, and model for America's development of its own bat-and-ball culture during this important period.[2]

This process of "modernization" had largely come to completion with baseball by the end of the Civil War and, in the estimation of the scholarly community, cricket, as an activity of significant American involvement, had effectively come to an end. By accepted consensus "in 1865 the fate of cricket in this country had been sealed," the game having been eclipsed by baseball in social popularity, and, consequently, was now largely confined to the immigrant English community where it was set on a slow but inevitable path to extinction within mainstream American culture.[3]

Though relegated to a permanently diminished demographic presence by the late 1860s, cricket would enter, over the second half of the 19th century, a second, significant phase of influence upon American sports, this one ideological rather than functional, as an alternative sporting ethos to the modern sporting world it had helped to bring about in America.

Sports, by its very nature, is social conflict. Someone is always, in some manner, trying to "beat" someone else, either individually or collectively. It's a social presence that encourages and releases aggression, hostility and emotions, and for those reasons had been, for generations, of questionable and suspect value to at least some Americans. Sports always faced the challenge of how such a personally detrimental activity could be "civilized" or "socialized" and incorporated into society as a positive social benefit. This issue became increasingly more significant during the emergence of "modern" team sports during the early 19th century with the rise of formal organization, specialization, mass participation, and financial interests becoming closely associated with a society's sports. "Modern sports" had unleashed and magnified the emotional interests beyond the single individual or event to the greater dimensions of teams, cities, and even entire regions. A new dimension of social engagement, in short, had now appeared, albeit overtly benign, but one that now had to be assessed as elevating or degrading in its social value. The response to the consequences of "modern sports" would coalesce around two sporting outlooks in 19th-century America, outlooks that, due to a number of social and historical factors, would largely, though not exclusively, become identified with baseball and cricket.[4]

In England, cricket had met the challenge of "modernization" in the early 19th century by evolving from a rough and tumble, largely working-class pastime rife with gambling and intense partisanship into a socially beneficial activity primarily through the game's adoption by the elite English public schools and universities. With the infusion of upper-class social values and behavioral expectations into the game, cricket was transformed into a "gentlemen's game" with a strict and prescribed code of propriety and sense of fair play. Cricket's ideology, from this point, became identified as "the spirit of the game," an outlook that ultimately justified sports for their contributing values towards positive personal development rather than towards an outlet for competitive success.[5]

In its earliest stages of development as a modern sport in New York City just before the Civil War, baseball seemed destined to follow much the same sporting ideology. Participation in the game was supported and encouraged because of its contributions to social harmony and good will. Games were played in the spirit of "friendly rivalry," their primary purpose being the health of participants and the occasion for friendly social interaction with the emotionally charged motives of winning or playing for "championships" being downplayed or outright discouraged.[6]

This sporting spirit, however, quickly changed in the years leading up to and immediately after the Civil War. Due primarily to the absence of an authoritative, established upper class that set moral standards for American society, as well as the emotional intensity generated by the game itself, baseball became increasingly dominated by an ideology of competitive success—that "winning is everything"—which took priority over any desirable character/moral benefits to participants. By the early post–Civil War years, cricket and baseball had not only diverged into two sports of competing participant allegiances but also two sports of divergent ideologies, representing two different sporting ethos—the "spirit of the game" as distinct from the "spirit of competition." For clarification, the elements of these two outlooks can be contrasted in relation to their more prominent sporting features via the following chart:

	"Spirit of Competition"	*"Spirit of the Game"*
Purpose of Sports:	Winning central motive. Competitive priority over personal benefits; "Winning is everything."	Personal and social benefits highest priority. Winning secondary to following prescribed behavioral norms; "How you play the game."
Excitement:	Determining importance. All game features to maximize emotional intensity for participants and spectators.	Subordinated to external values and ends, even to the diminishment of a game's emotional appeal.
Demographic Orientation:	Largely domestic, sporting experience culturally unique; limited transferability to other cultures.	Trans-national; sporting values recognized and adaptable to other advanced societies.
Personal Orientation:	Emphasis on specialization. Full-time involvement to develop expertise at the expense of personal benefit.	Non-specialized. Part-time involvement. Proficiency only to the extent of personal benefit.
Professionalism:	Primary actor. Controlling figure; strongly encouraged.	Contributing figure. Subordinated to non-professional in direction and control.
Change:	Welcomed and accommodated to the purpose of enhancing excitement.	Resists. Emphasis on sporting norms and retention of established "traditions."

These two sporting ethos would bring about two markedly different sporting worlds in regard to players, spectators, and social expectations of sports itself in the United States over the last half of the 19th century. Baseball would go from strength to strength, riding its emotional appeal to ever greater heights of popularity and organizational sophistication. The game's deepening appeal and increasing competitive intensity would also, however, leave a broad swath of undesirable social consequences by way of bitter, acrimonious sectional rivalries; gambling; and corruption among players and organizers.

With the cricket that continued to be played in United States over that same period, its participants and organizers would continue to uphold the game's ideology of the "Gentlemen's Game," a pastime that would draw its strength as an alternative to the tarnished sporting world associated with baseball. On the strength of this posture alone, cricket would continue to exert influence for years upon America's sporting culture greatly disproportionate to its diminished demographic presence, shadowing and beckoning the broader American sporting community not only to a different play form but also a comprehensive alternative sporting experience.

In one locality in America would this sporting ethos represented by cricket find its fullest expression and organizational strength: Philadelphia.

Since before the Civil War cricket had been, for various reasons which will be subsequently discussed, more popular, found deeper social acceptance and reached greater competitive proficiency with Americans in this city than anywhere else in the United States. From this beginning, the city's cricket community would build up an impressive sporting world over the next half century, a visible and imposing alternative sporting ethos within America's broader sporting culture. In short, the post–Civil War history of cricket in America is, for all intents and purposes, the history of cricket in Philadelphia.[7]

Far from seeing themselves as the "last stand" for cricket within the United States, these cricket-playing Philadelphians, to the very end, remained fully confident that the sporting ethos around which their game was built embodied the most desirable and beneficial contributions sports can have for society notwithstanding its limited participation among, or appeal to, the broader national populace.

The continued presence of this sporting outlook meant America's sporting culture which had been developing and advancing since the Civil War could not, historically, reach a state of finality until this alternative sporting outlook represented by Philadelphia cricket could be accommodated, absorbed or ... ultimately extinguished.

Prologue

* * *

I would like to express my deep appreciation and thanks to Kathleen Burns, Paul Hensley, Adam Blistein, and other staff members of the C.C. Morris Cricket Library for the many hours of generous help and assistance with the resources of their invaluable collection, without which this long-running project could never have been completed. A special thanks also goes out to Karl Suechting for his help with digital photos along with Gary Mitchem and the other editors at McFarland for helping make this project, twenty years in the making, come to reality.

A Note on Technical Cricket Terms

For the benefit of readers unfamiliar with cricket but, it's assumed, familiar with traditional American sports, I have adopted the procedure of explaining, in brackets, as briefly as possible, technical cricket terms immediately following their initial mention with analogies and comparisons to their closest equivalent in traditional American sports such as baseball, basketball, etc. Americanisms have been retained for commonly recurring terms (i.e., batter instead of batsman, pitch instead of delivery, etc.).

ONE

New York/Philadelphia Cricket and the Ball-Playing Spring of the 1840s

If not historically inevitable, it was highly probable that a bat-and-ball form of team play would become a central component of America's sporting culture.[1]

"Ball playing," if not strictly an historical tradition in America, had been among its populace since the country's earliest settlement. In almost all locations, among all classes, in varying degrees of organization and popularity, there had been a cultural continuity, in the New World, of "the desire of the Anglo-Saxon to arm himself with a stick and drive a small round body."[2]

This amorphous "ball playing" before the 1840s had assumed many different forms and expressions through the numerous bat-and-ball "folk games" such as "old cat," "rounders," "townball," and "wicket" found throughout the country.

Among this smorgasbord of early American ball-playing forms, cricket was well represented. The game had secured a place in America since colonial times, introduced and supported largely, but not exclusively, by the immigrant English community, which seemed to maintain some nominally direct trans-Atlantic contacts with, and influences from, the cricket played in the mother country. The individuals of the southern plantocracy who posed with their cricket bats for Benjamin West's portrait in the 1760s likely picked up the game during their studies in England and the members of the 1795 Richmond Cricket Club played by the official English rules of that period.[3]

The cricket club that was organized in New York City almost as soon as the British evacuated the city in 1783 and reportedly had enrolled in its membership some experienced English cricket players of the period could attract as many as a thousand spectators to its matches. This club, or its offshoot, continued an unbroken existence up to 1811 when the outbreak of war with Britain the following year presumably inconvenienced its English members and led to its disbandment.

What direct cultural contacts that had existed between American and English cricket up to this period seems to have diminished in the early decades of the 19th century. Whereas cricket in England continued to move forward in organization, technique, and social position to a "modern" state, what cricket that survived in its isolation in America remained an informal, unorganized, "pre-modern" game not much more distinguishable from other "folk" bat-and-ball games.

Thus the cricket that appeared in New York City in the late 1830s/early 1840s, organized by the city's resident English immigrants and reinforced by the formal establishment of the St. George Cricket Club on April 23, 1840, represented a significant departure from America's world of "folk" games. Here for the first time Americans found in their society a bat-and-ball team sport of advanced technique, formal organization, and well-established social standing. It was also a sporting institution identifiably nationalistic, an "English" game, a distinction that was largely absent in references to cricket in America prior to this period.[4]

The activities of the St. George club in America's largest city not only represented a disjunction from the country's own undeveloped folk ball-playing tradition but also ensured an American response to this novel social presence in the country by way of interest, attention, and participation, boosted in no small part by the inauguration of competitive contacts between the St. George and the Canadian cricket community.

It could only be expected that the New York immigrant English community would look to its colonial counterparts to the north for competitive opportunities, especially since it seemed some of the players/officers from the two locals shared educational or commercial ties with England. After some confused attempts in the early 1840s over proper arrangements, the St. George and Toronto cricket clubs began an annual series of matches between each other in 1844.[5]

The significance of the U.S.-Canada competition at this time and at this stage in the development and perception of organized sports in America should not be underestimated. Prior to this, sports play in the United States had been decidedly local and isolated in both interest and participation. There had been virtually no inter-city sporting contacts or competitions in the country before this. That grown men would actually travel six hundred miles to indulge in games was a revelation and wonder (as it was to William Rotch Wister) to American society, and this one single development could not but significantly transform the perception of and social attitudes towards sports play for Americans.[6]

But the significance of the U.S.-Canada cricket matches went far beyond the elevation of sports play to a trans-local status. It introduced into the American consciousness two elements indispensable for the rise of modern sports: (1) the phenomenon of a "following," the vicarious identification of an extended, non-participant segment of a population with a sporting experience, and (2) the element of "emulation," the incentive to replicate, mimic, and join in the accomplishments and perceived appeal of a hereto unknown and uninvolved social activity.

Prior to this, interest in sports play in the United States had been almost entirely non-extended. Interest rarely went beyond the direct participants and their immediate acquaintances or, at most, the local community. "Emotional capital" expended in such sports play extended no further than the single incident of the immediate game with no emotional "carry over" or expectations of future or cumulative sports occurrences.

With the beginning of the U.S.-Canada rivalry, the "emotional capital" expended on a sporting event now extended far beyond the bounds of a single occurrence. The series aroused excitement throughout and beyond New York City from individuals without a connection or familiarity with the teams or even the game itself. "The excitement during the continuation of the [U.S.-Canada] game," a contemporary observer noted, "is most extraordinary; it is the topic of the whole city, and every man, women and child seem as much interested as if the whole honour of the country depended upon the issue."[7]

The large attendance, along with the reportedly heavy betting involved in these games, impressed upon the public the emotional significance of the event, and, as a contest between America and a proxy to the mother country, this interest was further intensified by its perception as a challenge to national prestige.

The appearance of the U.S.-Canada cricket rivalry, in short, represented nothing less than the initial and most identifiable point of transition in America's sporting culture from a pre-modern to a modern sporting mindset, not simply the appearance of the objective expressions of "modernization" (organization, technique, media attention, etc.). One searches in vain for an example in U.S. participant sports before this where Americans displayed a mindset towards their sports play of personal identification, loyalty, and desire to promote or proselytize from their sporting experience. These all set in upon America's social mind as a result of this rivalry.

The series no doubt encouraged the formation of other cricket clubs in the New York area and beyond. Within the decade cricket clubs appeared in Boston; Syracuse; Newark, New Jersey; Chicago; Cincinnati; Baltimore; Washington, D.C.; Natchez, Mississippi; Louisville; and Charleston.[8]

These events collectively elevated sports interest to "a trend," an interest shared by unrelated, geographically dispersed followers that was, by the middle of the decade, "fast progressing throughout the land—in every city, town, and hamlet are [cricket] clubs found."[9]

Further reinforced by the growing interest and attention from the New York daily newspapers, along with the leading sports journals such as the *Spirit of the Times*, and publications of the English immigrant community such as the *Albion* and *Anglo-American*, this sporting "trend" extended beyond cricket itself, and it cannot be entirely coincidental that New York's earliest organized baseball clubs first appeared in the 1840s.[10]

America had, in short, entered its *Ball-Playing Spring*, a critical juncture when the country began to move beyond the pre-modern world of bat-and-ball play as an isolated, ad-hoc social occurrence, whose influence and attraction extended no further than the immediate incident with no objective beyond the single event and no cumulative influence beyond it. Sport was now on the threshold of becoming a social phenomenon with "significance" in interest, perceived importance, and value to extended society.

It would only be expected that Philadelphia—the country's fourth largest city in the 1840s, and one that had long been a favored destination for English immigrants, especially skilled workers attracted to the city's thriving textile/wool industries centered around the Wakefield Mills in Germantown and textile establishments in the city's Kensington area—would be caught up in the country's awaking cricket interest during this period.[11]

Cricket's presence in the city is known to have actually pre-dated the 1840s with mention of cricket activity among the city's English residents in the 1830s and evidence of an early match between English and American residents in the city and even of a challenge to New York.[12]

But little else is known of this cricket activity, which never seemed to have progressed to a state of permanent organization, and none of the reported names associated with the game at that time reappear in the city's later cricket organizations.[13]

Scholars of this period are fortunate to have at their disposal at least five firsthand accounts of the rise and development of cricket in Philadelphia before the Civil War. Consequently, we know more about early Philadelphia cricket than just about any other American team sport during this period, baseball not excepted.[14]

But all these accounts appeared decades after the material described (in one case, over seventy years later) and must not be accepted uncritically since, like all retrospective accounts from the distant past, they contain errors, some egregious.[15]

All these accounts assert, however, and independent contemporary sources confirm, that cricket in Philadelphia first took on a settled and permanent presence with the appearance of the Union Cricket Club around 1842, which seems to have been organized around the city's working-class English immigrant community. The driving force behind the club at this time is unclear, but the organization greatly benefited from the early involvement of the young English import agent Robert Waller whose business interests during this period seems to have taken him to New York, Philadelphia and England.[16]

Though he was never the president of the Union club (that position was held by Francis Blackburn, who may have been one of his business associates), Waller seems to have injected a measure of middle-class leadership into the predominantly working-class club, replicating the established leadership structure in English cricket at this time with the upper/middle class controlling a team dependent upon working-class player talent.[17]

Waller himself appears to have been a not untalented player, though, from contemporary accounts, he seems to have been a strong-willed personality, in one instance demanding, after an absence from the city, to captain the club's first XI (starting side), not the second team to which he had been demoted in his absence. This personality trait would have significant and even damaging consequences for antebellum cricket after he relocated from Philadelphia to New York and its St. George club in the following decade.[18]

If the organizational origins of the Union club may have been unclear, the avowed purpose of the club was not: it was to be a direct competitor to New York's St. George club, to give the country's leading cricket club "a hard struggle."[19]

The Union soon engaged the St. George in a number of highly publicized and highly competitive matches during the early 1840s and with the former's success in a number of these encounters seemed justified in its claims of competitive superiority with its New York rival.[20]

It was perhaps only logical that the St. George, which maintained full organizational control of the U.S.-Canada matches, would want to tap into the Union talent pool. But the inclusion of several Union players in the United States side that went to Canada in 1843 was rebuffed by their opponents on the grounds that these matches were to be between teams drawn exclusively from the St. George and Toronto clubs. This point of contention seems to have been ironed out by the following year, reportedly with the enrollment of several Union players in the St. George as "honorary" members. In addition, the United States side that met Canada in New York in 1844, in a highly publicized event generally recognized as the initial match of this historic series, included at least one Union player: Sam Dudson, a talented bowler (the "pitcher" in cricket).[21]

The organized cricket that emerged in New York and Philadelphia, as elsewhere around the country during the 1840s, seems to have been a largely immigrant movement, which had incited English residents around the country to revive and continue the game learned in their mother country. For some Americans of the period, this game was perhaps "becoming the rage in the country" but it still remained "little understood" among the wider American public that had limited direct involvement.[22]

Philadelphia, however, offered additional dimensions in its organized cricket.

The activities of the Union club seem to have attracted the attention of the prominent, Scottish-born Philadelphia doctor John K. Mitchell, and though it doesn't appear he was ever an active playing member, he was elected, or appointed, to an executive position in the Union club during this period. It may have been through Mitchell's encouragement that the person who would become one of the most pivotal figures in early Philadelphia cricket, William Rotch Wister, was introduced to the game.[23]

In his reminiscences, Wister claims Mitchell encouraged him to organize a team from among his fellow students at the University of Pennsylvania, an institution that was at that time "a small affair with some good people" and enrolled local residents almost exclusively. Wister himself had already, it seems, been exposed to the game through the immigrant English mill workers in Germantown and had even, he claimed, "filled a gap" by joining in some Union inter-club games when playing on its grounds in Camden, New Jersey.[24]

Wister also claimed the team he formed, the "junior club," was the first cricket club in the country composed entirely of Americans, a claim that, historically, was certainly not accurate. The game had been played by Americans as far back as the 18th century, and long before Wister's time, students were known to have played cricket at Dartmouth, Fordham, and even some far west colleges in Ohio. At almost the same time Wister claimed to be playing with his college classmates, future abolitionist, financier of the John Brown raid, Civil War general, and confidant of Emily Dickinson, Thomas Wentworth Higginson, was playing cricket with his classmates at Harvard.[25]

Wister, however, would play a far more significant role in Philadelphia cricket than as an early organizer. As a scion of one of the city's oldest and most distinguished families, this American teenager (Wister was only eighteen in 1845) would be the bridge between the working-class immigrant English cricket community, "in short sleeves and collarless," and "proper" Philadelphia society.[26]

This was the extended, inter-related network of old-line upper- and middle-class Philadelphia families who had controlled, or would significantly influence, the city's economic, social and cultural life from the colonial era into the early 20th century. Its involvement with cricket would be the most significant and determining development in the history of the game in Philadelphia.[27]

Wister, an "inveterate organizer," was assisted in his cricket activities by his brother John, who about that same time organized a team among his acquaintances in Germantown. The two sides played a series of nationally reported matches in 1845 that involved prominent future physician and novelist S. Weir Mitchell who won the prize bat in the first match offered by his father.[28]

All these developments— the emergence of the Union club as a competitive rival with the St. George and the involvement of native-born Americans—seemed to

William Rotch Wister, late in life. In his youth, this proper Philadelphian was the arch-organizer of cricket in Philadelphia and fully deserving of the title "Father of Philadelphia Cricket" (Germantown Site and Relic Society).

portend a promising future for cricket in Philadelphia. But a single incident far from the city would initiate a domino effect that would unravel much of the game's progress not only in Philadelphia but also the entire country.

During a critical juncture in the 1846 U.S.-Canada match played in New York City one of the Canadian batters, John Helliwell, while going for a run, ran into Sam Dudson, the bowler for the United States team, to prevent him from making a catch. Incensed by a perceived intentional interference, Dudson threw and hit Helliwell with the ball, causing an immediate disruption of the match. The Americans eventually apologized but the Canadians refused to continue playing and the match broke off unfinished. The ill-will generated from the incident seems to have lingered far past the match. Not only was no U.S.-Canada match held the following year (despite the inducement of a $1500 prize offered by the *Spirit of the Times*) but also representative matches between the two countries would cease altogether for the next seven years.[29]

The abrupt cessation of what had been one of the country's marquee sporting events at that time had immediate and long-lasting negative repercussions for the country's cricket. Dudson had been a member of the Philadelphia contingent on the United States team and an "uneducated" working-class mechanic at that. His violent reaction during the match was interpreted as an outbreak of what the genteel world of Victorian cricket most feared for its game: the intrusion of socially repellent working-class behavior.[30]

It can only be assumed that the St. George placed the blame for the disruption of the 1846 match and the subsequent breakoff of the U.S.-Canada series squarely on the Philadelphia contingent from the Union club. The incident almost certainly what was behind the end of competitive contacts between the two clubs and for the next nine years there would be no cricket contacts between any clubs from New York and Philadelphia.

The unfortunate occurrence at the 1846 U.S.-Canada match and the subsequent break-off of North American cricket's most prominent and highly publicized event also seems to have set off a downward spiral of disintegrating interest in cricket around the country.

In the New York area there was, over the next few years, a marked reduction in cricket activity, with the substitution of intra-club or married vs single matches for the higher profile inter-club matches. The St. George still remained active and for a few years tried to substitute the disrupted Philadelphia rivalry with matches against Boston. But the New England club wouldn't prove as competitive an opponent as the Union, leading the St. George to also resort to more intra-club games.[31]

Fears that, as a result of the 1846 incident, "cricket will receive a blow ... from which it will not speedily recover" soon seemed to be confirmed by a decline in cricket in other areas of the country. By the end of the decade, cricket activity seems to have diminished or outright disappeared from a number of its earlier locations such as Chicago, Cincinnati and several southern cities.[32]

All this seems to have brought to a halt, at least temporarily, a game that had, over the decade, been "fast progressing throughout the land."[33]

The ripple effect seemed to extend even beyond the cricket community, adversely affecting other nascent ball-playing sports of the period. It is perhaps more than coincidental that of the five baseball clubs known to have existed in the New York area in the 1840s, all but one vanished soon after the break-off of the U.S.-Canada series.[34]

For the next half dozen years, America's future national pastime would experience "a desperate struggle for existence," hanging on for dear life through the few intra-squad games played by New York's sole surviving baseball club, the Knickerbockers.[35]

America's promising ball-playing spring of the 1840s now passed into an ice age of noticeably diminished ball-playing activity, public attention, and interest that would last for a good five or six years. America may have been brought to the threshold of the world of "modern" team sports in the 1840s but it was not yet totally prepared, it seems, to accommodate this new sporting world.

The fallout from the disrupted 1846 U.S.-Canada and St. George-Union cricket rivalries impacted the game's very existence in Philadelphia as well, most noticeably with the Union club.[36]

Dissention seems to have arisen in the club at this time between factions representing historically antagonistic English localities, North and South—a baneful historical development within English cricket that had been transplanted to America, infecting the English immigrant cricket community in the United States with this traditional sectional hostility.[37]

Within the Union club this geographic animosity seems to have polarized around two factions represented by the John Ticknor family and the supporters of Sam Dudson (the club's name, the "Union," had reportedly been adopted as a gesture of peace and cooperation between the two factions).[38]

Perhaps exacerbated by the Helliwell/Dudson incident and the consequential break-off of Philadelphia/New York cricket contacts, any suppressed hostility within the club now seems to have burst forth. Whether this outbreak of intra-club hostility actually led to "hard blows" between its members, as Wister reports, or not, the club seems to have fallen into functional disarray.[39]

Without the moderating influence of Waller, who seems to have been absent from the city during this period, the "best people" reportedly abandoned the club, which, after a few intra-club matches in 1847, "passed away unmourned by the public," leaving John Mitchell, according to Wister, to cover the Union's $400 unpaid debts.[40]

The collapse of the Union, Philadelphia's leading cricket organization, also put a damper on the nascent American involvement with the game in the city. Without the direct competitive opportunities and assistance available with the experienced English players the American contingent that had formed around the Wisters noticeably decreased its activity.[41]

Wister reports only a few informal "pick up" games were played among his acquaintances over the next half dozen years, cricket being by now effectively "dead as a doornail" in the city.[42]

Jones Wister claimed "I do not know" why cricket activity with his American friends evaporated during the 1840s and the breakup of the Union should not, in itself, have had such severe repercussions in stifling interest, at least with Americans involved with the game. The continued involvement with the game in Wister's circle at a low, unorganized level seems to indicate this decline was due not so much from a loss of

American interest in cricket as it was an indirect reaction to the game's perceived negative influences.[43]

"Ball playing" by young men, throughout America up to that time, still carried an objectionable social image, an activity perceived to breed antagonism, disruption, and dissipation.[44]

It was an image, according to Wister, shared at that time by his strata of "proper" Philadelphia society which, for the most part, "looked down on" all forms of sports during that period. This perception must certainly have been reinforced with the circumstances surrounding the Union breakup, happenings that struck these Philadelphians as "too rough and repellent for Young America." To the proper Philadelphia families who witnessed the involvement of their sons with such a game, if even indirectly, such activity could hardly have been encouraged and likely positively discouraged.[45]

A more far-reaching consequence of the Union breakup, however, may have imprinted itself upon this stratum of Philadelphia society. The Union had been an English working-class club in the 1840s, when Philadelphia was being wracked by anti-immigrant riots and labor unrest, because of which this segment of Philadelphia society from which Wister and his other young associates came must have collectively concluded that not then, nor in the future, would their social class accept English working-class control of its cricket.[46]

It was a stance that would have profound implications for the future of cricket in the city. The Philadelphia Americans who remained involved with the game would continue to look to and welcome English assistance and competitive contacts. But never again would they allow English organizational or administrative control of their cricket, nor would they ever again entrust to the city's working-class strata of society, no matter how proficient or talented, the responsibility of upholding the moral integrity of the game.

These would become the uncompromising principles on which Philadelphia, over the next half century, would erect and sustain its cricket world.

Two

The Rise of Philadelphia Cricket and the Uncertainty of a Sporting Identity

The sudden and extended decline of organized bat-and-ball sports in America during the late 1840s was followed by an almost equally sudden and unexpected resurgence in the early 1850s, once again led by New York City and a revival that, this time, would usher in a revitalized and permanent presence for organized team sports in American society.

Why this happened and to the extent it happened at this time is unclear. The residual memory of, and the latent interest in, bat-and-ball sports certainly still simmered with the urban society of young men at that time, reflected in an expanding sports press such as the *New York Clipper*, which, soon after its establishment in 1853, became the country's most prominent sports journal.

Another development that same year must certainly have also boosted public interest in sports not only for passive observers but also for active participants: the revival of the U.S.-Canada cricket rivalry.

With the unpleasant memories of the 1846 incident having evidently faded, and new leadership at both the St. George and Toronto cricket clubs in place, the revived series, now between truly representative teams drawn from multiple area clubs, soon aroused so much public attention that, after the 1853 match, it was proclaimed, "a few more matches like the one recorded will make the pastime as popular here as in the mother country."[1]

In its renewed form, the rivalry quickly resumed its status as one of the country's premier sporting events, re-igniting not only local public attention but also interest in cricket that carried far beyond New York City. Cricket activity soon reappeared in numerous locations where it had previously existed such as Newark, New England, Chicago, Pittsburg (the city's spelling at the time), and upstate New York.[2]

These locations were now joined, in the early 1850s, by newly formed cricket clubs in Connecticut, Milwaukee, and Cleveland, the number of clubs increasing year by year to a point that granted credence to the *Clipper's* claim that now "a new era in popular amusements seemed to have set in with a rising tide."[3]

The cricket of the 1840s had been largely a phenomenon of the English immigrant community. The game, in its revived state, now began to spread to a much broader social spectrum, as a significant number of native-born Americans joined the sport. In the New York area, a number of clubs were organized, such as the Williamsburg cricket club in 1855, on the initiative of Americans, while other English-dominated clubs, such as those in Newark and Yonkers, began to attract greater numbers of Americans.[4]

All this interest, however, was far eclipsed by the students at the city's Free Academy (distant forerunner of City College of New York). The school went from two cricket teams in 1854 to three hundred of its five hundred students playing cricket by 1856.[5]

There was no more evident indication of cricket's prominence in antebellum America than the depiction of its marquee event, the annual U.S.-Canada match, on the front page of the country's most widely read sports periodical, the *New York Clipper*, in 1856 (*New York Clipper*).

Two. The Rise of Philadelphia Cricket

Philadelphia wasn't left out of this new trend. Cricket may have "slumbered" in the city over the half decade following the breakup of the Union club.[6] But the English immigrant working classes in the city had continued to play on an unorganized basis over these years, an interest that, by the early 1850s, took on a more formal shape with the establishment of the Kensington and Washington cricket clubs.[7]

These were soon followed by the Star cricket club organized by the talented English immigrant William "Buck" Jarvis who, acclaimed for his "perfection in batting," had recently relocated from Pittsburg, establishing a line of cricketers who would play a decades-long role in Philadelphia area cricket.[8]

For Philadelphia cricket at this time, the absence of a *dominant* English-controlled cricket club—one that stood above and apart in facilities, playing strength, and overall influence as compared to the city's other emerging cricket organizations—had present and future implications.

In most other large American cities during this period, a prominent English-controlled cricket club dominated the local cricket scene. The St. George was still the leading New York cricket organization, attracting the city's most talented players and continuing to hold a tight grip on the U.S.-Canada series. The club's status was further enhanced with its move, in the mid-1850s, to the area's premier sporting location: the Elysian Fields in Hoboken, New Jersey. A similar scenario could be found in Boston, Chicago and Baltimore: an immigrant English-controlled cricket club dominating the area's smaller, sometimes American/immigrant clubs in facilities and player talent.[9]

Not unexpectedly, American cricket interest in Philadelphia revived among that social strata which had been involved with the game in the 1840s: "proper" Philadelphians, some of whom had been part of Wister's earlier cricket circle.

Positive memories of their past experiences with the game, though perhaps faded, certainly hadn't been forgotten and, according to Wister, he and his social circle had, even in the years after the breakup of the Union club, maintained involvement with the game through informal and infrequent "scratch matches."[10]

Now with the uptick in cricket activity in the early 1850s "cricket began to be talked of" again in this segment of Philadelphia society.[11]

Wister and his friends, who had reached their middle and late twenties and were mature in judgment and independent in their choices, came together in 1853 and organized an "American Gentlemen's" cricket club.[12]

It would be a significant departure from the other cricket developing in the city. Wister and his social circle, as would have been entirely expected and logical, could have joined, or associated with, any of Philadelphia's immigrant English clubs. But memories of the Union fiasco, which had been precipitated by an unruly organization controlled by the working class, must have been still fresh in their minds. Consequently, Wister and his circle took the further step of establishing their own, more formal organization, the Philadelphia Cricket Club, at a meeting in Wister's law office on February 10, 1854.

The newly formed club had something of an amalgamated membership. Wister himself, along with his acquaintances who had been part of the old junior club of the 1840s, formed the "nucleus" of the organization. But the club also enrolled some "over the hill" English immigrant players, some complete novices, some "very scientific players," and at least one old Union club player: Thomas Facon.[13]

The joint American/English membership of the Philadelphia club was certainly not unprecedented among big-city cricket clubs at this time. The New York Cricket Club, second in importance to the St. George Club, had reportedly been formed specifically to attract American players.[14]

But there would be two significant differences with the Philadelphia club: this Philadelphia organization was structured to encourage a largely middle- and upper-class membership. The $12 membership fee and $5 annual fee alone would have largely deterred many working-class players from joining the organization.[15]

And the few who were allowed to join—like the Englishman Tom "Red" Senior, probably the best bowler in the city at that time, even at the age of thirty-seven, and hired as the club's "player/coach" to instruct its members as well as strengthen the team in its important matches—were, with their level of membership, not allowed to vote.[16]

The English immigrant William Bradshaw—who was also hired to coach and kept the team's equipment at his house next to the club's rent-free ground in Camden, New Jersey—probably also held a similarly second-class membership in the club.[17]

As Thomas Jable has shown, the membership of the Philadelphia Cricket Club at this time was predominantly professional and middle class, drawn primarily from the legal profession (attorney J. Dickenson Sergeant, and not Wister, was the club's first president).[18]

It was also clear that those American members, drawn from the proper Philadelphia social class, were, unlike other cricket club leaders in the country, going to maintain total organizational control of their establishment and wouldn't allow the class dissention that led to the demise of the old Union club to infect their club. From this point on, beginning with the Philadelphia club, the social strata of proper Philadelphians would assume complete organizational control of the city's top-level cricket and would never relinquish it.

The club was, however, competitively deficient in its beginning, receiving a "severe drubbing" by the English working-class teams it played during its first matches, as well as enduring another bad loss to another Philadelphia club, the Olympia.[19]

As the only Philadelphia cricket organization that seemed to own/lease its own ground at that time, and had the financial resources to hire professionals and travel out of town for matches, the Philadelphia club was, nonetheless, the one cricket organization in the city competitively strong enough to reestablish playing contacts with New York. Beginning in 1855, the club resumed playing the St. George club on a regular basis. It was a promising start for the new club and within a couple of years, its membership had grown to over a hundred, making it in fact, as well as in name, the city's premier cricket club.[20]

The Philadelphia Cricket Club had made provisions for junior members, but perhaps because of age differences or inaccessibility of the club's grounds in Camden, members from another branch of the Wister family, Jones and William, organized a club in Germantown on August 11, 1854. Drawn from local and mostly "inexperienced" residents, the club was more neighborhood based, playing on a plot of land owned by William Wister that could only be accessed by walking through corn fields.[21]

The club, at its inception, was composed mostly of young men in their late teens. As these members were under legal age, the organization enrolled the older Tom McKean, scion of a wealthy Philadelphia family destined to play a long and influential role in Germantown cricket.[22]

The new club was also slow to assert itself competitively and had to even rely on assistance from another Philadelphia club, the Delphian, at that time. Its first foray outside the city in 1859 took the team not east to New York, but west against the closer Pottsville cricket club.[23]

The Germantown Cricket Club established rivalries with New York clubs later that year and considerably improved its competitive prospects by enrolling a number of the city's more talented American cricketers such as Sylvanus Kephardt and Walter Newhall, and hiring its first professional, William Hammond. By 1857, its enrollment had sufficiently increased to a point that it could field two teams.[24]

More important to Philadelphia cricket was the rivalry that quickly developed between the Germantown and the city's senior cricket club, since it pitted predominantly American sides against each other. An exclusively American Germantown side registered a notable success with two wins over an all-American Philadelphia club side in 1856 and, by 1858, the two clubs would be playing each other in this format on an annual basis.[25]

Whether or not family connections between the Philadelphia and Germantown clubs had specifically brought the latter into existence is not certain. But they did play a part in the formation of the Young America cricket club, organized on November 11, 1855, with William Wister, Jr., enrolling younger relatives and friends ("mere children," it was claimed) of the Germantown club who had been barred from the older club because of their youth.[26]

This club, destined for future greatness, played its games on a plot of land owned by Thomas Newhall, thus establishing a connection with a Philadelphia family that would have deep and far-reaching influences not only on the Young America club, but all Philadelphia cricket for the next three decades.

Featuring a team of adolescents, the club had limited competitive opportunities. Though it was a separate organization, it seemed heavily dependent on its sister Germantown cricket club during its early years, even functioning as a "training ground" for Germantown's developing players, such as the talented Walter Newhall, who was promoted from the Young America to the Germantown club when he was only fourteen.[27]

The Young America didn't play an outside club on its own until 1857 (though it had taken on the Keystone Cricket Club a year earlier with the help of some Germantown players), would not play its sister club nor the Philadelphia club head-on until 1858, and would not beat the Germantown club until 1859.[28]

All this seemed to encourage a spirit of "self-reliance" which would be a hallmark of the club throughout its existence and a principle that would have significant repercussions for the club's future direction. Whether the Young America ever officially adopted an "American-only" membership policy—a step not taken by other Philadelphia cricket clubs—is unknown. But it did formally prohibit its members from playing for other clubs, a policy that *de facto* probably excluded all English immigrant players who insisted upon their cherished tradition of "revolving" (playing for more than one club). The consequence of this policy was evident in the absence of any immigrant English players on the Young America club at this time, even though two English-dominated teams, the Washington and Marylebone, used the Young America grounds.[29]

With the establishment of the Philadelphia, Germantown, and Young America clubs, three of Philadelphia's five future Halifax Cup clubs had now come into existence, all destined to become the city's largest, most affluent, and competitively dominant cricket organizations over the next half century. Because of this, historians have devoted most of their attention to these larger clubs and neglected the city's broader cricket landscape, providing an incomplete portrait.[30]

Historically significant as these larger clubs would become, they were barely the tip of the iceberg within Philadelphia cricket. By the mid–1850s, cricket may have been "extending itself to all parts of the United States" but nowhere was this sports "rage" so widespread and pervasive as it was in Philadelphia.[31]

Dozens of cricket clubs of various size and organizational sophistication sprang up alongside these three major clubs. The Delphian club may, in fact, have preceded even the Philadelphia club, as it claimed to have been founded in 1852 and reportedly had its own professional, which may have enabled the club to beat the Germantown club in the first match between the two sides in 1855.[32]

The Olympia cricket club was probably the equal in organizational standing and competitive strength of any club in the city at this time. It also had beaten Germantown, though its claim to have never lost a game before the Civil War was demonstrably false. Prominent within the club were members of the Graffen family. A member of this family, S.M. Graffen, would, after the Civil War, take his managerial skills honed on the cricket field to the St. Louis Browns professional baseball club, a pathway other early cricket players would follow.[33]

Below this tier of larger clubs was a plethora of smaller, less formal sides organized around neighborhoods or social groups. Almost all of these were overwhelmingly teams of young men. In contrast to the many immigrant-controlled cricket clubs with "old, fat, English" players, many of the Philadelphia clubs were gathering places for young Americans. The Olympic club was originally a team of seventeen-year-olds. The Hamilton and Empire clubs were high schoolers. The United cricket club had four thirteen-year-olds and the Jackson club was a team of sixteen- to twenty-one year-olds.[34]

Many of these clubs were loosely organized and short-lived, probably little more than schoolboy frolics, with players frequently moving from one club to another. Yet from these many smaller clubs would come individuals who would play prominent roles in elevating the standing, status, and pre-eminence of Philadelphia cricket long after their original clubs had passed out of existence.

From the Keystone cricket club came the standout players W.C. Morgan and Charles Barclay, the latter reported to have "no superior among the Americans" as a batter. Both would eventually move on to the Germantown club and win places on the Philadelphia side against Parr's All England team in 1859 and Wilshire's English professionals in 1868.

Considered one of the period's finest cricket players, Sylvanus Kephardt started with the Putnam club before migrating to the Germantown and Philadelphia clubs. Charles Vernou, "a really great player," would shuffle around between at least five different cricket clubs before joining the Young America, the start of a lengthy cricket career that would take him to all corners of America. Both were also on the Philadelphia team that opposed Parr's All England team in 1859.[35]

Three other standout American players—Richard Clay, who began with the Union cricket club; W.P. Johns, who first appeared for the Osceola club; and John Provost, originally with the Marylebone club, nicknamed "the wizard" bowler and reputed to be "as swift and straight as the celebrated Jackson" (the standout English bowler with Parr's All England team)—all eventually found their way onto the Young America club.[36]

With the Orient and Excelsior cricket clubs at that time could be found, respectively, scions of the prominent Pepper and Altemus families who would later play prominent roles in the city's cricket as members of the Germantown and Belmont cricket clubs. A founding member of the latter club, John P. Green, who would later gain stature as one of Philadelphia cricket's most dedicated and vigorous supporters after the Civil War, began as a member of the unpretentious Panola club.[37]

All this American involvement with cricket throughout the country injected a vibrant new spirit into the game so refreshingly different from the "old fogy [sic] school" identified with immigrant English cricket. A contributor to Amherst College's *Ichnolite* found cricket was intoxicating once practiced—"a true love of the game possesses him ... a zeal amounting to almost infatuation." Elliott Harrington of Waltham, Massachusetts, would recall that, during his youth in 1858, cricket "was the most absorbing and fascinating thing that could possibly come into a boy's life."[38]

At the same time, in 1857, that "on all the vacant lots of the city [Philadelphia] and suburbs there are cricket matches daily" and where the "Architectural Iron Works and Powelton Fair Grounds [in Philadelphia] never saw a week go by without two or three [cricket] matches being lost or won," dozens of cricket matches were also going on among the young Americans on the Boston Commons.[39]

Widespread as the cricket fervor may have infected Americans in other areas of the country, nowhere did it run as broadly and deeply as it did in Philadelphia during the 1850s. A city that observers liked to point out had a reputation for being "not much of a place for fun" was now a metropolis where "our people are cricket mad," with the number of cricket clubs in the city during this period estimated between forty-three and a hundred. To an extent unmatched in other areas of the United States, cricket interest in Philadelphia had assumed such a level of appeal that it had become a genuinely popular movement, spontaneously expanding through neighborhoods and social organizations, extending its appeal to the city's sports-minded populace to an extent to have "created a network dense enough to sustain a local cricket culture" that would endure for three generations.[40]

Philadelphia was clearly at the forefront, but certainly not the exclusive representative, of a nation-wide sporting trend. By 1857, the *Clipper* noted cricket was extending itself "throughout the length and breadth of the land," with Philadelphia's *North American* even portending, two years later, that cricket was "undoubtedly destined to be transplanted to this soil and become a national pastime."[41]

For these optimistic prognostications to fully come about for cricket, however, supporters of the game would have to resolve two significant internal challenges. As a sport that had been introduced, in its modern state, by the immigrant English community, cricket was still widely perceived, despite the increasing involvement of Americans, as a game tethered to this immigrant subculture. To reach a secure, sustainable presence within the broader populace the game's American supporters would have to (1) achieve a level of competitive proficiency in the game equal if not superior to the immigrant English community and (2) assume organizational control of the game, specifically in regard to arrangements, team selection, and finances of the more important inter-city and international cricket contests.

Individually American proficiency in the game was progressing most noticeably, though not exclusively, in Philadelphia. In addition to the above noted individuals, Walter Newhall—originally with the Germantown club, then lured away to the Philadelphia club—was developing into one of the outstanding players in the city. After making his initial mark as the top scorer in an American vs English match in 1857, the Philadelphia club match vs St. George in 1859, and U.S.-Canada match in 1860, he had now reached a point where, as a cricket player, he was "beginning to understand his great strength as a batter."[42]

While Newhall and other standout Philadelphia cricketers were coming forth in the 1850s, the veterans William Rotch Wister and Jones Wister continued to make their marks on the field of play. The former, though "lacking in style," was high scorer in a local Americans vs English in 1859 match while the latter was high scorer for the Americans in Philadelphia's match with Parr's All-England team that same year, hitting the English bowling "all over the grounds," all of which largely discredits Lester's claim that the Wisters "were greater in organizing cricket than in playing it."[43]

Improved American cricket proficiency was not limited to Philadelphia. Among the Eastern Seaboard cricketers could be found such "aspiring" Americans as John Holder of the Long Island cricket club; the Free

Academy student J. Davis; Isaac Jackson of the Amsterdam, New York, club; and Utica bowler John G. French, the last a player who reportedly could throw a cricket ball 103 yards.[44]

The ultimate test for any increased American proficiency, however, was in head-to-head competition between American and experienced English teams, but such progress was slower, even in Philadelphia.

The Philadelphia cricket club was, in its earliest years, uncompetitive against the city's English immigrant cricket clubs and had to heavily rely upon its own English members such as Tom Senior, William Bradshaw and even at one point Sam Dudson of 1846 U.S.-Canada infamy. Even then, the club frequently had to play the English teams at odds (one team allowed more players than the other). The competitive gap between American and English teams, however, noticeably closed by the end of the 1850s. The Germantown Americans' win over the English Star club in 1857 effectively and permanently established the superiority of the city's American cricket players over their English residents at least on a club vs club basis.[45]

In representative matches, American sides in Philadelphia, at least when playing at odds, were beginning to get the best of the city's English sides by 1858 and later that same year passed a significant milestone by beating an all-English side playing without odds. In 1860, another American side further confirmed the city's competitive superiority by beating a combined team of Philadelphia and New York English players, a result that brought "no small degree of pride and pleasure" to the Quaker city. Lest there be any further doubt these Americans were getting better at the game, another team of Philadelphia Americans followed up with another win later that year.[46]

It was a different story against teams outside Philadelphia, specifically against clubs from New York, still the acknowledged center of American cricket. With much less frequent American participation in the game, New York cricket remained firmly in hands of the immigrant English community. St. George still stood as the country's premier club, keeping ahead of its seemingly more American-friendly rival, the New York Cricket Club. The Newark cricket club had even arranged the New York area's first American vs American match against the New York cricket club in 1854 and had followed this up with a match against an all-American Philadelphia side a year later. But the disproportionate number of American cricketers in Philadelphia and New York area cricket clubs made a continuation of these matches impractical and the primary competitive direction for the country's cricket remained American vs English.[47]

The resurgence of cricket in the 1850s did, however, revive the Philadelphia/New York cricket rivalry and it would soon become a rivalry between Philadelphia's American-dominated cricket clubs and New York's English-dominated clubs, a rivalry that was, at the start, largely one-sided.

During this period, neither the Philadelphia (effectively Philadelphia's primary cricket organization) nor the Germantown club was able to beat the St. George when that club was at full strength. Philadelphia might lay claim to having the best American cricket players, but it could still make no claim to having the country's top cricket club.

Because of this competitive imbalance, the rivalry between the American and English cricket camps, beginning in 1856, would be played out on a representative, rather than individual club, basis through an annual match between representative American and English teams which pitted the best American players from the Eastern Seaboard—primarily Philadelphia, New York, Newark and upstate New York—against the top English players from New York/Philadelphia clubs.[48]

Even when playing at odds of 18 vs 11 (the latter being the number of players on a regulation cricket team), the American sides lost the first four of these matches though by decreasing margins and increasing confidence on the part of the American players ("not a nerve was relaxed" in the closely contested 1858 match).[49]

The breakthrough win for the Americans came in the 1860 match, this one held on the Philadelphia cricket club home ground in Camden, the consoling "pats on the back" of former defeats at last giving way to the exuberant satisfaction and pride of a solid and convincing win over their English opponents.[50]

The accomplishment was, for the American team captain Richard Stevens of the Philadelphia club, "the proudest moment of his life" and for more than one reason. The game had been, in effect, a win by and for Philadelphia cricket. All but one of the team's eighteen players were Philadelphians, the depth of the American cricket talent in the city evidenced by the fact that these seventeen players were drawn from no fewer than six different clubs: Philadelphia, Germantown, Young America, Union, Southwark and Hamilton. The entire affair represented, in effect, the at least temporary ascension of Philadelphia cricket itself over the country's immigrant English cricket community.[51]

The match was the most explicit and undeniable evidence of the increasing and extended influence of Americans in all aspects of Philadelphia cricket. The Philadelphia and Germantown starting teams were now predominantly American, the Young America entirely American, and by the eve of the Civil War the city's leading cricket clubs were becoming less and less dependent on their English members apart from their professionals.[52]

Any lingering doubts about Philadelphia's increasing role in the leadership of the country's cricket had actually been dispelled a year earlier in its match against the All-England team that toured the United States and Canada in 1859. The Philadelphia match, though lost by the host team, was the closest of all those played by the powerful All-England side during this team's North American tour, largely due to the contribution of the thirteen Philadelphians on the twenty-two man team. The English tour manager Fred Lillywhite was certainly impressed with what he saw, noting that in that city's cricket populace, there was very much "material for making good cricketers."[53]

If Americans in Philadelphia and elsewhere were steadily, if slowly, closing the competitive gap with their English opponents, as well as weaning themselves from a dependence on English assistance, progress was not much slower in expectations for assuming the management and direction of the game.

The English immigrant cricket community always seemed willing to support and encourage American participation and involvement in its game but were much less willing to concede control to its American cousins, being intent on keeping the game, even in this foreign location, as an institution "run for and by Englishmen."[54]

As noted, the distinct feature of Philadelphia was the early assumption of American control of the game. The Philadelphia cricket club had been administered and controlled by its American members from the time of its establishment, an arrangement that also applied to the Germantown and Young America club as well as possibly with a number of the city's smaller cricket clubs. The English immigrant cricket community in the city, though still maintaining a competitive presence, was largely confined to a periphery of working-class clubs that didn't have their own grounds or the financial resources to travel out of town or hire professionals.

This scenario within Philadelphia cricket didn't, however, go unchallenged. Robert Waller himself, now domiciled in New York, still seems to have had enough personal or business dealings in Philadelphia to try and reassert his influence over the growing cricket interest in the city. In 1858 Waller, or an intermediary, organized a "Boys Cricket Club," recruiting to the team some of Philadelphia's best American cricket players with the intention, it can probably be assumed, of reestablishing a measure of English direction over the growing number of talented American cricketers in the city. The club, however, was short lived and if it had been Waller's intent to reassert English influence over the city's cricket, it would not be successful.[55]

A more significant English assertion also came about in 1858 with the formation of Philadelphia's own St. George cricket club, which seems to have been, like its New York counterpart, organized around the city's

Two. The Rise of Philadelphia Cricket   29

middle class, rather than working class, English immigrants. This club also attempted to recruit some of the city's best American cricket talent, including the future baseball stars Dick McBride and Tom Pratt, though if its intent was also to re-establish English influence on Philadelphia cricket, these efforts seem to have been more narrowly focused on a single event.[56]

This much is suggested in the club's involvement with the All-England match that was held in Philadelphia in the fall of 1859. With the All-England visit exclusively arranged and financed by New York/Canada English cricket authorities, it was understandable that the English cricket community in Philadelphia wasn't going to let the promotional and financial benefits of this major sporting event pass into American hands. This appears evident when the St. George, a few months before the match, hastily erected its own ground at Camac Woods with $800 in improvements on the expectation that this location, rather than the fine "picturesque" and readily available Camden ground of the Philadelphia cricket club originally slated for the event, would be the site of the match.[57]

What exactly transpired over this issue isn't fully known, but it seems certain it aroused some antagonism between the city's American and English cricket communities. This at least is indicated from the anonymous letter published by the *Clipper* whose author bitterly complained of the "slanderous" attacks upon the St. George for what seems to have been its aggressive tactics in securing the match site. In the end, the match committee (made up of representatives from the larger Philadelphia area and St. George clubs) agreed to hold the match at the Camac Woods grounds, possibly as a trade-off for the inclusion of more Americans on the representative Philadelphia side.[58]

The All-England visit was a one-off event. More contentious would be control of the annual U.S.-Canada match. From the series inception in the 1840s, the St. George club of New York had held a firm grip on the event, staging the match on its own ground and selecting the United States players, giving priority to its own members and, in all matches up to 1858, selecting only two Americans.

Dissatisfaction with this arrangement had been building even within the broader English cricket community, led by New York City's second most important club, the New York cricket club. In 1860, after what must have been an extended period of contentious and acrimonious negotiations, this club eventually succeeded in wresting control of the match from the St. George.[59]

Both nineteenth-century observers and contemporary scholars have maligned the St. George Club of New York for its role in American cricket during this critical period in the game's history. As the most prominent and influential cricket organization in the country, the St. George should have been in a position to almost single-handedly direct the course of the game, and in this capacity, it failed in the eyes of almost all concerned.

The English immigrant community in America at this time had long been reputed to be the most insular of the country's numerous immigrant nationalities and the St. George did little to dispel this image. Its membership was widely criticized for being "clannish," a membership that "burrowed" into positions of inflexibility and stubbornness in dealing with other cricket clubs and outsiders. Along with an attitude of "insufferable insolence," St. George members were criticized for their "ingratitude towards the source of their ... riches," the country in which many of its members were enjoying healthy financial returns. Even in the 1840s the organization had "never been popular" with the greater cricket community and was the constant target of criticism from Henry Chadwick, the *Clipper's* cricket reporter.[60]

Some of this criticism was clearly unwarranted. The St. George did seem to evidence a *bona fide* desire to extend interest among Americans and assist them with cricket. The club generously offered coaching to the students at the Free Academy, did have some American officers in the organization, and made it known it was ready at any time to go to West Point and assist the cadets with the game.[61]

But the St. George failed to grasp in its own time what cricket authorities have failed to grasp to this day: a desire to interest Americans in cricket is not the same as the ability to do so.

The Americans associated with the St. George, and other English-dominated cricket clubs during this period, always seemed to have been marginalized and subordinated to the interests of their English members. Waller himself was roundly criticized for not allowing the talented American baseball player James Creighton, who as a member of the St. George was equally proficient at cricket, to bowl in club matches even though it was palpably clear to all observers the American was far more talented than many of the club's English players. The English cricket community at large was also excoriated for its subordination of novice American members, one of whom angrily complained that during practice sessions "the weakest have to go to the wall for they are bowled out [if the bowler throws a pitch past the batter and hits the batter's wicket—three, short, upright poles just behind him—the batter's immediately out, equivalent to a 'strike out' in baseball] on, perhaps, the first ball, and then are compelled to fag in the field on both sides," adding the ominous warning "this kind of one-sided thing Americans won't submit to."[62]

So it must have been with considerable satisfaction to the extended cricket community that the St. George's rival, the New York cricket club, wrested control of the 1860 U.S.-Canada match away from the dragon

Two. The Rise of Philadelphia Cricket

slayers. The president of the New York club, Henry Sharpe, was an immigrant English glass stainer who, as a Chartist, had fled to the United States in the wake of that movement's conflicts with the British government in the 1840s.[63]

As someone in the English cricket community who had been, for years, personally dedicated to attracting Americans to cricket (he tried to get the Americans in his own company to take up the game), Sharpe made the unprecedented decision to include five Americans on the United States side for that year's Canada match, all Philadelphians, an acknowledgment of the high caliber of that city's cricket talent and a marked progression from the two Philadelphians, William Rotch Wister and Walter Newhall, who had been selected for the previous year's U.S.-Canada match. As a further gesture of confidence in the Philadelphia contingent, Sharpe promoted several of the American players up the batting order, allowing Walter Newhall and Charles Vernou to score, respectively, 27 and 22 runs to lead the United States team to a win. Little wonder that Sharpe "was very popular with the Philadelphia cricketers of his day."[64]

In the eyes of Henry Chadwick, the whole affair surrounding the 1860 U.S.-Canada match was the most significant game-changing development for cricket in the United States, this longtime cricket advocate seeing here the achievement of his highest hopes: the transcending unity of the American and English cricket communities into a single sporting culture in purpose, objective, and cooperation.

In what would be one of his most effusive and emotional declarations as a sports reporter, Chadwick now proclaimed that, as a result of this match, the hereto separate English and American cricket communities "have so completely affiliated themselves with American interests and American ambitions as to incorporate themselves into the American ranks, to intertwine their hopes and join their labor so fraternally with us that hereafter we can know no separation of nationality, but must look upon all those as members of our own democracy of cricket. Then when in the future a question of American vs any other cricketers comes up they are of us inseparably."[65]

If Chadwick had hoped and believed the 1860 U.S.-Canada match signified the obliteration of the American/English fault line that had long plagued the game, that all cultural differences had now been subsumed into a great American cricket "melting pot," and that from this ethnically indivisible sporting unity it could be declared to all the country's cricketers that "you are now in your legitimate place," he would soon be disillusioned of these euphoric expectations following the annual United States Cricketers Association meeting two years later.[66]

As a result of cricket's surge in popularity during the 1850s, supporters had called for a national body that would bring together all clubs and individuals for the purpose of developing, organizing, and coordinating the game's growth, a move that brought about, in 1857, the formation of the United States Cricketers Association in New York City.

The first few annual meetings of the association proved to be relatively harmonious, if not necessarily productive. But the fault lines between the American and English cricket camps began to again raise tensions at these meetings, initially between parties that wanted to prioritize efforts to popularize the game with Americans and the English community's insistence on organizing international matches and strengthening representative teams with imported professionals. This tension led to an open rupture at the 1860 meeting over control of the U.S.-Canada match, the faction led by the New York cricket club successfully removing control of the event from the St. George club that year, a development that led the St. George to distance itself from the national association.[67]

Philadelphia had been represented at the initial 1857 convention by one of the Philadelphia cricket club's English members, Thomas Facon, and Philadelphia's growing influence eventually brought the association's annual meeting to the city itself in 1861 without, however, attendance by New York's St. George club, tantamount to that club's declared disassociation from the organization.[68]

An effort seems to have been made to reassert English influence at the 1862 convention, now back in New York, resulting in an acrimonious and contentious meeting. What exactly transpired during that meeting is rather sketchy, but it seems that the faction led by students from the Free Academy turned back efforts by an unnamed faction, but possibly the St. George, to assert a contrary position and policies. The gathering ending in animosity and division among attendees, with Chadwick, who had attended the meeting, declaring the whole affair to be a total "farce." The association would never meet again.[69]

As a result of the 1862 fiasco, Chadwick must have now realized how impossible was his vision of American cricket as a bilateral sporting culture of English and American elements somehow held together in a workable harmony and that a time of reckoning would come when cricket, to have a viable presence in American society, must be, in direction and organization if not in participation, either entirely English or entirely American.

It was no mystery where Chadwick's sympathies were in this matter. The country's most influential cricket reporter, though born and raised in England, firmly believed cricket's prospects would be best served if the game was "more in the hands of American players." He would live to see, in his lifetime, these intentions come true in at least one location in America.[70]

Three

Post–Civil War Cricket and Baseball and the Divergence of a Sporting Culture

For all the apparently ineradicable ethnic/nationalistic tension within American cricket before the Civil War, this didn't seem, in itself, to be an insurmountable obstacle for the game's continued growth and acceptance with Americans. Left on its cultural trajectory from the early 1850s, American cricket could, theoretically, have followed the same historical pathway the game would take in British colonies such as India or the West Indies where it was also an external cultural import that native participants eventually adopted to an extent that would culturally subsume its English character.

With the further boost from the All-England cricket team visit in 1859 which had incited "intense excitement throughout the length and breadth of the land," cricket, it seemed, was "destined to become popular there can be no doubt," a sport that was steadily settling into the minds of Americans as a social presence "not something to be wondered at but a reality, a living institution." All this gave its supporters at that time the not realistic expectations that, on its current track, cricket "is undoubtedly destined to be transplanted to this soil and become a national pastime."[1]

Among Americans of the 1850s "a new era in popular amusements seemed to have set in with a rising tide" that had not only opened the door for cricket but also for a wide variety of other bat-and-ball play forms Americans had known for generations.[2]

"Ball playing" had been a feature of America's vernacular play culture since colonial times, with numerous low-skill, unorganized and irregular "folk" bat-and-ball play conducted throughout the country.

This bat-and-ball play existed in its most elementary and unsophisticated form with such pastimes as trap-ball or old cat but also in more organized team forms that existed under numerous and often geographically specific names such as townball, Massachusetts game, rounders and baseball.

This class of bat-and-ball forms of play shared the same basic features of short spells at bat and scoring by the circumnavigation of several stations. But that was all they shared. In all other respects (number of players, forms of out, length determination, etc.) the games differed.[3]

The appearance of organized cricket clubs in New York City during the 1840s almost certainly acted as some form of catalyst for Americans to also develop and elevate some of these pre-modern bat-and-ball games up to an organized level comparable to cricket.

Only one of these pioneer New York baseball clubs, the Knickerbockers, survived the ball-playing "ice age" that set in during the late 1840s. But by the early 1850s the country's renewed sporting fervor had brought forth a handful of newly formed baseball clubs in New York City. By mid-decade, the number of baseball organizations in the city was "noticeably increasing" and it soon became evident this new game was emerging as a serious rival to the more established cricket for popular attention.[4]

The most serious obstacle to baseball's advancement at this period, the diversity of rules under which the game was played, was eliminated at the conventions of New York area baseball clubs held in 1857 and 1858, from which emerged a game played by a single, uniform set of rules. Dubbed, in this format, "The New York game," it was to become the "King's English" among the diverse variations of bat-and-ball play and, bolstered by the cultural influence of the country's largest city, would within little more than a decade sweep away all other variations of baseball from the face of the land.[5]

Baseball had appeared in Philadelphia by the late 1850s but its progress was slow and not without resistance. In addition to cricket, which had an established presence in the city, the New York version of baseball had to contend with Philadelphia's most popular pre-modern baseball form, townball, which had been played in the city on an organized basis since at least the 1830s (Wister and his friends had all been townball players before they took to cricket).[6]

The first baseball game in Philadelphia under the New York rules was reportedly not played until June 11, 1860, and the city was not even represented at the national baseball conventions held annually in New York until 1865.[7]

Once the game had secured a foothold, however, the baseball "mania" began to sweep Philadelphia in 1862 and within three years the game was "all the rage" with "more than a dozen" baseball clubs established in the city by the following year. Among them would be Philadelphia's most prominent baseball organization, the Athletics, originally a townball club that had converted to the New York rules in 1860.[8]

The competition for Philadelphia's bat-and-ball allegiance was now on and over the next few years, while the nation was locked in a bloody civil war, Philadelphia was locked in the less pretentious struggle over which ball-playing form would dominate the city's sporting landscape.

In the beginning the contest seemed evenly balanced, uncertain, and not necessarily a contest for sports dominance as much as the establishment of mutual co-existence between two play forms that, each in its own way, offered equal satisfaction to its participants.

Throughout the city cricketers were now playing baseball and baseball players were also playing cricket. The Camden cricket club played cricket and baseball interchangeably with the Camden baseball club while the Magnolia cricket club got the Keystone baseball club to try its game in 1863. The Olympic cricket club, that same year, along with the Chippewa cricket club, also played baseball with the Keystones. At least one member of the Shibe family, destined to play a long and prominent role in Philadelphia baseball, was at this point playing for the Enterprise cricket club.[9]

This strange gray world of mixed ball-playing loyalties that was unfolding in Philadelphia during these years is probably best seen in the career of the two most talented ball players in the city at that time: John Dickson "Dick" McBride and Thomas Pratt. The first, a lifelong resident of Philadelphia, the latter a transplant from Massachusetts, both began their ball-playing careers with cricket. Numerous "McBrides" appear on the rosters of Philadelphia's smaller cricket clubs in the late 1850s—for example, Frank McBride is listed as the president of the Atlantic cricket club. Dick McBride can first be positively identified as a member of the Ashland cricket club in 1860, though he may have been playing with the Wyoming cricket club as early as 1857 as a ten-year-old. Pratt first appeared with the St. George cricket club of Philadelphia and the Franklin cricket club in 1860.[10]

The ball-playing talent of the two players soon became widely known. McBride, in particular, was not only a fast, deadly, underarm bowler but a fine batter, something that "astonished" the Young America club in its loss, in 1861, to McBride's Chippewa club. The two players were in such high demand that they often appeared in tandem, playing for multiple cricket clubs and routinely contributing outstanding performances such as high scoring (Pratt 43 runs, McBride 21) in their team's match against the Zouaves military regiment recruited by Philadelphia cricket player C.H. Collis in 1862.[11]

By the early 1860s, however, the tide was turning against cricket in Philadelphia. The sporting press couldn't ignore the fact that, by 1863, "young men preferred [baseball] to cricket" throughout the city. Individually more and more cricketers were transferring loyalties, among them the pride and joy of Philadelphia cricket, Sylvanus Kephardt, who, by 1865, had transitioned from the Germantown cricket club to that town's baseball team. Making the most of their transferable bat-and-ball skills, experienced cricket players were now, it was claimed, getting into the starting lineups of area baseball clubs after just a few games.[12]

Eventually these defections extended to entire teams. The Bachelor cricket club, all "old cricketers now persuaded it should be their policy to follow the American trend," migrated *en masse* to baseball in 1865, as the Atlantic cricket club had done as early as 1860. The Camac Woods ground, host of the 1859 All-England cricket match and, up to this time, a site shared equally by area cricket and baseball clubs, had, by 1862, been largely "surrendered" to the city's growing number of baseball clubs.[13]

Inevitably McBride and Pratt also determined that their bat-and-ball skills would have greater career prospects within the city's burgeoning baseball community. Whether the Athletics' baseball club captain D.W. Moore actually recruited McBride and Pratt, as it was claimed, "straight off the commons when they were playing cricket" to his baseball club or not, these two standout cricket players were, by 1862, soon appearing on the city's leading baseball club, the start of long and outstanding baseball careers for both.[14]

Baseball's ascension over cricket in Philadelphia would, however, never be as thorough, complete, or final as it would be in New York City and other metropolitan areas such as Boston and Baltimore. By 1865, the local press conceded most of the city's young men had "thrown aside cricket for baseball," the English game diminishing to a point where now only "five cricket clubs were in the city for every fifty" before the Civil War. This, however, still amounted to eleven known clubs, giving supporters encouragement that "the baseball people haven't quite run the cricketers into the ground."[15]

Cricket still held an allurement, if diminishing, to the city's top bat-and-ball talent. McBride and Pratt continued to linger on the fringes of game, both still playing for the Chippewa cricket club in 1865 and together taking all wickets (got out all the opposing batters) in their club's match against the Olympic cricket club in 1865. McBride evidently still welcomed the competitive opportunity provided by the game, helping the Philadelphia cricket club win its match against the New York cricket club a year earlier. All things considered, the historical record seemed to indicate that baseball, by the end of the Civil War, hadn't so much superseded cricket in Philadelphia as it had "merely surpassed it."[16]

In the span of little over a decade, from the mid–1850s to the end of the Civil War, Americans probably experienced the most far-reaching developments and changes to its sporting culture than it would at any other period in its history. Cricket—the game that in the early 1850s seemed well on course to secure an extensive presence in America and even national status, a sport of established standing and advanced development that originated from the most powerful country in the world—had been completely eclipsed by the unheralded and underdeveloped bat-and-ball game of baseball.

The course of events that had led to all this must have puzzled observers of that time as much as it has scholars to this day, and an explanation of cricket's "failure" as an American sport remains one of the most puzzling perplexities in all sports history.

On a macro-analytic level the rise of cricket and baseball to cultural prominence is far more conveniently explained than the divergent paths subsequently taken by the two games. If it is agreed that cricket and baseball had been the earliest American team sports to emerge as "modern," exhibiting the same features—organization, statistics, role differentiation, uniformity of rules, etc.—that would characterize all future American team sports, and if it is also agreed both games developed under the same changing social conditions in America at that time—increased urbanization, changes in social attitudes towards sports, the growing influence of a sporting press, etc.—the perplexing question immediately arises how these identical inputs of "modernization" that elevated to prominence such structurally similar and socially fulfilling bat-and-ball team sports of cricket and baseball could concurrently bring about such radically different outputs in cultural popularity and acceptance of the two sports?[17]

Because of these interpretive difficulties, other scholars have pursued more narrowly focused explanations within this broad "modernistic" framework, some of considerable analytic sophistication. Of these the most widely circulated are (1) "elitism," that a strata of upper-class "gate keepers" controlled and restricted cricket's popularity to a small segment of American society; (2) "facilities," that cricket's requirement of more specialized playing facilities (well-manicured pitches) than baseball handicapped the game's accessibility; (3) "cultural leaders," that certain prominent and influential individuals associated with baseball were more successful in proselytizing their game with the American public than cricket; and (4) "want of a national pastime," that Americans, as a matter of cultural necessity, demanded a homegrown game, rather than a sport of "foreign origin," as their national pastime.[18]

Though all these constructs have their merits, none have proved to be entirely persuasive and, consequently, no clear consensus, it can be said, has emerged as to why cricket "failed" as an American sport. The subject remains one of the more enduring enigmas of sport history.[19]

The author has long maintained, and continues to maintain, in contrast to these largely conditional interpretations, that the most plausible explanation for cricket's decline vis-à-vis baseball lies in the alternative excitement experiences that are generated from the differing structural character of the two sports, an explanation firmly supported, in contrast to many other interpretations, by the most compelling evidence: the direct testimony of participants and observers of that period.

It can't be denied specific extraneous factors influenced Americans' choice of what sport they would, or would not, play during this period: social class, national identity, ease of access, publicity, etc. But cricket and baseball are both games, and, as with all sports, it ultimately becomes a matter of the emotional appeal of, and expectations from, that sport's core excitement experience. Whatever extraneous obstacles or deterrents an American may have encountered in his involvement with cricket during this formative period, none should have been insurmountable for his continuation in the sport *if he wanted to play cricket.*

The cultural battle between cricket and baseball during this critical juncture in American sports history would be played out on the emotional rather than the conceptual level, ultimately determining which of the two sports' excitement experience would come to successfully "dominate a country's emotional attachments."[20]

To adequately understand and appreciate this interpretation it's necessary to examine, in some detail, the playing structure of the two games and the excitement experience that they respectively generate.

Contrary to long-standing popular perception, cricket and baseball are virtually identical in their core structure and objective: two bat-and-ball team games in which sides alternate batting and fielding, with players on the batting side trying to hit a ball thrown by a player on the fielding side and score runs while the fielding side tries to prevent runs by getting the opposing batters "out." "In cricket or baseball," as one contemporary observer duly noted, "a player runs, strikes, watches, catches, throws, must learn quickness of hand and eye, must learn endurance as well."[21]

Both sports equally offer participants and spectators the thrill generated from the "crack of the bat," the thrill of the "big hit" (home run in baseball, six in cricket), the thrill of the pitcher defeating the batter (strikeout in baseball, bowled in cricket) and the thrill of acrobatic catches and pinpoint throws. In both games the defense begins with the ball and both are played without a clock (to name two features that baseball has traditionally claimed exclusively for itself. Cricket, during this period, was played up to a set time but there was no limit for either an individual's or a team's time at bat).

Although this "generative principle" of action, as a contemporary observer noted, was identical and "equally balanced" in both games, the content of this action (tempo, duration, rhythm, etc.)—what another contemporary observer termed the "superficial differences" within the two game's shared playing structure—unfold very differently.[22]

In baseball the batter must run after hitting a fair ball, which, in some instances, also requires a teammate, if on base, to also run. This requirement immediately initiates a classic "chase scenario," generating the instantaneous excitement of the fielding team trying to beat the batter to the base—what another contemporary observer dubbed "critical occurrences." With the batter's objective to get just a single hit during his time at bat, followed in short sequence by all other batters on his team, this structurally ensures "constant quick change," with a "rapidity with which the sides change" (which occurs regularly with 54 total outs in a baseball game, while there's only twenty outs in a one innings cricket match) and numerous opportunities for put outs, all contributing to the "high pressure" character of baseball with its "numberless varieties and changes." This also ensures that excitement in baseball is generated with a continuous, frequent, though brief, flow of action which "increase the excitement of the player and the zest of the looker on."[23]

In cricket, by contrast, there are no balls or strikes, nor does the batter have to run when he hits the ball. Add to this the cricket batter's limitation of only one time at bat (or, at the most, twice in a two-innings match) in an entire game means that batting excitement here is generated as a more continuous flow rather than a staccato of short batting outbursts. Whereas the baseball batter, being required to run if he hits a fair ball, must adopt a "sledge hammer" approach to batting almost out of necessity, trying to hit every good pitch as hard as he can, the cricket batter, since he bats only once, must often bat carefully and defensively, frequently just blocking pitches from hitting his wicket.

If the cricket batter is facing a talented, hard-to-hit bowler, he may have to bat this way for an extended period of time, resulting in little or no excitement from hitting, running, and scoring. As a Haverford College cricket player of this period pointed out, if the cricket batter just has a mindset of always trying to "send a ball over the fielder's heads," his turn at bat will quickly come to an end from "a ball that coolly takes his wicket" (gets him out).[24]

Every sport is only as exciting as the individuals who are playing it, and this is especially true in cricket. Here the excitement level very much depends on the skill and mindset of the individual batter. If the batter adopts a stance of playing carefully and cautiously, few runs will be generated and fewer chances for put outs occur, leading to the "slowness" widely attributed to cricket. An American humorist of this period, Mortimer Thompson, writing under the pseudonym of

Q. Philander Doesticks, lampooned this situation in his widely circulated account of a cricket match during this period, denigrating the game as "a solemn ceremony periodically performed by deluded Englishmen who think they're having fun."[25]

There is, however, a flip side to all this. Unlike his baseball counterpart, the cricket batter doesn't come out after scoring a run but continues to bat and score runs until the fielding team can get him out. To best illustrate this feature, an analogy with basketball is more appropriate. Just as the star basketball player thrills spectators (and presumably himself) by scoring as many points as possible in a continuous, unbroken sequence of action over the entire game, defying all attempts by the opposing team to stop him, so a talented cricket batter can thrill crowds by scoring continuously over an extended period of time, defying all attempts by the opposing team to get him out and thus providing a continuous stream of batting excitement that baseball is incapable of duplicating.

This has always been one of cricket's most powerful appeals and one certainly recognized and appreciated by Americans involved with the game during this period. George Wright—star shortstop for the Boston Red Stockings in the 1870s and future Baseball Hall of Fame inductee, who began and ended his sports career playing cricket and thus became one of the few players of both sports at the highest competitive level—personally found this the most compelling appeal of cricket: "There is really more science and enjoyment for the player in cricket. There are a hundred points in batting that one has to bear in mind and the avoidance of a difficulty or the accomplishment of a pet stroke gives much pleasure to the player. I do not think the spectator has much of this pleasure. Give me cricket to play and baseball to look at."[26]

Though starting from almost identical, basic, ball-playing structures, baseball and cricket, it should now be clear, can generate very different bat-and-ball excitement experiences in tempo, duration, and episodic frequency. As the late 19th-century Philadelphia cricket star Frank Bohlen summarized it, "the main interest [in cricket] lies in method; in the other [baseball] in action."[27]

Significant as the interior action of a sport is for its appeal, just as critical is the game's length determination: over what period of time is the excitement generated by the game to be carried to the satisfaction of both participants and spectators. Historically, both baseball and cricket struggled with this issue. Baseball, early in its organizational development, came to a satisfactory resolution; cricket, even to this day, has not.

In traditional cricket, the fielding side must get out ten of the eleven batters on the opposing team, one after the other, before it can come to bat. Since batters continue to bat until they are out, a team with many skillful batters can extend the time at bat over a long period. And when the fielding team comes up, it, as well, bats through its entire order the same way. Although, in theory, an entire cricket side can be put out in as few as ten total pitches (just as an entire baseball team can, in theory, be put out in just twenty-seven total pitches), a match in cricket's traditional format at this time might have to be extended over several days to allow both teams to have all their batters come up, bat, and be put out. And if both sides don't have an opportunity to bat completely through their orders by the end of the agreed-upon playing time, the match ends at that point and is declared a "draw" without a winner no matter what the score, a very unsatisfactory conclusion for all involved.

Baseball established its length determination over an extended period of trial and error. In many of the pre-modern "folk" versions of baseball the game was played under a "target score" arrangement, with the first team to reach a pre-determined run total—sometimes as high as a hundred runs—the winner.[28]

The drawbacks with such an arrangement were obvious to players and observers even at that time. Between mismatched sides the game could be decided in an unsatisfactorily short time. If the teams were evenly matched, the game might extend over an unacceptably long period of time before it could be concluded (if, for example, modern baseball games were decided by the first team to score, say, six runs, this total might be reached in only two or three innings of play—or it might not be reached until twenty innings had been played).

The pioneer New York baseball club of the 1840s, the Knickerbockers, ameliorated this drawback somewhat by playing their games to a target score of only twenty-one runs. Yet the game was still played under the handicap of an open-ended and, hence, indeterminate length of time and many early baseball games of this period were completed over the widely variable lengths of between two and sixteen innings.[29]

This flaw was remedied at the New York baseball conventions convened by the city's baseball clubs in 1857 and 1858. Tasked with putting together a set of single, uniform rules for all the area's baseball clubs, the convention discarded the Knickerbocker target score of twenty-one runs for a total determined by nine, three-out, innings per side.[30]

It was probably the single most significant development in the entire history of baseball. Although getting 54 total outs was still, in effect, an "open ended" game determination, since the batters were required to run on every fair hit, this arrangement structurally ensured baseball games would henceforth be completed over a length of time that would provide sufficient, but not excessive, activity for the enjoyment of both players and spectators.

In 1872, a reporter for the New York *World*, in one of the few objective and non-partisan evaluations of baseball and cricket at this time, drew the correct and logical conclusion from all this: "On the whole it must be apparent to every unprejudiced critic that these games [baseball and cricket] are equally balanced. One is weak in one place and stronger in another than its rival and there is no very decided superiority or inferiority at any one point in either."[31]

With two such bat-and-ball excitement experiences available to Americans in the 1850s, each with its own excitement content, the question immediately arises: why did Americans almost instinctively prefer the excitement experience generated by one game over the other? Why would Americans prefer the excitement experience of baseball over cricket, while Australians, South Africans, and New Zealanders, who came from a British colonial background and shared so many other cultural values and preferences with Americans, would prefer the excitement experience of cricket over baseball? Why did the British journalist covering the American baseballers touring England in 1874 find the action of this American bat-and-ball game "monotonous," while Robert Fitzgerald, manager of the English cricket team touring the United States two years earlier, fully concede that, despite cricket's technical sophistication, Americans "are not charmed with monotony, even if it is high art"?[32]

To observers of the time, this was attributable to the "American temperament." Americans were just "predisposed" to the quick ebb-and-flow excitement pattern generated by baseball, and cricket's extended, methodical excitement pattern was "at variance with the Americans temperament" and out of sync with the "inclinations of volatile Americans."[33]

Recourse to "national temperament" or "national character" as an analytic tool has always been suspect, if only because of its imprecieseness and anecdotal character. But since "historians tend to see themselves as dealing with real people and events rather than abstracted texts and phenomena," this imprecision does not mean non-existence, and here the assertion may have some validity on the basis of two compelling observations: (1) the pervasive presence of "safe haven" and "cyclical" forms of bat-and-ball games in all areas of the United States from earliest times and (2) the uniformity of response and attraction to this form of bat-and-ball excitement with Americans of all ages, classes, backgrounds and geographic locations who, conversely, have uniformly shown a revulsion to the excitement experience associated with cricket. This cultural posture has remained resolutely unchanged over six generations.[34]

Although many more abstract reasons may be put forward to explain this persistent and pervasive sporting preference, any such claims, in the words of George Wright, now speaking as a baseball player, "have not consulted our common human nature" and would be at odds with, and contrary to, observed behavior. If human culture, as the renowned German historian Jacob Burckhardt defined it, is "the millionfold process by which the spontaneous unthinking activity of a race is transformed into considered action" Americans unthinking sense of excitement had fully emerged as their "considered action" in modern baseball.[35]

American cricket supporters, of course, could have tried to modify cricket's traditional laws (officially called "laws," not rules) to alter the games excitement structure, but two things stood in their way. The English immigrant community viewed the rules of their game as sacrosanct, rules that had endured over centuries, and strongly resisted any proposed alterations. Perhaps because of their standing as novices in the game, and awed by cricket's revered traditions, Americans during this period complied with this stance. When he and his acquaintances played in the 1840s, Philadelphia cricketer Barnett Phillips recalled "we dared make no innovations" to accepted cricket rules. Additionally, whenever Americans played against English sides, either domestically or against visiting overseas English teams, they would, and could, only play by the officially recognized laws of the game without modification. In short, if Americans wanted to play the game against the best English teams, they would either have to play the way the English played or not at all. As we shall see, Philadelphia cricket would struggle mightily with this issue throughout its history.[36]

Baseball, by contrast, developed under no such extra-cultural constraints. The game would undergo many modifications and changes over the 19th century through trial and error, all with the sole objective of settling onto a form that optimized bat-and-ball excitement by Americans for Americans. The significance played by this cultural "malleability" which made it possible for baseball to assume "national characteristics" without conformity to any trans-national standards or authority should never by underestimated in the game's ascent to the status of a national pastime.[37]

If this interpretative model is accepted, it could then, perhaps, be more correct to claim cricket didn't so much "fail" because external conditions or obstacles prevented or deterred Americans from playing the game as much as it was the cricket community's refusal, or inability, to comply with American society's ultimatum: *Either bring your sport into conformity and alignment with America's specific expectations of bat-and-ball excitement or fail.* Do this or doom cricket, as the *New York Times* would later explain it, to forever be "led off in the wrong direction."[38]

With cricket, Americans had, in the mid-1800s, been bequeathed a complete, fully developed sporting culture: a modern, highly organized, and technically advanced sport of established social value. Here was a game that had liberated Americans from their pre-modern sporting existence of "puerile child's play," constrained by a "miss nancyish morality" for a new reality of sports as "manly" and "scientific," a powerful new social force—according to the *New York Times*—that would "form a very distinct element of social and national life" in the country's future.[39]

All this the immigrant English community presented as "an inducement held out to our Americans friends to join heart and hand."[40]

But America would decline to enter this sporting world, and what has been interpreted as America's "rejection" of cricket was, more correctly, a *selective accommodation*. America jettisoned the excitement content of cricket yet fully retained many other features of this "foreign" sporting experience (competitive structure, social justification, "scientific" technique, etc.) necessary for a modern bat-and-ball sport to secure a permanent place in American society. Cricket's influence would, culturally, extend no further than providing Americans with the *cultural confidence* to build up, from their own pre-modern ball-playing traditions, an impressive bat-and-ball sporting culture of their own, anchored solely and entirely on their own expectations of bat-and-ball excitement. It would quickly become a sporting world so intensely emotional and satisfying that this appeal would alone trump all the impressive inducements cricket could hold out to Americans.[41]

Four

Guardian of a Sporting Alternative

As the accepted cultural expression of America's bat-and-ball excitement experience, baseball, following the Civil War, rapidly swept across the country in one of the most impressive social movements in United States history, an unstoppable engine propelling forward what was now clearly America's established sporting culture.

But baseball now faced the challenge of dealing with the consequences of its popularity, especially with its perceived moral purpose and benefits for its participants, something that, as would soon become apparent, radically altered in just a few years.

Here extreme caution must be exercised not to fall into the temptation of projecting the contemporary mindset Americans have towards baseball that has accumulated over five generations—a game of unquestioned positive social value—onto the mindset of this, the very first, generation of Americans towards baseball—an appealing yet novel activity of still uncertain social standing and value.

During its antebellum years baseball was a game played largely for its motives subservient to competitive superiority. Here was an "innocent" pastime indulged in for its benefits to health and as an occasion for positive social interaction, motives that had themselves long been identified with cricket.[1]

These sporting motives, however, were increasingly giving way to the intensifying emotional pressure of competitive success, a trend clearly becoming evident in a letter to the *Philadelphia Inquirer* in late 1860. Taking issue with an earlier letter that espoused baseball's equivalence to cricket as a "noble game," the correspondent derided baseball's identification with such a "Quixotic affectation." Americans didn't play this game to duplicate the "tedium and ceremony of cricket" but primarily as "an effort to take advantage of your opponent whenever you can." Baseball was, to be sure, a game, like cricket, of "uncommon manliness," but it was, above all, a field of action for those participants "whose perception is alert to the opening in his opponent's armor through which he can thrust his lance."[2]

The specter of fanaticism was settling in upon baseball and the "eminently social" character of its sister sport cricket was being rapidly cast aside with increasingly visible and disconcerting consequences.

Charles Newcomb, one of the first American "intellectuals" to turn his attention to sports, pinpointed the crux of the matter, declaring "excitement is, in itself, wildness," a dangerous element that can quickly transform sports into an experience of "emotional hostility." The *Philadelphia Inquirer*, as well, was troubled with the spirit of "revengeful retaliation" seeping into the baseball in its city by 1865. Years earlier the *Clipper* had seen the same signs in the baseball games it now observed. The spirit of factionalism and hostility was "replacing kindly feelings with hated and manly emulation and generous rivalry with revengeful retaliation," seeing in these degrading developments nothing less than a social retrogression to the "riotous proceedings that have been recorded for a hundred years past."[3]

There may no longer be any doubts over what baseball *was* to Americans: a wildly exuberant, emotional, activity. But as the excesses of this emotionalism came more and more to the forefront, there was a growing chorus of concern over what baseball *was doing* to Americans.

The *Clipper* may have consoled the public with the assertion "if anything is carried to the extreme, baseball is certainly the most harmless" even when this was also so palpably leading straight to a very harmful "spirit of faction." All this must have raised serious doubts whether sports were fulfilling the expectations of contributing to that social improvement with Americans envisioned by the *Clipper*, one where "a vast improvement in the character of the race is now coming upon the carpet ... more fearless and independent in action and more deserving the reputation for intelligence and ability which has always been their boast."[4]

Mesmerized by baseball's meteoric growth immediately after the Civil War, sports historians, though well aware that with the game's rising popularity came a not "unambiguous moral image of organized baseball," have also been mildly oblivious to the depth and extent that baseball was, during these years, "in an unstable condition" morally, a state that not only raised doubts about the game's social desirability but also its very legitimacy as a "national pastime."[5]

Like all social movements of intense partisanship and fanatical following, baseball quickly became a magnet for the Victorian underworld of gamblers and con-men, further tarnishing the game's standing and reputation with increasing accusations of corruption, thrown games, and dishonest players. By the late 1860s, sports observers were repelled by how baseball was descending into a "carnival of betting," turning many clubs into "little more than gambling operations."[6]

The emergence of professional baseball in the 1870s seemed to only compound the game's disfavor with the public, such a perfect storm of corrupt clubs, players, and administrators that it led the Detroit *Free Press* to outright proclaim that "what is called our national sport is only a species of individual degradation—a gamester's pursuit—outraging athletic exercise and insulting to the good manners of intelligent people."[7]

The *New York Times*, not a particular friend of baseball during this period, went a step further, calling into question the game's very claim to national status. "Baseball is not, in itself, considered a subject of positively national importance ... its claim to be considered a peculiarly national game does not rest upon a very strong foundation." Doubts about the very presence of a game of such moral degradation had been raised years earlier by the Philadelphia *Evening Telegraph*, which outright declared that it "would be better to have no game than what we fear it will become."[8]

As a sport, baseball was, above all, an activity of personal participation and observers directed their harshest criticism towards the baseball-playing fraternity, especially the heretofore unknown phenomenon in American team sports, the professional ballplayer.

Here was an individual who no longer participated in sport for the honorable motives of health or personal pleasure but as an unapologetic means of livelihood. As such, the professional baseball player was viewed as the portal for all the game's ills, eminently vulnerable to corruption in his occupation and immorality in his character. Here were individuals "recruited from the idle, shiftless, and yet ambitious class of mortals," in most cases "men without social standing, perhaps without character, depraved, ignorant" who should be "completely suppressed."[9]

None of these critics were completely placated by the baseball reformers who masterminded the formation of the National Baseball League in 1876. Albert Spalding and William Hulbert who, for all their high-profile moves to rid their new league of corrupt influences, never carried this to the extent of jeopardizing the commercial viability of the organization. To Spalding himself, the first obligation of every baseball player, at least a paid player, was not social conformity but competitive performance. "When a baseballer," according to Spalding, "dons his Base Ball suit he says good bye to society, dofts his gentility and becomes—just a ball player."[10]

With baseball falling far short of its anticipated and promised social benefits, some sections of the American sporting public inevitably began to look to alternative sporting experiences more worthy of involvement. Some observers of the time believed that they could find this in cricket.

After a further decade of continued degradation with the country's national pastime, the *New York Times*, still the *bete noire* of baseball, offered its most protracted anti-baseball editorial, extending its earlier criticism of baseball to an outright call for an alternative to the national pastime and declaring that "the time is now ripe for the revival of cricket.... Our experience with the national game of baseball has been sufficiently thorough to convince us that it was in the beginning a sport unworthy of men, and that it is now, in its fully developed state, unworthy of gentlemen."[11]

This was, of course, only the voice of America's moral leaders, the "better part" of American society that had been most repelled by baseball and, as such, could, and would, be effectively ignored by the country's sporting majority.[12]

For other sports-interested Americans, however—those who, by agency or perceived self-appointment, qualified as the moral guardians of society—cricket became viewed as a very viable sporting option. Over the balance of the century the game was looked on as a desirable alternative team sport for these Americans, a sentiment that took institutional expression in the formation of the more selective and affluent cricket clubs that emerged in the country's largest metropolitan areas such as New York, Boston, Pittsburg, Chicago, Detroit and, above all, Philadelphia.

The sporting ethos that sustained cricket at these American clubs was largely an extension of that which had emerged in English cricket over the first half of the 19th century. There cricket, like early baseball, had endured a period of social disfavor, beset by gambling and the appearance of professionalism over the 1820s to 1840s.[13]

English cricket, however, underwent considerable transformation and social alteration during that period when Britain's upper classes began to take the game under their wing through the elite public schools and universities, stripping cricket of its competitive excesses so that the game "was able to be absorbed more readily into a culture of refinement and restraint." Thoroughly identified with fair play, gentlemanly behavior, and obedience to authority, cricket would now become an institution "synonymous for all that is fair and above board," a game in which it was "better to lose right than win wrong."[14]

The role of professionals in English cricket also underwent significant change. At mid-century English professionals largely operated as independent practitioners, organizing teams and fixtures among themselves and playing in well-attended matches throughout the country. With the rise of large, heavily patronized, county cricket clubs this independence declined and professional players had to increasingly find employment with established clubs. Here, however, they were forced to play with, and were under the captaincy of, the club's amateur players, who were almost invariably individuals from the country's elite public schools, universities, or even peerage and ensured the moral standards of the game were rigidly maintained. They effectively relegated professional cricket players to a status of moral, and economic, subordination.[15]

This arrangement had, in its general features, been largely replicated by the larger immigrant English cricket clubs in the United States, such as the New York St. George club, whose middle- and upper-class members hired and oversaw their club's predominantly working-class professionals and also ensured the game's moral standards were maintained.

In Philadelphia the moral leadership of the game was, with the establishment of the Philadelphia cricket club, assumed not by the English, but by the city's American upper and middle classes who, though they also enlisted the assistance of English professionals, regarded themselves as the sole guardians of the game's moral integrity. It was a social arrangement all Philadelphia's other large, propertied cricket clubs would effectively duplicate.

It shouldn't be assumed that the divergent sporting ethos that was developing around cricket—the "spirit of the game" as opposed to baseball's "the spirit of competition"—was simply an orientation along class lines or economic status or the differentiation between amateurism and professionalism. Those in the cricket community saw in the game and its traditions nothing less than the most legitimate and socially desirable arrangement for all individuals involved with sports.[16]

The *locus classicus* that explains and delineates the differing outcomes and expectations from these two sports ethos can be found in H.J. Whigham's article in the September/October 1909 issue of *The Outlook* magazine, which discusses the differing attitudes of the British and Americans about sports.[17]

Starting from the premise that "keenness to win is as characteristic of one race as the other," the author squarely identifies the differing sports outlook of the two nations in their differences regarding the "real attitude of mind towards sport." The preoccupation of Americans with winning encourages, even requires, extreme specialization and hence the prevalence and encouragement of the "expert" in their sports, the professional, who must, in his pursuit of the highest level of sporting proficiency, subordinate all his energies and life activity to this single end. For the English athlete, this orientation is "all wrong" because it inherently diminishes the athlete's personality and "it is essentially the mark of a bourgeois mind to specialize." To Whigham, the primary purpose of sports is to provide a field, an outlet, for the full development of the individual's full range of capacities and abilities, not just one. For an individual to submit to the intense, all-consuming demands of specialization represents a subversion of the personality "for that would upset all the balance of character." The highly specialized athlete, in the process of his all-consuming athletic end purpose, diminishes himself as a man because "the man who practices desperately hard [is regarded] as a poor kind of creature." The severest criticism of the highly specialized (almost invariably professional) athlete is not that he pursues his sport under an extraneous motive, either financial or otherwise, but that it retards him in his full development as an individual. "You cannot acquire great proficiency in any game without" Whigham claims, "sacrificing some of the attitudes of a well-balanced mind." Ultimately the author sees in the more undesirable features of American sports something that goes far beyond the field of play: attitudes that "are contrary to all his [English] conceptions not merely of sport, but of the right way to live."[18]

To the cricket community, including its followers in America, to be an "amateur" wasn't a matter of engaging in sports without compensation or even "for the love of the game" (a motive that can be fully shared by a professional). It was to engage in sport as *the physical expression of the overall accomplished individual.* In modern, sports-minded society, this was becoming an increasingly noteworthy field of personal accomplishment, but only a complementary one, never to be subverted by an over-consuming attention and preoccupation that distorts and restricts the overall higher capabilities of man.

This sporting ethos identified with cricket, in short, was perceived as a training regimen of the personality that put the participant on a path of independence, leadership, and moral rectitude, an inclusive experience that "builds up a finer man altogether."[19]

From start to finish, the proper Philadelphia cricket community would support, adopt, and defend this sporting outlook, a sporting world in which its participants "strive not only to be good cricket players but good men—in fact, gentlemen," and one that ensured that their sport could stand before the scrutiny of society as the "only athletic game ... in which all degrading influences have been carefully eliminated." Little wonder that in its inaugural issue on June 20, 1877, the *American Cricketer* proclaimed on its banner head "No selfish, conceited, lazy, irritable man can be a first class cricketer."

Not only did cricket, in the nature of its play, inherently reinforce these desirable individual/social qualities but it also assumed these qualifies with its adherents to the game. In both instances, cricket was valued as a game that elevates an element in its play above and beyond the immediate excitation of play excitement.[20]

Above all, these Philadelphians valued their cricket as a preparation, an enculturation, towards the higher obligations of their class. Whereas experience was demonstrating, among many top baseball players, "excellence in professional play tends to unfit him for any useful sphere hereafter," whose sporting involvement contributed little to what Philadelphia cricket player Charles Newhall termed the "collateral scope of life," the cricket played by proper Philadelphians was always viewed as "a preparation for a higher game of some sort," an activity where "young men can attain mastery in athletic sports without neglecting any of those duties which makes them useful members of society." It was always assumed, by this cricket-playing strata, that those who gave a good account of themselves on the cricket field would invariably give "a good account of themselves in the more serious duties of life."[21]

Probably more than any other single American sporting fraternity in the 19th century did the Philadelphia cricket community personally come to exemplify this sporting outlook of the "gentleman athlete," the individual whose highest athletic accomplishments were a pathway to, not a disqualification from, these "more serious duties" of personal and career accomplishments.

A sampling: Among Philadelphia's standout international cricket players, George Patterson and Frank Bohlen, both of the Germantown cricket club, would go onto distinguished legal careers, the former in the city attorney's office and the latter as a law professor at the University of Pennsylvania and author of a highly respected work on torts. Percy Clark, also from the Germantown club, would go onto a successful career in law and banking (one of his daughters would marry Nelson Rockefeller). J. Henry Scattergood of the Merion cricket club would hold directorships in numerous companies and help found the Alpine Club. His Merion teammate, John Lester, after receiving his PhD from Harvard, settled into a career in academia. Reynolds Brown, another Germantown cricketer, would also become a law professor at the University of Pennsylvania. Fred Sharpless and J. Allison Scott would become physicians, the latter appearing in the famous Thomas Eakins painting *The Agnew Clinic*.[22]

Among the Halifax Cup cricketers, George Wharton Pepper of the Germantown club would represent Pennsylvania in the United States Senate. John P. Green, of the Belmont cricket club, would become a vice president of the Pennsylvania Railroad while his teammate, John Colahan, would become president of the Pennsylvania Bar Association. Howard McNutt of the Young America club would compose music for light opera while William Foulkrod, Jr., of the Frankford cricket club, would become president of the Southwark Bank. Milton Work, also of the Belmont club, would attain something of a celebrity status as one of the country's foremost bridge experts.[23]

To the proper Philadelphia society that played or supported the game it may have been that "professionalism is a repugnant idea to American cricketers." But professionalism had been part of American cricket from its earliest years as an organized sport, even in Philadelphia, and was, as such, a sporting presence that had to be accommodated.[24]

The larger Philadelphia cricket clubs that could afford to hire professionals generally adopted, at the outset, the English model of subordinating the professional (in all instances, professional cricket players in the United States were either resident English immigrants or players recruited from England) to a role of strengthening teams of predominantly amateur American players. This model had been established by the Philadelphia cricket club from its very beginning with the hiring of Tom Senior before the Civil War, who was succeeded after the war by Job Pearson. The Germantown club followed suit by hiring William Hammond. The Young America club, true to its purpose of "self-reliance," would not hire a professional until 1883, and even then, he would be confined to coaching the club's junior players.[25]

With duties that also included individual coaching and training these club's junior players, the cadre of English professionals was tasked with elevating the overall standard of cricket playing in the city; in effect, to minimize the very need for professional reliance, which seemed to be the tacit intention of the Philadelphia cricket community. Only Americans were on the side that played the English MCC team that stopped in the city during its North American tour in 1872 as well as the Philadelphia side that played in the Halifax, Canada, tournament in 1874.[26]

Any expectations of rapid competitive advancement with only Americans players, however, received a hard dose of reality in the city's crushing loss to Wilshire's team of English professionals that visited Philadelphia in 1868. Nor had the competitive gap between the city's American players and English professional players significantly diminished by the time Lord Harris brought an English team to America eleven years later. This "rump" team of English professionals stopped in New York in its "spare time" on the way home from Australia just long enough to administer, even without four of its starting players, including Harris himself, a sound thrashing to a combined New York/Philadelphia side. Philadelphia's competitive deficiency was further exposed that fall of 1879 when another team of English professionals, captained by Richard Daft, testing the North American market as a potential post-season source of income, made "mince meat of their American cousins," easily defeating the Philadelphia side, even with the home team allowed to play fifteen against eleven.[27]

This long, discouraging procession of defeats forced the Philadelphians to concede that, against top English pro cricketers, it was "useless for our unpracticed resident cricketers to attempt to play foreign professional teams with any hope of winning." An additional source of cricket talent had to be tapped and the Philadelphia cricket community had little choice but to turn to that class of cricket players it had traditionally shunned.[28]

The decision, at some point in the late 1870s, to boost the city's competitive prospects by bringing on board more English professionals was made easier because the move had been encouraged by Daft himself who was confident that Philadelphia cricket would be materially improved with the assistance, by way of coaching and direct participation, of some good English professionals. Philadelphia heeded the advice and in 1880 or 1881 the Germantown club hired George Bromhead, the Philadelphia cricket club Henry Tyers, both personally recommended by Daft himself. The Belmont cricket club independently took on the talented Nottinghamshire cricketer Arthur Wood while the Merion club had already hired English professional Charles Braithwaite.[29]

Expectations that this infusion of professional talent would immediately boost the prospects for the city's representative sides against foreign competition were, however, soon dashed. Alfred Shaw's team of English professionals, stopping over in North America en route to Australia in 1881, routed a combined Philadelphia/New York/Boston side that was assisted by no fewer than seven professionals, four of whom were out for ducks (a score of 0), the three Philadelphia professionals hired a year earlier contributing a meager nineteen total runs. A greater disappointment came the following year when a representative Australian side, stopping in Philadelphia on its way home from England, inflicted a severe defeat on a home side that included three professionals. It was a particularly bitter defeat, since the Philadelphia side that had managed to secure a draw against largely the same Australian team four years earlier had only included amateur players.[30]

These results must have initiated some intense soul-searching within the Philadelphia cricket community and a close re-evaluation of the decision to enroll professionals into its representative sides. Who was spearheading this movement is not known, but the Young America club (or likely the club's Newhall brothers who, as well as being among the city's best amateur cricket players, were also known for their highly pro–American leanings) was most likely involved.

The Young America club was well justified in its hostility towards professional players. The organization had been victimized numerous times by professionals on the opposing Philadelphia clubs it played in the years after the Civil War (Philadelphia club professional Job Pearson and Germantown's Martin McIntyre had almost single-handedly beaten the Young America team numerous times) and the club's suicidal attempt to take on Daft's professionals with even sides only resulted in a disastrous and humiliating loss. The Young America club even preferred to cancel its scheduled match against a side of visiting Irish amateurs in 1879 rather than play against a team that was going to let a professional player, Arnold Rylott, umpire the match.[31]

After what was reportedly a period of intense debate, Philadelphia cricket authorities adopted a new policy sometime shortly after the Australian match in 1882. Even though it was now evident that "amateurs can never meet professionals on equal terms in any undertaking whatsoever," the decision was made to ban professionals from all representative Philadelphia sides and from that point in time to the very last days of Philadelphia cricket no professional would ever again play for representative Philadelphia teams against foreign opponents.[32]

With the adoption of this radical all-amateur policy, Philadelphia cricket had set itself on a path of total reliance upon the development of homegrown talent, fully aware of, but willing to accept, the competitive consequences. No matter how discouraging the competitive results were to be, the city's cricket community would never alter its determination that "it would be better for this country to continue to play ... cricket than to improve the game by hiring men to devote their whole time to it." To further emphasize what their cricket now stood for, Philadelphia's representative teams would, from this point on, only play under the title of "The Gentlemen of Philadelphia," a purely amateur team that would compete with no assistance from, or partnership with, professional players.[33]

The anti-pro sentiment, however, didn't stop with the selection of representative teams. After what must have been further considerations of the long-term future of the city's cricket, the decision was made to also ban professionals from the Halifax Cup and, beginning in 1885, no professionals would be allowed to play in the city's premier cricket competition.[34]

If there had been any opposition to this policy of barring professionals from representative sides, it didn't seem to be significant. Not so with the plan to extend the ban to the Halifax Cup matches. With all but one of the clubs that competed in that competition employing professionals, the ban would have immediately affected a shift in the competitive balance among the participating clubs. The Young America, with no professionals, would have been the most obvious beneficiary. Belmont would have suffered the most, as it seemed to be the Halifax Cup club most welcoming to foreigners (its American vs English members match in 1882, so common with other American cricket clubs at this time, seems to have been the one and only such match of its kind ever played in Philadelphia). The Merion club, with three professionals on its staff, threatened to outright withdraw from the competition if the policy was adopted.[35]

The sentiment in favor of amateur reliance, however, was by now

Four. Guardian of a Sporting Alternative

becoming irresistible and all the Halifax Cup clubs eventually came on board, as did a number of smaller non–Halifax Cup clubs, which, following the trend, voluntarily barred pros from their matches as well. The city's anti-pro stance reached its finale three years later with the prohibition of pros from also playing in matches for the Club Record Cup awarded to the club with the best combined 1st, 2nd, and junior team results, as well as the disqualification of any professional from receiving the Childs Cup awarded annually to the city's top batter and bowler.[36]

Having started from English cricket's model of socially segregating but competitively integrating professionals, Philadelphia had now gone to the radical extreme of total disbarment of professionals from all its significant domestic and international competitions.

The professional cricket player in Philadelphia now saw his playing horizons limited to non–Halifax Cup matches, inter-city matches and the occasional American vs English contest (often styled, à la England, as "Gentlemen vs Players" matches). With the primary responsibility of their professionals now confined to the assigned roles of coaching, grounds keeping and umpiring (the anti-pro drive had not denied them this important function), Philadelphia cricket had sent a clear message to the English cricket community, at both home and abroad, that any professional who contemplated a move to the Quaker City would have to virtually abandon any aspirations for a career in high-level cricket competition.[37]

Not surprisingly, this marginalization didn't go unopposed by Philadelphia's cadre of professional players that declared the intention, in 1882, of forming its own national all-pro cricket team, contemplated a tour to Australia, and even planned to form its own national association. But these countermoves were half-hearted and never progressed any further than a few local matches and a game between an all-pro team and Baltimore.[38]

Individually Philadelphia's professional cricketers adjusted to these diminished competitive horizons in their own way. George Bromhead seemed content to accept his prescribed role as coach, umpire, and groundsman, even accompanying the Gentlemen of Philadelphia side on its 1903 tour of England as team manager. Rare among the resident English professionals, Bromhead would pass his entire life in Philadelphia and end his career as a revered figure in the city's cricket community, a personality known for his "clear soul and inner nobility."[39]

Some, like Arthur Woodcock, hired as Haverford College's cricket coach in 1889, found a happy medium, spending his spring coaching and even playing alongside his American students and returning to England in the summer to resume his first-class playing career.[40]

Others, however, would bounce around from club to club in the larger American cities, going where the opportunities would arise. Such was the path followed by Germantown's first professional, William Hammond, who moved on from Philadelphia to New York, eventually ending his career, in 1870, as manager of the Boston baseball club grounds.[41]

As America emerged from the Civil War, it had firmly institutionalized its emotional attachments to the sporting experience contained in baseball, unconditionally accepting that "the furor of base ball playing rises superior to all obstacles." But as undesirable social consequences began to arise from this unchecked intensity, a certain stratum of American society would continue to identify with an alternative sporting ethos, one that demanded that the intense emotional attachment of sports be subordinated to higher social purposes, and this social strata would look to cricket to satisfy these expectations.[42]

Just how sharply contrasting were the sporting realities that could arise from these alternative outlooks were demonstrably revealed to the Philadelphia public with two major occurrences in the 1870s.

The first was a cricket match in fall 1872 between a representative Philadelphia side and a visiting team from the Marylebone Cricket Club, the governing organization of English cricket at that time (and always referred to as "the MCC"). The sporting public witnessed a close, tense, and exciting match where, at its dramatic finish, "the atmosphere was electric," according to W.G. Grace, a member of the English team and at the start of a career that would make him the greatest of all English cricket batters. This intensity, however, was always moderated by a spirit of cordiality and propriety, where "utmost good humor prevailed" among players and spectators and "not one single question arose," MCC manager Robert Fitzgerald recalled, "between us and our antagonists to disturb the harmony." Followed by an enriching post-match reception and entertainment, the entire event exemplified what cricket supporters always honored in their game: an activity that, above all, was to "harmonize a people."[43]

Three years later, the Philadelphia public witnessed the realities of a far different sporting world unfold around the city's flagship professional baseball club, the Athletics. Chronically plagued by mismanagement, player/owner antagonism, and accusations of corruption, the club, also infested with "the influence of meanness or vulgarity," slid into organizational chaos and disintegration. By 1876, the organization that had excelled under Dick McBride's leadership was outright expelled from the professional baseball league despite its championship win during the league's inaugural season five years earlier.[44]

For the next half century, Philadelphia, with its cricket, would almost single-handedly champion, build, and exemplify this alternative sporting world, a world built around a game that epitomized society's and the individual's highest moral purposes, attributes that, in their estimation, more than compensated for their sport's limited popular appeal.

"They say that cricket is a slow game," conceded the *Philadelphia Times* a decade on, while also reminding the American sporting public, with the stinging rebuke, "but they do not say that cricket games are bought or sold."[45]

FIVE

Young America, the Hargreaves Family, and the Assertion of Nativism

Cricket's presence in the United States in the latter half of the 19th century was in an unusual state of affairs. The game had been, and would remain, predominantly an institution of the English immigrant community. In other English colonies such as Australia, New Zealand, and South Africa this immigrant identity would be subsumed, even obliterated, as cricket, with no bat-and-ball rival, was progressively absorbed into the local populace, a pathway baseball's dominant presence largely made impossible in America.

Cricket, in effect, now existed in the United States as something of a sporting *imperium in imperio* and Americans involved with the game faced the decision of affiliating with the game's English community or attempting to assert a distinctly American identity and direction. It would unfold as one of the greatest challenges Philadelphia cricket would face.

Though cricket in Philadelphia had been "superseded" by baseball in popularity and public attention by the end of the Civil War, the game's more dedicated followers continued to involve themselves with the sport, even harboring the now unrealistic expectations that their game "bids fair to again become as popular as it was when the great international match was played in Camden [sic]." Cricket's antebellum popularity had permeated to such a depth that the game was, even now, still seen as an activity as worthy of local emulation and pride as baseball, the local press, in 1865, demanding Philadelphia "must fly the whip [championship pennant] in cricket as well as baseball."[1]

The city's three leading antebellum cricket clubs, Philadelphia, Germantown, and Young America, quickly revived with the return of peace, rebuilding their war-depleted membership rolls (the Philadelphia club had increased its membership from 58 in 1864 to 179 by 1868). As further evidence of the game's renewal, General George Meade—native son and Gettysburg hero—even dedicated the new and improved Germantown club grounds at Nicetown in 1865.[2]

Other antebellum clubs also revived and re-organized, such as the Olympic club, the leading non–Halifax Cup organization, as did the Osceola, bringing the number of identifiable post-war cricket clubs in Philadelphia to at least eleven.[3]

Nor was the era of cricket expansion yet over.

On October 5, 1865, a small group of young men in the northwest part of the city, led by Maskell Ewing and William Montgomery, founded the Merion cricket club, following up on an idea reportedly hatched on a walking tour in the Bryn Mawr hills. The young men, most of whom "had never played cricket before," signed on to play once a week. Their club was the last of a long line of Philadelphia cricket clubs initiated as "little more than a frolic of a few merry boys," but one that would endure far longer and play a much greater role in Philadelphia cricket.[4]

Memories of their antebellum enjoyment with cricket probably led John P. Green and fifteen friends to organize the Belmont cricket club nine years later on September 3, 1874. Located in west Philadelphia, closer to the city than its sister suburban clubs, the Belmont club would become known as "essentially a neighborhood club," more attractive to members of the city's business, rather than professional, class.[5]

With its establishment, the Belmont club rounded out, with the Philadelphia, Germantown, Young America and Merion clubs, what would become the "Big Five" cricket clubs of Philadelphia: the largest, wealthiest, and American-controlled clubs in the city which would dominate, for the next four decades, the city's cricket, monopolizing the best players, selecting representative city teams and controlling the overall direction of the game in Philadelphia.

The face of Philadelphia cricket had also changed by this time. The hordes of teenagers that had crowded the city's antebellum cricket clubs were now gone, as was the chimerical hope that cricket would again generate "as much excitement ... as it did before the rebellion." Philadelphia cricket had now become a game of young and middle-aged professional men, smaller in number but more affluent, settled, and equipped through social influence to fully secure and maintain the standing and progress of their game despite its reduced demographic presence.[6]

Though now nationally acknowledged as "the head of cricket on the American continent," Philadelphia still continued to be the destination of choice for significant numbers of English immigrants during this period (a quarter million in the 1880s alone), swelling and strengthening the already considerable English presence among the city's second-tier cricket clubs, something Daft's English players clearly recognized during their visit to Philadelphia in 1879.[7]

Resident English cricket in Philadelphia continued to find its greatest concentration at the working-class level among the still large number of textile mills centered around the Kensington and Wakefield districts. Many of the cricket clubs formed here were small and loosely organized, but a number of prominent English-dominated cricket clubs soon emerged after the Civil War, such as the Girard club, founded around 1869, followed by the Wakefield club in 1872 and the St. Timothy in 1875. The first two were even deemed strong enough to gain admission, for a few years, into the Halifax Cup competition.[8]

With this infusion of English immigrants came some individual cricket players of sufficient ability and talent to find themselves a place on other Halifax clubs.

The most prominent cricket-playing family within the English immigrant community of this period was the Hargreaves family. Originally from Leicestershire, the family would have no fewer than seven members playing high-level cricket in the city, with Joe, John, Robert and Tom acknowledged to be the most talented. Three of the brothers were born in the United States, grounds for qualification as "American" in playing status, though the family always seemed to identify, for cricket purposes, as of "English stock." Expectedly, the brothers initially gravitated towards the city's immigrant English cricket clubs, such as the Lillywhite club, but by 1868, after spending a few more years with the Wakefield club, most were now playing for Germantown as their permanent organization.[9]

By the late 1870s, these "devoted cricket players" had become "the backbone" of the Germantown team with as many as five of the brothers on the club's starting side. Their presence, at least at this time, evidently was welcome and uncontested, with one member, Joe, even becoming a director of the Germantown club.[10]

Polar opposite was the composition of Germantown's rival only four blocks away, the Young America club. This organization had progressed from its antebellum character as a club of teenagers (many not in the war because of their youth) to a team of mature young men with considerably improved competitive abilities.

On its avowed commitment to "self-reliance" in cricket matters, the club reasserted its policy of not allowing members to play for other clubs after the war, effectively ensuring its membership would remain exclusively American, an arrangement that endowed the club with a specific and symbolic mission.[11]

The return of peace (and even a little before) had also made possible the revival of the country's oldest and most intense cricket rivalry between

Five. Young America and the Assertion of Nativism

Philadelphia and New York. The St. George still held fast to its claim as not only being New York's most prominent club, but also as the organization that still "stood at the head of cricket in every respect" in the land.[12]

The St. George regularly played the Philadelphia and Germantown clubs, but its matches against the Young America club attracted the greatest public attention. The rivalry—fierce but usually cordial—assumed intense nationalistic overtones from the start: this youthful, all-American side against the country's long-entrenched citadel of immigrant English cricket, with the winner invariably settling the "question of supremacy" as the unofficial national cricket champion.[13]

The Young America club had announced its competitive ascendancy even during the Civil War with a win over the St. George in 1864, a feat even noticed by *Bell's Life*, Britain's leading sporting journal at that time. This was followed by a decisive Young America win the following year, the St. George being "outplayed at all parts of the game" by the American side, and a result hailed as "the most important match since the All-England visit." To observers, it was evidence that Philadelphia, on the accomplishments of this one club, had unquestionably superseded New York as the country's leading cricket city. The claim, however, wouldn't go uncontested. The St. George swung the balance back with wins and a draw against the Young America club in 1867 and 1868 and inflicted a severe defeat on the American club in 1877, getting the entire side out for only 39 runs.[14]

An 1867 match in progress at the Young America Cricket Club's ground at Turnpike Bridge, where the trend-setting Philadelphia club launched itself into national prominence in the 1860s and 1870s (Germantown Site and Relic Society).

The overall trend, however, was palpable and relentless. The Young America club gained further wins over the St. George in 1869, 1870 and 1875, with the American side further confirming its superiority over the English cricket community with a win, to boot, over a combined team of Philadelphia and New York English players in 1869, the last hailed as "the best played game in years." The Young America club topped this off by also inflicting a massive loss on a visiting immigrant English team from St. Louis in 1873.[15]

The driving force behind the Young America club since its inception had been the Newhalls, one of Germantown's oldest, though not necessarily influential, proper Philadelphia families. No fewer than seven members of the extended family played for the Young America club starting side from the time of the club's formation to its merger with the Germantown club in 1890. The family was, in effect, the very heart and soul of the Young America club, providing a generation of talented players for the club itself as well as core leaders for all representative Philadelphia sides throughout the 1870s and 1880s.[16]

Four members of this cricket-obsessed family in particular stood out: George, Charlie, Daniel and Robert.

George, at the age of only thirteen, was thrilling crowds with his skillful bowling, winning acclaim as the "little wonder" before the Civil War. When he batted, his square cut (hitting balls down the "right field line"), it was claimed, had "never been equaled," and in his maturity he had developed into a "thorough cricket player." His demeanor on the field was "quiet, unobtrusive," but effective, and over his career he would become "a household word" throughout the city's cricket community.[17]

Charles, "Chuck" Newhall would, over his career, develop into the premier fast bowler for the Young America club and the city, as well as, many thought, for the country. He even won the praise of W.G. Grace himself after he bowled Grace for only fourteen runs amid an "explosion of applause" during the MCC match against the Philadelphians in 1872. It would be the first of four times this American would claim the wicket (get out) the 19th century's greatest cricket batter.[18]

Robert, the youngest of the four brothers, was portrayed as the "most dangerous batsman" in the city, with a reputation largely secured by his determined 84 runs against the visiting Australian national team in 1878, though his more patient and tenacious 40 runs against Alfred Shaw's English team three years later was often identified as a "better piece of work."[19]

Of the brothers, Daniel was considered to be the most accomplished all-round cricketer. As a batter his hard hitting against Roller's visiting English side in 1885 brought a grin to umpire George Wright's face "so wide that his teeth glistened in the sunlight." In the eyes of the visiting Irish cricketers he was also "the trickiest of tricky bowlers," always on the lookout to "Mankad" ("pick off" in a fully legal, but devious, manner) opposing batters as he did to one of their players during a match in 1879.[20]

Said to have "took up the bat when he dropped the bib," Dan Newhall seemed to exhibit an inherent will to win unmatched by any of his contemporaries, someone to whom cricket was nothing less than a "strife for existence," and who, on the field of play, "does not know the meaning of the word *fail* in his cricketing vocabulary." Newhall was a "popular cuss" to his teammates, with a reserved yet demanding leadership style as captain, directing and commanding his team with "no noise, no demonstrations; a simple nod of the head or wave of the had did it all."[21]

Together and in succession, the Newhall brothers would build, mold, and lead their Young America club to the competitive pinnacle of American cricket, the club winning 163 of its 200 total matches and putting as many as eleven of its members on representative Philadelphia sides, as it did in the city's match against the MCC in 1872.[22]

From the time of their crushing win over arch rival Germantown in 1867, when their 330 second innings total "awakened them [Young America] to the sense of their position in the cricketing world," the Young America club would stand above and beyond the rest of Philadelphia cricket in demonstrating that this team of all Americans "has succeeded in its effort to show that those who love cricket and organize to make it popular may conquer all obstacles."[23]

The very spirit, method, and character of the club's style of play impressed and amazed opponents and observers alike. Collectively the players on this club exuded an "esprit de corps" and as a team its "movements on the field are scientific, catlike, and clever." In the eyes of *Forest & Stream* magazine what made the Young America the model cricket club was "correct and early training that enables this team to play so charmingly together ... a system is observed and a discipline maintained ... the spirit of encouragement shines out and good humor is the order of the day. In fact, this method is a beacon to all teams that would succeed." All things considered, the Young America club seemed fully deserving of the acclamation that this single Philadelphia organization "has since its inception probably done more to forward the interests of the game than any other organization in the country."[24]

Recognized in their time as the two leading "cricket families" in Philadelphia, the Hargreaves men and the Newhall brothers would also come to stand for two competing pathways for the advancement of the city's cricket: continued reliance upon, and assistance from, experienced immigrant English players or encouragement and development of inexperienced, but potentially much more talented, American players.[25]

From the very beginning there had always been tension and uneasiness between advocates of the two pathways. Before the Civil War William

Rotch Wister had expressed displeasure that team selectors for representative matches were staffing these sides with immigrant English players, "mostly well in years," even when it was evident "some Americans were better at the game than the English." His brother, Jones Wister, was less diplomatic, straight out declaring this was because "the English of that day had regarded the Americans with contempt."[26]

There was little movement, however, to alter this arrangement, since the city's larger clubs, Philadelphia, Germantown, and Merion, though controlled by Americans, with considerable say over their competitive arrangements (scheduling, team selection, etc.), were, at this time, still locked into a relationship of reliance upon immigrant English players, both professional and amateur.

The national integrity of their cricket had always been a sensitive issue for the Philadelphians, especially with representative teams, and the sentiment seemed to intensify after the Civil War. Two identifiably English players were on the Philadelphia side against Wilshire's professionals in 1868 and three Hargreaves men were on the Philadelphia team that played the MCC in 1872, though their presence didn't alter MCC manager Robert Fitzgerald's impression that the Philadelphia game was his team's "first experience of a genuine American match."[27]

Philadelphia cricket authorities, however, were becoming more sensitive about the national purity of their representative teams and adopted, for the city's team that traveled to Halifax, Canada, two years later, an explicit policy that this team "shall consist wholly of Americans born who have acquired cricket in this country." The policy, however, wasn't absolute at the time, with two Hargreaves men on the Philadelphia side that played the Canadians during their return match in the city the following year.[28]

The success of the Young America club, with its reliance exclusively on American players, must, however, have further stimulated this nativist feeling and with the loss of confidence in any meaningful competitive benefits from enlisting English professionals, the feeling seems to have reached a point of serious policy consideration by the early 1880s, at least with one Philadelphia cricket club.

This seems to be the most probable explanation why the entire Hargreaves contingent, in 1880, suddenly and unexpectedly left the Germantown club and migrated, *en masse*, to the English-dominated Girard cricket club. It's unclear what specifically was behind this sudden and wholesale departure, later sources only mentioning, in passing, that the "outlook was very dark" for the Germantown club at that time (Lester is silent on the incident). The likely influence of the Young America club in this matter can't be ruled out. The grounds of the two clubs were only blocks apart and though membership in their respective cricket teams was separate, there must have been considerable social interaction and policy discussions between the two clubs.[29]

In any event, whatever sentiments or feelings may have led to the Hargreaves exodus, they seemed to have been deep and intense, since no member of the Hargreaves family would ever again play for Germantown or any other Halifax Cup club, though members of the family and their descendants would continue to maintain an extensive presence in Philadelphia cricket into the early 20th century, playing for numerous, but always English identified, city clubs.[30]

Germantown's noticeable shift towards a greater reliance upon its American members seems, however, to have been more of an intention than actual policy at this point. At least two other immigrant Englishmen continued to play for the club, Joseph H. Rastall and T.C. Cuppitt, the latter a descendent of another extended antebellum immigrant English cricket-playing family. Almost as soon as the Hargreaves men had departed, a recently arrived English cricketer from Warwickshire, A.E. Radliff, had secured a place in the Germantown lineup. Yet even these English players must have increasingly felt that they were not entirely welcome. Rastall, within a few years, would migrate to the Belmont club, Cuppitt to the Girard club (Radliff would prematurely die, at age 34, in 1890). The result was that, by the mid-1880s, the Germantown first team had been completely purged of all immigrant players and from that time on fielded an exclusively American-born team.[31]

Leveraging its standing as the club on whose ground, Nicetown, all Philadelphia's international matches were played during this period, Germantown now seemed to be in a position to also set the rest of Philadelphia on a path of total American self-reliance, fully implementing the declared principle that "the English may beat us, but they cannot help us." In the beginning, this self-reliance led to discouraging results. Germantown itself, now without its talented English players, saw its competitive strength sharply decline, with a bad loss to the Staten Island cricket club (New York's successor club to the St. George) in 1880, while the Hargreaves men inflicted an embarrassing loss on their former club by leading their adoptive Girard club to a convincing win over Germantown in 1882.[32]

The competitive consequences of going it alone with only American players had been readily apparent to the club years earlier, when a Hargreaves-less Germantown side was overmatched in a game against a visiting Detroit team stopping in the city on an eastern tour in 1878. Much of the damage to the Philadelphians was administered by Tom "Jumbo" Dale, this deserter from the British army in Canada and bigamist destroying the Germantown batting lineup with his destructive fast bowling. Four years later, "demon bowler" Dale again brought "dismay" to Philadelphia cricket as a member of a Western XI team drawn from the best British/Canadian players in Detroit, Chicago, St. Louis and Pittsburg, a team that won all its games against the city's Halifax Cup clubs. A "United States" team made up entirely of immigrant English players further exposed the deficiency of native reliance by soundly beating an all-American Philadelphia team in 1883.[33]

Yet Philadelphia, led by Germantown, an area of the city long reputed to have "an individuality of its own," persevered in its nativist policy, especially with its representative teams. Its policy received a welcome boost with the nominal success of the representative city team that toured England in 1884, which was the first Philadelphia cricket team—one with an entirely American side—to travel overseas.[34]

Though only playing against strictly amateur English sides, the Philadelphians returned home with a winning record, an accomplishment that was immediately hailed as a watershed in America's long quest for competitive parity against cricket's bellwether power. Not surprisingly, the loudest acclamation came from a Newhall.[35]

In his article on American cricket that appeared in *Outing* magazine shortly after the tour, George Newhall brashly proclaimed that the threshold had now been passed where an "American team can beat the ordinary English team with ease," leaving no doubt, in his estimation, that, at least in this American city, "the English residents have been left far behind in the race" for competitive supremacy in the game.[36]

Within the given limitations of amateur opposition which the Philadelphians only played during their English tour, these claims, coming, as they did shortly after the embarrassing loss to Australia in 1882, seemed to be supportable. Especially after the following year, when Philadelphia defeated a visiting English amateur side captained by W.E. Roller. The press was so enraptured by this, the city's first win over a visiting English cricket team, that it proclaimed "the names [of the Philadelphia team] shall be written on the scroll of fame beside that of the Puritans." The result seems to have been even more satisfying, since there appears to have been intense pressure to strengthen the Philadelphia side by including resident English players.[37]

A clean sweep by all the Halifax Cup clubs over a visiting West Indian side in 1886, a win over a visiting Irish side two years later, and a moderately successful record by another American-only Philadelphia side during a second tour to England in 1889 must have finally laid to rest any doubts that representative Philadelphia teams could win with only American players. Philadelphia had by now firmly, confidently, and irreversibly settled upon its policy that hereto only strictly American sides would represent the city and for the next twenty years no unqualified immigrant cricketer would play for any Gentlemen of Philadelphia side.[38]

Having been denied access to the city's highest competitive level put Philadelphia's amateur English cricket community in an even greater quandary than the ban on its professional cricketers. Many migrated to the fringe of smaller, English-dominated cricket clubs that populated the city, and an "English Residents" cricket association was even formed in 1885 as something of a rival to the Halifax Cup competition.[39]

For the more talented resident English players, it meant a more or less forced abandonment of any prospects or hopes for competitive advancement in their adopted country. This was a fate that befell the talented English cricketer Fred Suttcliff of the North End cricket club. Acknowledged as "one of the best bowlers in America" at this time, native or immigrant, the Englishman would spend his entire career playing for only minor city clubs, advancing no further than as a net (batting cage) bowler for the Merion club.[40]

However, Philadelphia's standout resident English player, Arthur Wood, would fight this policy, forcing the city's cricket authorities to modify their restrictions. Having removed one obstacle to his hopes of playing for representative Philadelphia teams by reverting to amateur status at his Belmont club in the early 1880s, Wood immediately ran into another with the ban on all resident foreigners. Protesting, through letters to the *American Cricketer*, the injustice of a policy that denied an amateur English resident, who had lived and played cricket in Philadelphia for almost a decade, the opportunity to play for his adopted city, Wood seemed to have pressed city cricket authorities to establish formal qualification standards for selection to representative sides.[41]

These qualification standards, formally outlined in 1891, that stipulated those not "free born" or "naturalized citizens" be residents for a minimum of five years (much more stringent than the two-year requirement in English cricket and seek American citizenship, finally allowed Wood, at the age of thirty-one, to begin his international career in the 1892 U.S.-Canada match. From that time, when he debuted with an impressive 129 runs, the Belmont standout would go onto a long and productive international career for his adoptive city.[42]

The policy clarification would also open the door for the English-born John Lester, though not without objection from the Germantown club, which questioned his national loyalties in 1896 as it also had with Wood. Like his predecessor, Lester, once qualified, would go onto a long and distinguished cricket career not only as a standout player for the city's representative teams but also as a life-long supporter, advocate and ultimately chronicler of the game.[43]

Germantown's nativist motivated policy that, at least with the city's representative teams, insisted "victory over our cousins, to be real, must be native," seems to have become settled policy among the rest of the Halifax Cup clubs by the late 1880s. But the selection philosophy would face one more significant challenge.[44]

Very likely sensing a business opportunity with the increasing success of the city's international sides, Ernest Crowhurst, cricket editor of the *Philadelphia Inquirer*, hatched a scheme early in 1890 to create an "All-American" cricket team, bringing together what he envisioned to be a truly national United States cricket side of the best cricket players—pro and amateur, American and resident English—from cricket clubs throughout the country, not just one city. According to his plans, such a team would undertake a grand, extended tour with twenty-four matches in England.[45]

The scheme, from the time Crowhurst personally pitched it to the English County Cricket Council, seemed to catch fire with cricket authorities around the world. The English loved the idea, W.G. Grace himself personally assuring Crowhurst such a team would be enthusiastically welcomed by all the county sides (professional English cricket clubs are designated by counties). The Australians were also on board, promising the American team some matches after they had finished their English tour. George Wright fully endorsed the idea while another future baseball Hall of Famer, Cap Anson, who had top scored in the cricket match his team of professional baseballers had played in Australia the year before on their around-the-world tour, wanted to play for the team.[46]

The suggestion that any representative American cricket team would include pros and non–Americans, however, immediately ignited opposition from Philadelphia cricket authorities. The dispute spilled over into the national press, exposing an intense, and partisan, division of opinion and emotions. Philadelphia's "American-only" policy had never been without its critics, the *American Cricketer* itself, as early as 1879, decrying the "Know Nothings" advocating this restrictive stance, which, in the eyes of the publication, seemed blatantly "contrary to American principle and spirit."[47]

In a role reversal to antebellum English exclusiveness, Philadelphia cricket authorities were now accused of being "too clannish," a letter to the *American Cricketer* complaining that "there is more class and caste shown here [in Philadelphia] than on the green sward of old England." It was a stance that the Philadelphia cricket community certainly didn't attempt to conceal. "The presence of resident English cricketers," it was acknowledged, "is the signal for scarcely concealed resentment," a radical nativist sentiment that ran so deep some of its advocates "declare that they would rather see their club lose every game than win through the instrumentality of English members."[48]

What all observers must have known, if unwilling to acknowledge, however, was that, by now, American cricketers in Philadelphia had progressed to such a point of competency that they were head and shoulders above almost all resident English cricket players, even the most objective critics conceding there were, outside the Quaker City, only three cricketers of any ability in the entire country: M.R. Cobb and J. Rose of New York, and J.C. Davis of Chicago, all English residents. In addition to the issue of inclusiveness, there had to be considered the matter of popular appeal, the Philadelphians knowing full well that "if foreigners are masquerading as American cricketers, Americans will look upon the scheme [of the All American team] with absolute indifference."[49]

With the Philadelphia cricket community firmly and irrevocably opposed to any of its players on a team that would be a "heterogeneous mixture of foreign hirelings," a stance with which the *American Cricketer* eventually came to agree as well, the All-American scheme never advanced beyond the planning stage (Crowhurst himself had never been authorized by Philadelphia cricket authorities to even pursue the matter) and it eventually withered on the vine. Philadelphia would remain, as it had been, *de facto*, since the late 1870s, as the sole representative, spokesperson, and decision maker for United States cricket.[50]

If any ill-will surrounding Philadelphia's uncompromising insistence on the national purity of its representative teams continued to linger, the efficacy of the policy would at last be decisively confirmed during the national cricket championship of 1891.

The idea of staging an officially recognized national cricket championship, floated as early as 1887, became a reality in 1891 with the arrangement of a knock-out tournament to be played that year between representative teams from the country's major cricket-playing cities: Boston, New York, Baltimore, Philadelphia, Detroit, Pittsburg and Chicago. With Philadelphia and Chicago advancing to the championship game played in Philadelphia that fall, the contest was unavoidably seen as a contest between advocates and critics of Philadelphia's nativist stance.[51]

The all-resident English Chicago team had good reason to believe that it could beat its all-American opponent, as it had beaten both the Germantown and Belmont clubs during their visits to the Windy City earlier that summer, and must have been further motivated by Philadelphia's long-running criticism of Chicago's attempts to actively recruit English immigrant players to its city cricket clubs.[52]

The contest, however, turned out to be a complete walkover for the Philadelphians, the home side rolling up 478 runs in its single innings on the way to a crushing and humiliating innings and 138 run win over their immigrant player–dominated opponents (a team in cricket that, batting once, scores more runs than their opponents do batting twice wins "by an innings"—always a lopsided margin of victory, equivalent to a basketball team scoring more points in one half than their opponents do in the entire game). Never before, or after, would an American cricket team so badly beat a team of resident English players. With this "success of native talent over the English players," Philadelphia's American-only policy now stood confirmed and indisputable, and all cricket among the Halifax Cup clubs would henceforth be conducted, organized, and arranged "entirely in the interests of American cricket."[53]

Controversial since its inception and paved with years of competitive disappointment, Philadelphia's radical native-only policy with its cricket would be, without question, the single most significant and far-reaching decision in the city's cricket history, opening an unobstructed pathway for the development of Philadelphia's native-born cricket talent. Even before the exodus of the Hargreaves men, Germantown was moving towards a stance where "the development of native talent comes first," pushing forward with an intensive junior program. By 1881, five former junior players were on the club's starting XI. From this "cradle of the new school of cricket" would soon follow the future international players George Patterson, Frank Bohlen, Frank Ralston and Reynolds Brown.[54]

Other Halifax Cup clubs soon followed suit and during the 1880s future international players such as Percy Clark of Young America, as well as Henry Bailey and John Thayer of Merion, would begin their cricket careers in the junior programs of their respective clubs. Eight of Belmont's starting XI began their careers in that club's junior program while on the Tioga cricket club's junior team another teenager was cutting his teeth, one destined to become America's greatest cricket player: John B. King.[55]

These and other young American players who were now moving up, encouraged and fully supported, through the junior ranks during this period would become Philadelphia's greatest generation of cricketers and, over the next two decades, carry the city's cricket to its greatest competitive heights.

Six

Intern to Internationalism

Every sport, like every religion or every political persuasion, inherently wants to bring the value system contained within its experience to new populations, to expand and extend the appeal of its social content to other peoples.

As the two team sports that developed earliest into an advanced, "modern" form, cricket and baseball—one in England, the other in the United States—very quickly came to be identified as social expressions of an "advanced culture," historical confirmation that "the governing races today are races of sportsmen; the people who are inheriting the earth today are the people who play games."[1]

As such, advocates of both bat-and-ball sports who accepted this declaration soon came to view their respective "national pastimes" not only as expressions of domestic prominence but also as desirable conduits for extending their "civilized" features far beyond national boundaries.

Cricket was in a particularly advantageous position for acting upon this perceived mission, as it was the sport of the world's most powerful country during the 19th century. The game followed, *pari passu*, Britain's expanding colonial empire, establishing new pockets of cricket activity wherever English immigrants settled. Through the expansion of their game, cricket supporters came to view their sport as a significant instrument for the advancement of two geopolitical objectives.

First, cricket was an activity that served to "consolidate" Britain's far-flung colonies, keeping the English diaspora in Australia, Canada, New Zealand and South Africa in active contact while reinforcing trans-national loyalties through cricket tours and rivalries. Second, advocates, both within and outside the game, believed that cricket, as an institution that embodied the most worthy and desirable English social values and norms, could be a powerful tool for "cultural diffusion," one of the "Three Cs"—Christianity, the classics, and cricket—with which England equated "Anglo-Saxon" civilization, all of which could be exported and enlisted in the desirable cause of "elevating" the indigenous non–English peoples within its far-flung empire. Under this perceived scenario, "the civilizing mission of cricket," according to England's most impassioned cricket imperialist, Lord Harris, was far more than the exportation of an advanced entertainment form but the world-wide dissemination of Anglo-Saxon values.[2]

Baseball advocates as well, especially after the explosive, coast-to-coast post–Civil War growth of their game, came to view their national pastime as embodying all the values and traits that were propelling the United States towards its manifest destiny as a future great world power.

But any aspirations for baseball's expansion beyond national boundaries faced several obstacles. As a game that was at the time only played by a single country, baseball was constrained by its every claim of cultural uniqueness. If baseball was, in fact, "America's game," a sporting experience that, culturally, was "national only as far as no other country plays it," and that "Baseball and the United States were made for each other," then, by inference, no other people or culture would be able to fully enculturate the game or play it at a proficient level. Additionally, America didn't have a colonial empire with readily available and extensive trans-national populations to which the game could be exported.[3]

None of this, however, deterred the game's most dedicated impresario of the era, Boston Red Stockings star pitcher and future Chicago White Stockings part-owner Albert Spalding, from an obsessive, lifelong belief that baseball was destined for worldwide popularity.

It was the driving motive behind this future sporting equipment magnate's organization of his two overseas baseball tours in 1874 and 1889, the first to England, the latter an "around the world" trek, both undertaken in the expectation that America's national pastime could become "the universal athletic sport of the world."[4]

Forced to concede that among all countries other than the English-speaking nations there was, at this period, "utter indifference to athletic sports," and meeting a cool reception at stops in his target markets of England and Australia, Spalding realized his grand scheme for baseball's world pre-eminence wasn't playing out as expected and, consequently, baseball would remain, for the most part, on the sidelines during the international expansion of sports over the last half of the 19th century.[5]

Baseball would, over time, establish its own trans-national spheres of influence, primarily in the Far East and the Spanish-speaking Caribbean (the English-speaking Caribbean would remain thoroughly cricket playing), but Spalding would go to his grave never having achieved what he most craved and desired for baseball: the blessing of the English nation, the *fons et origo* of all bat-and-ball sports.

Despite, and probably because of, its modest following in the United

States, American cricket supporters continued to look beyond national boundaries for their game's inspiration, competition and resources, viewing themselves as very much a part of cricket's expanding international presence, a game that was "justly regarded as cosmopolitan in its character, especially among the English speaking nations of the world."[6]

This was certainly the posture of the Philadelphia cricket community, and its radical nativism should not be interpreted so much as an anti–English sentiment as much as an anti–English reliance. To the proper Philadelphia social strata cricket always remained a "splendidly Anglo-Saxon" institution, nurturing an indivisible "bond of sympathy" between the cricketers of their city and England, with a shared esteem and admiration for the game's sporting values and traditions.[7]

It was a sentiment happily reciprocated by the English cricket community, which was always hopeful America, or more correctly its proxy Philadelphia, would develop into a full-fledged cricket power that would, someday, join the leading cricket nations on an equal competitive footing. Commenting on Philadelphia's first English tour in 1884, Lord Harris, a lifelong friend, supporter, and well-wisher of Philadelphia cricket, fully expected that "by bringing Englishmen into the friendly competition of the cricket field with Americans," this would be "good to all the English speaking peoples of the world, by bringing them together in friendly intercourse and honest, beneficial, rivalry."[8]

The *Pall Mall Gazette*, in its own review of the Philadelphians' English visit thirteen years later, in 1897, carried this sentiment even further, viewing America's participation in high-level cricket as the capstone to the game's mission of Anglo-Saxon worldwide cultural unity: "This admitting of America to the full graces of the ancient and ever glorious game of cricket was the one thing needed to prove to the world that the Anglo-Saxon race is one race, no matter by what distances, long or short, the several branches are divided."[9]

For Philadelphia to rightfully assume this perceived role as the United States representative in the growing world of international cricket, it would have to overcome essentially the same obstacles that had stood in the way for establishing its domestic leadership: (1) control of the country's international cricket arrangements and (2) elevation of its play to a trans-national competitive caliber.

The "United States" participation in trans-national cricket before the Civil War was largely limited to its annual match against Canada, an event firmly controlled by New York's St. George club. Dissatisfaction with this arrangement that arose in 1860 was largely due to the absence of any officially recognized national governing cricket body, which may have led to the second disruption of the rivalry after 1865—one that would last fourteen years.[10]

If American cricket was to have a permanent presence outside of the country, it would need an officially recognized existence within the country and, in 1878, largely on the initiative of Philadelphia, a formal United States Cricket Association came into existence.[11]

Though "national" in name, the association was, for all intents and purposes, a Philadelphia-controlled organization. Most of the member clubs and most of its officers were from Philadelphia and over the life of the organization only once, in 1883, was its annual meeting held outside the Quaker city. This also enabled Philadelphia to progressively take control of the U.S.-Canada series which the association revived in 1879. The "United States" team was always top-heavy with Philadelphia players, especially for home matches, which, with the single exception of the 1886 match played at the Seabright Lawn Tennis and Cricket club in New Jersey, were always held in Philadelphia, an arrangement that continued up to the very end of the rivalry in 1912.[12]

The revived U.S.-Canada rivalry, however, never resumed the status it had enjoyed before the Civil War, the series progressively becoming overshadowed by the increasing interest in, and importance of, the growing number of matches against overseas teams, contests that were looked on as a more accurate barometer of Philadelphia's competitive progress.

These matches against overseas teams were, as well, initially under the control of the English immigrant cricket community, primarily the St. George club. New York's leading cricket club had arranged the All-England tour of 1859, Wilshire's visit in 1868, while English cricket authorities in Canada had initiated the MCC tour of 1872.[13]

With its rising stature, especially in relation to New York cricket, Philadelphia couldn't be excluded from this important facet of the country's cricket for long and for numerous reasons.

From the time of the All-England match with Philadelphia in 1859 overseas teams found, in this American city, not only the strongest opposition, the best facilities, the largest crowds, the most cordial hospitality, but, above all, the best match arrangements. Not until its stop in Philadelphia did the MCC, in 1872, find serious opposition, while Daft's professionals, seven years later, felt for the first time on their North American tour that "we were among friends who understood and appreciated our national game." One member of Daft's entourage, on arriving in Philadelphia, went so far as to proclaim "like Rip Van Winkle I rubbed my eyes and wondered whether they could be dreaming" in finding themselves among such fine cricket facilities so far from home.[14]

From the late 1870s on Philadelphia leveraged these advantages to assume increasingly greater control over the arrangements of all matches against overseas teams. Philadelphia cricket authorities had been sub-contracted by the St. George for Wilshire's visit and it may have been on the city's initiative that the Australians were persuaded to visit the United States in 1878. In steep decline by the late 1870s, the St. George club was effectively relinquishing, by this time, its role as the lead organizer for visiting overseas teams. The matches in 1879 with Lord Harris' English team and the Irish amateur team seem to have been the last such events arranged by the once prominent New York cricket club. Henceforth, Philadelphia would be the sole initiator and organizer of all future visits by foreign cricket teams, effectively assuring the city's uncontested claim to being America's sole representative on the stage of world cricket.[15]

Philadelphia soon learned, however, that it was going to be a far more difficult and extended task to find a respectable place on this expanding world sports stage.

Foreign teams had, to be sure, always found their toughest opposition against Philadelphia sides. Only here was the All-England side extended into a second innings on its North American tour in 1859. Wilshire's professionals, nine years later, found their match in Philadelphia "the best and most hotly contested" of their American tour while the MCC side, locked in "the match of matches" in its contest against the Philadelphians, had to struggle to make the modest 34 second innings runs needed to beat the American side in 1872.[16]

Despite these commendable showings, the Philadelphia sides, as the local press clearly recognized, "have a great deal to learn" about the game. The Philadelphia bowling generally impressed the English visitors; its batting and fielding much less so.[17]

These Philadelphia cricketers were, even years later, still hitting their wickets (getting themselves out) when batting, stopping balls with their feet when fielding, things that would be expected from players who, up to this point, had to learn their cricket "partly by natural instinct, partly by copying other players and ... partly by book study."[18]

That English cricket authorities seemed to have had, at this period, a lukewarm assessment of the city's cricket potential can only be inferred from the fact that, after the MCC visit in 1872, no overseas team would visit America for another six years, the longest stretch without a visiting foreign team Philadelphia would experience. Even vigorous attempts to induce an English team to participate in the country's Centennial celebrations in 1876 were rebuffed.[19]

If England, for the time being, seemed to be ambivalent towards Philadelphia as a worthy cricket opponent, the city's cricket authorities were able to persuade a team from the cricket world's newly emerging power, Australia, to stop over for a few matches on its way home from an historic series in England in 1878.

The historical/cultural backgrounds of these two countries would seem to have portended a natural and cordial sporting relationship through cricket. Here were two young, rising, cricket-playing countries, former and soon-to-be-former colonies of a mother country towards which neither had any special affections (though for different reasons). Yet no two countries probably initiated their sporting contacts as acrimoniously as did the United States and Australia at cricket.

The Australians, who had astonished the cricket world that summer by beating some of England's top cricket clubs, unexpectedly found themselves struggling to beat a far inferior New York team in their first match and in another difficult tussle against Philadelphia in their second, the latter playing, for the first time, against a foreign team with even, 11 against 11, sides.

Having barely avoided the follow on (the team batting first in cricket, if it has a big lead after their opponents have batted, has the option of switching the batting order in the second innings, forcing their opponents to immediately bat again—"follow on"—and play catch up), the Australians were gaining control of the match in the second innings until the Philadelphia umpire, Hazen Brown, made such a blatantly bad call in favor of the home team that the Australian captain, David Gregory, immediately took his team off the field.[20]

Attempts to reconcile the two sides only seemed to escalate tensions. The Australian team—"a rough side, rough in their behavior, rough in their attitudes" that would become even worse in America—demanded that the Philadelphia umpire be replaced. The Australian manager John Conway, a "belligerent and forceful" personality in his own right, further offended his hosts with the insinuation that the Australians were not in "a civilized country" and strongly hinted that if this demand was not met, the visitors would not resume the match, to which Philadelphia captain George Newhall angrily replied that the Australians could leave "anytime they wanted."[21]

Threatened with non-payment if they abandoned the match, the Australian players took a vote and, by a majority of one, reluctantly agreed to resume play. Too much time, however, had been lost to complete the match which ended in a draw (a cricket game that cannot be played to completion is declared a "draw" with no winner whatever the score). Even after the match concluded, tensions between the two sides seemed to persist. Australian wicket-keeper (catcher) Jack Blackham's post-match brag that "We got the best of it" was angrily rebuffed by Dan Newhall's "Are you sure?"[22]

Despite these unpleasantries, the Philadelphians had discovered, from this initial encounter with the Australians, the challenges they faced trying to balance their game's moral expectations with the intense competitive demands of international-level cricket. In the eyes of the Philadelphians, these Australians, who "were accepted as amateurs although they never pretended they were" and were led by an "obnoxious" captain, struck the Americans as "grasping and penurious," a gang of "sharps" displaying "poor character," completely contrary to the expectations of proper Philadelphia cricket. The Philadelphians consoled themselves that, if they weren't better cricket players than their opponents, they were at least "better sportsmen." In short, the Australians were not what the Philadelphians took to be "gentlemen" athletes and should, it was even suggested, be best avoided in the future.[23]

Yet the Philadelphians, tacitly and perhaps reluctantly, must have recognized that the cricket exhibited by these Australians was the cricket of the future and the standard to which Philadelphia would have to aspire. For all their perceived moral deficiencies, these Australians were the "champagne cricketers of the world," with their exceptional batting abilities, a side that, in its energetic style, played with "something of the dash of the New World." The Australians took their cricket "in deadly seriousness" and impressed their hosts with their "tremendous pluck and grit," and "never give up" resilience displayed throughout the match. In short, the Australian cricketers were everything that the Philadelphians wanted their cricket to become, and the Americans must have hoped, if not expected, an established cricket rivalry between the two countries would help bring this about.[24]

It would be, however, a largely one-way cricket relationship. Though the Australians had concluded from this 1878 match that these Philadelphian cricketers were "not a team to be despised by any means," they would never avoid the suspicion of not taking their American opponents seriously and, from the start, seemed skeptical of Philadelphia's future prospects in world cricket. The Philadelphians would never get from the Australians the positive reinforcement the English cricket community so readily extended to its American cousins. These Australians were "all business" with their cricket and weren't particularly interested in playing the role of nurturer to upcoming, but unworthy, opponents.[25]

The bad feelings between the two parties, nonetheless, seemed to have subsided enough for the Australians to return to Philadelphia in 1882, although the motive may have been "payback" for 1878—highly suggested since their match in Philadelphia would be the only one played by the Australians during their visit to the United States. This powerful side, by general consensus one of the "best that ever visited [England]," thoroughly outclassed the Philadelphians, squelching the Americans' slim hopes of salvaging another draw when the visitors easily and effortlessly hit off the required fifty-three runs to win the match in just thirty minutes. Having convincingly reclaimed their competitive honor, the Australians, for the remainder of the decade, effectively ignored Philadelphia cricket, turning down numerous invitations from the Americans during this time. Fully eleven years would pass before an Australian side could be persuaded to return to Philadelphia.[26]

This, however, was in the future. For the Philadelphians, the 1878 draw against the powerful Australians had been "in every way an exceptional event," providing an unexpected yet much needed boost to the morale of the city's cricket community, not the least because the encounter was the first time that a Philadelphia side had not lost a match to an overseas team.[27]

The result also seems to have caught the attention of the English cricket community which may have been induced to take a second look at America as a place where competitive cricket could be found, not to mention its potential as a future source of post-season profits. The season following the Australian visit would be "the revival year" for Philadelphia cricket, with no fewer than three overseas teams visiting the city in 1879. With the U.S.-Canada series also revived that year after a fourteen-year break, the year would give the Philadelphians extensive opportunities to accurately gauge their standing in world cricket.[28]

The first of these overseas sides, Lord Harris' English team, on its way home from a controversial tour of Australia, made a passing stop in New York that spring to take on a combined New York/Philadelphia side. Even without a full complement of players (Harris himself was visiting Niagara Falls and several other English players passed up the match to return home), this contest was easily won by the English side, a portent of discouraging times for Philadelphia cricket.[29]

The second team, Richard Daft's strong team of English professionals, arrived in Philadelphia that fall. Like the Australians, this team was also "all business" and easily defeated a representative Philadelphia side in its first match followed up by an equally one-sided win over the Young America club, which had played under the "foolhardy" belief that it could contend against this powerful side of professionals with even teams of eleven per side. The visitors then proceeded to further underscore their demonstrated superiority by following these humiliations with a "see how the experts do it" exhibition match between sides drawn from the English team's Nottinghamshire and Yorkshire players.[30]

If Daft's visit hadn't sufficiently impressed upon the Philadelphians how "hopeless" it was for their city's cricketers to take on experienced English professionals, it was driven home even more emphatically by Alfred Shaw's team, also a fully professional side, two years later.[31]

Passing through America on its way to Australia in the fall of 1881,

Shaw's team effectively repeated the results of its predecessor, overwhelming its Philadelphia opponents, even with the Americans given the odds of playing twelve against eleven. This English side then added its own insult by insinuating that the wins were so effortless, it had "let them [Philadelphians] down easily."[32]

The Philadelphia cricket community had little choice but to concede that, for its amateur, weekend athletes, it was utterly "useless for our unpracticed resident cricketers to attempt to play foreign professional teams." Even the city's best cricketers were clearly in over their heads against this level of competition, just not "far enough advanced" with their game to successfully compete against fully professional sides. With Shaw's departure, no all-professional English cricket team would ever again be invited to play in Philadelphia.[33]

The more appropriate competitive level, Philadelphia had come to accept, was against comparable amateur sides. This had been largely self-evident from the time of its close match against an exclusively amateur MCC side in 1872 coupled with the city's success against the amateur Irish team that toured the United States in 1879, the third overseas team to play in Philadelphia that year.

The Irish matches in particular were contests that fulfilled everything Philadelphia expected from its cricket. The Irish team, on a "pleasure tour," a leisurely working vacation through Canada and the eastern United States (the tour doubled as the honeymoon for one member and his wife), was relaxed and laid-back, in sharp contrast to the cold, hard-nosed approach of the Australians and English professionals. Relations between the two sides were cordial and friendly, both on and off the field, the beginning of a long and harmonious sports rivalry between the two cricket countries that would continue for three decades. Above all, here was an overseas opponent that Philadelphians could beat, which they did that fall in a close, evenly contested game, as would be the case in almost all future encounters between the two sides. More significantly, for the first time in its cricket history, Philadelphia, in its 1879 match against the Irish, had defeated an overseas side.[34]

Accepting of, and working from, this more realistic evaluation of their cricket abilities, the Philadelphians, in 1884, made the decision, after playing host for a quarter of a century to overseas teams, to send their own representative side on a tour of England. With this "daring experiment," Philadelphia would debut on the overseas cricket stage becoming only the second nation to send a representative cricket team to the mother country.[35]

Unlike their Australian predecessors, the Gentlemen of Philadelphia wouldn't come to England from a position of strength. These

Americans would only play against amateur sides and, aware of the limited appeal their cricket would likely have with the English public, financial self-sufficiency would be required. The Philadelphians would pay their own way from a subscription fund raised among supporters back home and, as they would with their second English tour five years later, generously donate what few gate receipts they received to English charity. It was a gesture that guaranteed the Americans a "hearty welcome" from the English cricket community, but compared to the profitable, if not lucrative, returns the Australian and English professional teams reaped from their American tours, these arrangements were, in effect, a financial give-away. Yet they were arrangements to which the Philadelphians essentially would agree in all future English tours.[36]

The Gentlemen of Philadelphia, by open admission, were coming to England "not to conquer but to learn," and to learn at "the fountain head" of cricket, a view that seemed to be shared by their hosts. The Philadelphians' reception by the British public was subdued, their abilities unknown. The British press was initially dismissive of these Americans, who, after some early losses, "had come, and seen, and been conquered." Over the course of the tour, however, this estimate would more than once be modified, as it would in all future Philadelphia visits.[37]

The Philadelphians received a warm welcome during their match in Ireland and a decidedly impolite one from Scotland. Somewhat humorously, they also found themselves as the transfer agent for the veiled hostility between the England and Australian teams that summer; the Australian players privately confiding to the Americans their hatred of English players, the England players secretly confiding their contempt for the Australians.[38]

Playing against teams that varied widely in strength and stature, from full-fledged county sides to less dominant service and local teams, the Philadelphians had their ups and downs. An impressive 168-run win over Gloucestershire, a match in which Charles Newhall twice claimed the wicket of England star batter W.G. Grace, and a "good uphill fight" that got them past Surrey with ten minutes to spare, the first of what would be a succession of memorable encounters between these two sides, were perhaps the highlights of the tour. A bad loss by an innings and 171 runs to an MCC side was probably the low point, the first of what would be several disappointing losses to England's flagship cricket club.[39]

In the end, the Gentlemen of Philadelphia would finish the eighteen-match tour, the most extensive ever undertaken by a Philadelphia team, with an 8–5–5 record. Though modest in its accomplishments, the record, at least on the basis of raw results, would, however, be the best of any Philadelphia senior team to visit England.[40]

Though their opponents were all amateur sides, and some admittedly sub-par, the Philadelphians, or at least the *American Cricketer*, with characteristic American bravado, saw these results as the graduation of the city's cricket from mediocrity to a competitive status fully comparable to the best amateur cricket in England. Lord Harris, commenting on the tour in *Lillywhite's Cricketers' Annual*, politely but firmly disillusioned the Philadelphians of their assessment. These Americans, according to Harris, were solid, competent cricketers, but as they did not have to face professional bowling during the tour, they could hardly claim parity with England's top amateur sides. Only one member of the team, slow bowler William Lowry, did Harris consider to have "a very good chance of being selected in most English county elevens." To Harris, Philadelphia certainly had a future in high-level cricket, but that future was not now.[41]

The whole experience, however, seemed to have infused Philadelphia cricketers with a new confidence in their abilities, which became evident the following year in their first match against the English amateur side brought over by E.J. Sanders, most probably arranged during the English tour. Before more than seven thousand spectators on the last day of the match, many rushing onto the field in celebration at the match conclusion, Philadelphia achieved its first win over a visiting English side. With critics declaring that "never had such good all-around cricket been witnessed before" by the home players, the team's accomplishment was interpreted as an "immediate outgrowth" of the experience acquired by the Philadelphians in England.[42]

Nor did losses in the two matches against Sanders' stronger English team that returned to Philadelphia in 1886 significantly shake this growing confidence, since it was offset by the Philadelphians' clean sweep of a visiting West Indies team that same year. Playing individually, not as a representative side, the Germantown, Merion and Belmont clubs clearly demonstrated, with their wins, that this future world-cricket power from the Caribbean, at this point in time, was "not up to the form of the leading [Philadelphia] clubs."[43]

Philadelphia re-confirmed its claim as North America's leading cricket power by providing the majority of players to a combined Philadelphia/New York/Boston team that paid a return visit to the Caribbean the following winter, this far from strong side still managing to win a majority of its matches, including a win that could arguably lay claim to being the West Indies' first test match (match between representative national teams).[44]

This was followed, in 1888, with a further sweep of the second Irish team to visit North America, both matches following the by now established script for Philadelphia/Ireland matches: close, evenly contested games ultimately won by the Americans.[45]

The city's cricket was clearly maturing and progressing to a point that Philadelphia cricket authorities felt fully confident and justified in their decision, the following year, to send the Gentlemen of Philadelphia to England for another extended tour.

This second visit was scaled back from eighteen to a dozen matches and English cricket authorities were only willing to grant their American visitors two days for most contests, not enough time to allow the Philadelphians to complete more than half their games during the tour. This visit, as well, had its ups (a draw with Surrey that had a combined 1,150 total runs—the most ever on Surrey's home ground, the Oval, and probably the Philadelphians' best performance) and downs (another bad loss to an MCC side that always seemed intent on fielding some of its strongest sides against the Philadelphians—probably the Philadelphians' worst performance). If the Philadelphians' overall record of 4–3–5 could be interpreted as evidence that Philadelphia cricket had not materially improved from five years earlier, it at least clearly indicated that it had not retrogressed.[46]

To English observers, there could no longer be any denying these Philadelphia cricketers had "thoroughly mastered the grammar" of their national pastime while to other critics, these Americans now showed enough proficiency at cricket that they could have been "born on the village green." All this pointed to the fact that by the final decade of the 19th century, Philadelphia had undeniably elevated its cricket from "a noncompetitive leisure activity to a first-class sport." The Quaker city, by every right, could be confident in the future of its game now that it had reached a point where its players and supporters "no longer anywhere expressed fears that cricket will succumb to the many disadvantages it has hereto labored under."[47]

In the context of the times, when the future cricket powers of South Africa and New Zealand were only in their "infancy," still playing, and losing, to visiting England teams at odds, while Philadelphia was beating Ireland, the West Indies, and Canada on the field of play multiple times (beginning in 1888 the Philadelphians would beat Canada five straight years), the Quaker City could, with full justification, look on itself as the world's number-three cricket power after England and Australia.[48]

More significantly, with these accumulating trans-national accomplishments, the Philadelphia cricket community was, year by year, demonstrating the full validity of its sporting ethos where it most mattered: on the field of play ... not only to the city, but to the nation, even the world.

Seven

Clubs, Players, and the Flowering of Late 19th-Century Philadelphia Cricket

Philadelphia had built its cricket world on the three pillars of amateurism, nativism, and internationalism, and as the last decade of the 19th century approached, all these elements were converging in a "fullness of time" for the city's cricket. A commitment to the first had firmly established the ethos and purpose of their sport; the second was its committed development pathway; and the third would be its ultimate measure of accomplishment.

To cricket historians, the period from 1890 to 1914 has long been proclaimed as the "Golden Age" of their sport; a period over which all earlier trends and developments in the game came together to create the edifice of what would be modern cricket, in organization, technical advancement and worldwide presence. In the leading cricket countries of England and Australia, this would be the period that saw the establishment of formal national championships along with more sophisticated administrative bodies, not to mention the appearance, during these years, of some of the game's greatest players. As summed up by the distinguished cricket historian Rowland Bowen, "It is difficult to think of any other period of the game's history when so many important things happened."[1]

Philadelphia would largely mirror and duplicate these trends with its own cricket, though in its own way and largely as a reflection of the impressive overall growth sports were experiencing in the United States itself during this period, maturing and deepening its permanent presence throughout all areas of American society.

All of America's major sports had, or would, also effectively come into existence during this period. Following fast on baseball came gridiron football, basketball, golf, and tennis, whose popularity grew and spread exponentially through a proliferation of clubs and leagues, reflecting an ever expanding sports interest and participation through schools, colleges, athletic clubs, and numerous other social institutions. America's interest and participation in sports of whatever kind, by this period, seemed insatiable.

Despite its minority status as an American sport, cricket wasn't absent from these developments, certainly not in Philadelphia.

The number of active cricket players in the city by 1888 was estimated to be at least 2700, a number that most likely doubled over the next decade if correlated to the increased number of matches and clubs.[2]

From a total of 94 in 1887, the number of reported cricket matches in Philadelphia rose to 103 in 1888, dipping slightly to 90 in 1889 (most probably due to the Gentlemen of Philadelphia's England tour that year), rising to 111 in 1890, then doubling to 225 in 1891. The following year, 239 matches were reported, increasing to 279 in 1895 before peaking at 275 in 1898 and holding steady at 272 in 1899.[3]

Germantown alone could field, in 1895, eight different teams (first, second, third and fourth elevens; first and second junior teams; along with a summer and a veterans team), sides that would play 77 total matches in 1897. On at least one occasion, in 1899, the Belmont club could be found hosting two matches on their ground at the same time.[4]

The city's cricket continued to be dominated by the old, established "Big Five" clubs of the Halifax Cup competition and their membership numbers reflect the popularity of the game at this time.

The largest club, Germantown, claimed 1340 members in 1894, followed by Merion with 1137 members. The Philadelphia club had about 600 members and Belmont 557. The largest non–Halifax Cup clubs, the Tioga and Belfield, had an estimated membership of 500 each. The Pennsylvania Railroad and North End cricket clubs claimed, respectively, 200 and 150 members.[5]

Organizationally, the Halifax Cup, still the city's premier cricket competition, was now joined by several additional leagues set up by the city's many smaller clubs, such as the Quaker City league. By the turn of the century, at least half a dozen such non–Halifax leagues were active in the city.[6]

With full justification the *American Cricketer* could claim, by the mid-1890s, that the growth of cricket in Philadelphia had been "more brilliant and phenomenal" than in any other country outside of Australia.[7]

Among the city's numerous cricket clubs Germantown continued to stand supreme, not only in membership and facilities (all international matches involving representative Philadelphia sides had been played on its grounds at Nicetown since 1868), but also competitive strength, a status that was significantly enhanced with its merger with the Young America club in the late 1880s.

Such a merger between these two Germantown area clubs was, for several reasons, logical. The two organizations were just blocks apart and the lease on both grounds was about to expire, sparking rumors and then informal discussions about combining the two clubs as early as 1886. Despite the economic advantages of such a move, suggestions of a merger were initially opposed by both clubs until it became evident that Germantown had, by the late 1880s, effectively assumed the Young America's very *raison d'être*, namely, as the bastion and champion of the city's "American-first" policy.[8]

With its ability to attract and develop the best young American players in the area, Germantown was also slowly surpassing the Young America as a competitive force. By the late 1880s, the Newhalls were coming to the end of their playing careers, making it harder for the club to attract and retain younger members. By 1888, the Young America club was "down at the heel," as was becoming evident when the once dominant club lost by 162 runs to Belmont. The club was, by this time, losing to such weak sides as the Manhattan cricket club of New York, and even outright defaulting on some of its matches. The handwriting was clearly on the wall with the club's loss to Germantown by the hereto unheard of margin of an innings and 266 runs.[9]

The Young America club was clearly "going backwards" as a viable organization and resistance to any merger eventually weakened. The two clubs informally agreed to merge in 1889 with the union officially finalized on March 17, 1890, the new organization retaining the Germantown name while adopting the Young America club colors of blue and white.[10]

"Higher and higher seems to have been the aim" of this newly created cricket club, an organization whose members soon decided would require a new facility appropriate to the club's elevated status, and in 1890 a magnificent new $25,000 clubhouse was erected on a plot several blocks from the old Nicetown ground. Hereafter always referred to as "Manheim" from the street on which it was located, the facility fully reflected its member claims that here was a cricket ground that was the "finest in America and probably the world."[11]

The Merion club was also on the rise. The organization had advanced competitively from its modest early matches against college teams, to its first match away from Philadelphia in 1872, to a breakout win against Young America in 1877. The club had achieved something of an "international reputation" by beating, in 1880, a Canada team that had, a few days earlier at Nicetown, beaten a representative United States team.[12]

Two years after Germantown opened its new grounds Merion relocated from Ardmore, its home since 1873, to Haverford and as the only major Philadelphia cricket club to outright own its ground, erected an impressive new $25,000 clubhouse of its own that was fully comparable to Germantown.[13]

Tragedy struck in 1896 when the clubhouse caught fire and burned to the ground (destroying, among other things, the club's original charter), a calamity that would befall almost all Philadelphia's major cricket clubs during this era of oil lamps and nonexistent sprinkler systems. Disaster revisited the club when another fire barely six months later heavily damaged the rebuilt clubhouse (one "replete in every detail" with amenities). This wouldn't prevent Merion, however, from hosting one of the matches with the visiting Australian team that fall, nor handicap the club, by the end of the decade, from reaching a stature in membership and competitive reputation fully equal to Germantown.[14]

After years of location insecurity, the Belmont club also, during these years, settled into its own new and improved facilities while also enjoying an enhanced competitive standing. The club had always been of a slightly different stamp from the other Halifax Cup clubs. Domiciled in West Philadelphia, rather than the city's Northeast suburbs, the Belmont club catered more to a middle-class business, rather than professional, clientele, with a membership reputed to be "not so much a fashionable as it is a cricket loving throng."[15]

The club took its competitive lumps early in its history, once losing to the St. George club, in 1877, by the embarrassing score of 340-27. But its playing strength rapidly improved in the 1880s, the local press noting "its vigorous growth in the past few years has been a matter of surprise to the older cricket organizations" and the club's various teams were, by 1890, playing as many as 56 total matches in a single season.[16]

Belmont's location, however, made it vulnerable to the incursions of Philadelphia's expanding railroad network, and the right of eminent domain forced the club to relocate twice in the span of three years, from its original grounds at 49th and Baltimore to 58th and Woodward in 1893 and, after clearing trees and brush from an undeveloped plot, finally finding a permanent home at 49th and Chester in 1885.[17]

In 1888, the organization's clubhouse was also damaged (though not entirely destroyed) by fire but also quickly rebuilt and, in 1893, it was greatly expanded, bringing it up to a standard fully comparable to those of its Halifax Cup rivals.[18]

For the city's apostolic cricket club, the Philadelphia, these were, by contrast, unsettled times both logistically and competitively. Hard times began when the club lost its old antebellum ground at Camden, New Jersey, in 1872, another cricket casualty to railroad expansion. For the next seven years, the Philadelphia club had no permanent home of its own, playing its games as an alien tenant on the Germantown and

Seven. Flowering of Late 19th-Century Philadelphia Cricket   87

The Belmont Cricket Club during the time of its location at 58th and Darby. It would be the only "Big Four" Halifax Cup club not to survive to this day (courtesy Library Company of Philadelphia).

Young America grounds. It was a handicap that contributed to the club's steep competitive decline, the organization having to resort, during these years, to playing non-members for some of its matches, as it did in 1879, or not playing any official matches at all, which happened in 1880.[19]

For all practical purposes, the club should have probably disbanded and allowed its members to join more stable and viable organizations. A lifeline, however, was thrown to the Philadelphia club in the early 1880s through an arrangement to merge with the Chestnut Hill cricket club in Wissahickon (earlier attempts to merge with the Germantown club had been rebuffed). The merger was facilitated by the plans of wealthy Philadelphia businessman Henry Houston, who must have realized that the presence of the city's oldest cricket club would enhance the quality of life for area residents.[20]

The merger was finalized in 1882 with the newly amalgamated club retaining the Philadelphia name and, in 1885, the organization celebrated its rebirth by also erecting, that year, a fine new clubhouse.[21]

Improved facilities and organizational stability, unfortunately, didn't translate into improved competitive performance for the Philadelphia cricket club. After its "long rest" from high-level competition, the club formally entered the Halifax Cup competition in 1886 but would linger for years as a perennial also-ran. The club had difficulty fielding full teams for some of its 1888 matches and experienced a humiliating 243–41 loss to Germantown that same year, eliciting the sarcastic comment that the match "might just as well been forfeited" by the losing side. Nor did the club's first win in the Halifax Cup in 1889 portend better times. For years, the Philadelphia club continued its persistently losing and neglectful ways: failing to show for its scheduled matches against Haverford College for three straight years, forfeiting some of its second XI matches in 1890, and seeing its junior team score an abysmal two total runs in a match against the Germantown juniors.[22]

The city's oldest, once most revered, cricket club remained, during these years, wallowed in "an unfathomable sea of difficulties." Yet such was the dedication to its legacy that club members persevered through these times and eventually surprised the city's cricket community by beating the powerful Germantown club twice in the Halifax Cup in 1894, even finishing third in the competition the following year, its highest finish to date. The impressive new clubhouse erected by the club in 1897 at least allowed Philadelphia to lay claim to being the only city in the world at that time that now had fully four first-class cricket grounds.[23]

"What with the building of clubs, extending grounds, strengthening clubs that were previously anything but weak," the *Philadelphia Inquirer* proclaimed in 1890, "there should be such an infusion of interest among cricket circles as to render the coming season an exceptional one." This "infusion" of interest would, in fact, carry through for a full decade and propel Philadelphia cricket, over that time, to its most impressive period of growth, influence, and competitive accomplishments.[24]

Nationally, the city's head-and-shoulders cricket superiority was unassailable, and any outside cricket club that ventured into the lair of Philadelphia cricket over the last two decades of the century were routinely sent home, one after the other, with overwhelming, often humiliating, defeats. The Longwood cricket club, Boston's premier cricket organization fully comparable, in status and organization, to Philadelphia's Halifax Cup clubs, lost all three of its matches during a visit to the Quaker City in 1881 and suffered an identical fate during its return visit three years later. The Staten Island cricket club, which, since the late 1870s, had succeeded the St. George as New York's leading cricket organization, was also swept in its three Philadelphia matches in 1882. The Baltimore cricket club—the most socially vibrant but competitively weak of the country's major metropolitan cricket clubs and an organization known more "for the excellence of the lunch than the cricket"—also left winless following the four matches it played in Philadelphia in 1880, including a 357–65 humiliation at the hands of the Young America club.[25]

A largely identical fate befell visiting cricket clubs from farther afield. The team of cricket-starved English residents that journeyed to Philadelphia from Virginia in 1876 returned home with a 310–63 loss, but this would be less embarrassing than the 443–25 annihilation that the Pennsylvania Railroad company cricket team pinned on another Virginia club from Roanoke in 1893, with Arthur Wood, playing for the company team, scoring 278 runs. The Canadian cricketers from Winnipeg who visited the city in 1890 were not rewarded for their long trek, posting three straight losses.[26]

Smaller out-of-town clubs that dared challenge Philadelphia's top-tier clubs at full strength were routinely and invariably punished for their over confidence, as was the case with the Trenton cricket club in 1901. Obliging the New Jersey club's insistence that it field a full-strength side, the Belmont club proceeded to thrash its outclassed opponent 290–55.[27]

Philadelphia cricket clubs would occasionally lose to out-of-town opponents, but these losses did nothing to cast doubts on the city's national cricket dominance. Any thoughts of reaching competitive parity that New York may have entertained after upsetting Germantown in 1895 evaporated when a representative Philadelphia team, five years later, administered a crushing innings and 349 run loss to a team of New York's best cricketers. With full justification, Philadelphia believed, by 1890, that the city had to look for competition overseas, since there just weren't any "American teams that could teach [Philadelphia] anything."[28]

Now reaping the rewards of its "American-first" policy, along with the benefits of improved facilities and an ambitious leadership, Philadelphia cricket would, above all, be propelled forward on the achievements of what would be its most talented and experienced generation of cricketers.

From the late 1880s through the first decade of the 20th century, Philadelphia would produce numerous talented cricket players, though objectively evaluating their merits and abilities is difficult given the widely varied strength of their opposition. At least six individuals, however, would stand out, by general consensus of the most knowledgeable cricket observers, both domestic and foreign, as unquestionably first class (professional level), several of international caliber, and one of unquestionably all-world ability.

Lester dubbed the period of Philadelphia cricket from 1890 to 1897 the "Patterson Period." It's always a distinguished, but usually disputable, honor to have an entire era identified with one individual, but Lester's declaration, within the context of the times and the man, seems to be largely justified.[29]

The son of a University of Pennsylvania law professor, George Patterson was very much the product of the Philadelphia cricket "system" during the 1880s. Beginning his cricket at the Germantown Academy, he followed the prescribed *cursus honorum* for the proper Philadelphia cricketer: Haverford College, Germantown's junior team, University of Pennsylvania law school (graduate-level students, at that time, being allowed to play for university athletic teams), the Germantown first XI and, ultimately, the Gentlemen of Philadelphia.[30]

Patterson's cricket abilities first drew attention when, as an eighteen-year-old, the "little wonder" displayed a tenacious batting stand in Philadelphia's loss to Thornton's visiting English side in 1886. Over the next eleven years, he would be an automatic selection for, and eventually captain of, all representative Philadelphia sides for which he was available. He topped his team's batting averages during Philadelphia's English tour in 1889 as well as made the top score in the city's historic win over Lord Hawke's English team in 1891. The bat with which he made his impressive 109 runs against Frank Mitchell's Oxbridge team in 1895 was displayed at the Colonnade Hotel for the admiration of the public.[31]

"Slow-gaited, slow of speech," Patterson was "not a sensational batsman but was steady and consistent." In the estimation of Frank Mitchell (always an unflattering critic of Philadelphia cricket), he was the one Philadelphia cricketer of unquestioned English first-class batting standard and, according to his longtime teammate John Lester, the one player who would stand as "a model for Philadelphia cricketers for the next fifteen years."[32]

Different in style and following a slightly different cricket pathway was Patterson's teammate Frank Bohlen. Like Patterson, Bohlen began playing serious cricket as a Germantown junior in the early 1880s but developed his skills at St. Paul's school in Concord, New Hampshire, a school with a long cricket-playing tradition, though more as a feeder for cricket clubs in Boston and New York rather than Philadelphia. Nor was the start of Bohlen's career as impressive as Patterson's, the future international scoring 0 and 1 run in the first match with his Germantown club in 1885. He had, however, worked his way onto that club's first XI by 1889, his "breakout" coming the following year when he scored an unprecedented four centuries that season (scoring 100 runs or more in a single time at bat; not all that astonishing since a cricket batter can score as many as six runs with one swing of the bat).[33]

"His defense," according to one English observer, "is superb and ... his method of adapting himself to the circumstances is particularly admirable." From the time of his *annus mirabilis* in 1890, and for the next eighteen years, he would be, as well, an automatic selection for all representative Philadelphia sides when he was available. Probably the finest of his many outstanding batting performances came against the visiting Australian team in 1893, when his "commanding style" saw him top score for his Philadelphia side in all three innings he played.[34]

One of the few Americans to hold membership in the MCC, England's most revered and prestigious sporting organization at that time, Bohlen was one of the even fewer Americans to actually play for team, considered England's flagship cricket club. A "stylish batsman with a strong off-drive" (able to hit to "right field" with power), according to Lord Hawke, "and an enthusiast to bargain," Bohlen was on the MCC side in its match against Leicestershire in 1894 and, that same year, had the honor of opening (batting "lead off") with the legendary W.G. Grace in its match against a visiting South African team.[35]

For all their declared preference for native-born American cricketers on their representative teams, Philadelphia cricket authorities couldn't ignore the talent among their resident English cricketers, two of whom could not be denied a significant and standout role in the city's cricket history.

Arthur Wood, unquestionably the city's most talented resident English cricketer from the time he was hired as Belmont's professional in 1881 until Lester's appearance, had patiently endured the city's American-first policy until he was finally qualified for selection to Philadelphia's representative teams in 1892. Over the next sixteen years he would confirm his place as one of the most reliable and consistent scorers on the city's representative sides. A batter who was "effective, not graceful" in style, Wood would amass, over his career, 7,157 runs in the Halifax Cup competition, more than any other individual and, at the age of forty-seven, would top the batting averages for the Gentlemen of Philadelphia on their final first-class England tour in 1908.[36]

Justice wouldn't be so long denied Philadelphia's other Anglo-American cricket star, John Lester.

Emigrating to Philadelphia in 1892 to join his family, and enrolling at Haverford College as a mature student of twenty-one, Lester was soon marked as the "best player the college has ever had"—the top scorer, by a wide margin, for his college side during its first England tour in 1896.[37]

Despite opposition from Germantown, he couldn't be denied a place on the Gentlemen of Philadelphia side that played the visiting Australians that fall, and from that date on, he, too, would be an automatic selection for, and sometime captain of, every representative Philadelphia side for which he played.[38]

"His success as a batter," (Lester referring to himself in the third person), "was based on sound defense ... his hitting was hard and clean all around the wicket." Captain, by unanimous consent, of the Philadelphia teams that toured England in 1903 and 1908, Lester was Philadelphia's top run maker during the first tour when he won adulation from English critics as "the one [Philadelphian] batsman who may almost [be] described as great."[39]

Despite its immersion within a sporting culture fixated on batting balls and scoring runs, Philadelphia cricket would never, however, be able to carry this facet of its cricket, which should have been so instinctive and natural for baseball-bred Americans, beyond this limitation of "almost great." From the city would come, over the decades, a succession of talented, some unquestionably first class, batters but Philadelphia would never produce a batting star comparable to a W.G. Grace, the Cambridge University–educated Indian Prince Ranjitsinhji (always referred to by contemporaries as "Ranji") or Victor Trumper, three of the greatest cricket batters for English and Australian teams of that era.

The story would be different with bowling. The Philadelphians would develop this facet of their game, despite its unnatural (to Americans), stiff-armed, javelin-type, throwing motion, to a standard of proficiency and skill fully equal to the best of that era.

It was a proficiency that Americans seemed to evidence from their earliest involvement with the game, and in all areas of the country. Before the Civil War John G. French, from Utica, New York, was widely reputed to be the fastest bowler in the country, English or American, once throwing, it was claimed, a cricket ball 103 yards.[40]

Probably even more talented was the standout early New York baseballer James Creighton, whose exceptional ability soon had him doing double duty playing baseball for that city's top baseball clubs and cricket for the St. George club, allowing him to lay claim to probably being America's first two-sport star before his tragic death at the age of twenty-one.[41]

Another baseballer-turned-cricketer, Edward Sprague, rose to prominence in New York cricket in the 1870s. This former star player for the Eckford baseball club greatly unsettled the powerful Australians in 1878 with his archaic, yet effective, underarm throws, "the most puzzling kind of balls" that "caroms over the ground with fearful hop and skip" (the bowler in cricket can throw the ball to the batter on the bounce as well as on the fly), deliveries that completely "placed them [the Australian batters] upon the defensive."[42]

Sprague's bowling was equally "destructive" against the Irish amateurs the following year, the ex-baseballer finishing with figures of 4–56 (he got out, during his time bowling, four of the opposing team's ten total batters during their innings—turn at bat—while allowing 56 runs. The more batters a bowler gets out and the fewer runs allowed, the more outstanding the bowling performance). Later that fall, this American bowler gave Daft's English professionals the same treatment, bowling the English captain himself for only five runs, confirming the Englishman's declaration that "the bowlers we met in America were superior, as a rule, to the batsmen."[43]

Another American, J. Lawrence Poole, also brought his bowling talent to New York over the following decade. This St. Paul school alumnus soon rose to prominence as the city's outstanding bowler, his fast deliveries "breathed death" against Sanders's English team in 1885, where he returned figures of 7–44 and, against the visiting West Indies team the following year, 6–35.[44]

With the Baltimore cricket club was Kelsey Mallinckrodt, "a genius for disguising pace," according to English batting star Gilbert Jessop, who personally witnessed this American bowler go 9–103 against his visiting English team in 1897.[45]

Even in distant Detroit, word was circulating that the American F.C. Irving, playing for the city's Peninsular cricket club in the 1880s, was emerging as "one of the most destructive bowlers in America."[46]

By the early 1880s, English cricket observers had seen, or personally experienced, enough of the bowling strength of their trans-Atlantic cousins to concede "American bowling, while far below the English standard as a general thing, is frequently strong and very puzzling."[47]

If American cricketers, in general, were developing a special knack for good quality bowling, the cricketers of Philadelphia would develop and elevate one particular style, fast bowling, into a veritable tradition. Before the Civil War, John Provost had stood out as the city's outstanding bowler with his fast and uniquely deceptive style, and was succeeded, in the immediate postwar years, by the left-handed Philadelphia cricket club fast bowler Spencer Meade. In the estimation of MCC team manager Robert Fitzgerald, this son of the Union commander at Gettysburg was "by far" a better bowler than his more celebrated teammate Charlie Newhall.[48]

No less talented was Warren Duhring of the Germantown club who, by 1886, was widely recognized as the premier fast bowler in the country, succeeded, in 1891, by another standout fast bowler, Charles Palmer, who shared the stage with the young, gifted, Tioga cricket club fast bowler Fred Bates. The last mentioned was considered by many a player "fully competent to fill the shoes of King or Lester." Though he wouldn't live up to these expectations as a member of the Gentlemen of Philadelphia teams to visit England in 1897 and 1903, Bates actually outperformed his more famous bowling teammate, John B. King, in several matches during those tours.[49]

The supply of high-quality fast bowlers in Philadelphia during this period seemed limitless. At the Belmont club was the "left handed phenomenon" George Jump; at the Philadelphia cricket club was Silas Climenson, a "truly remarkable bowler" who returned figures of 5–41 as a member of the Philadelphia Colts side against P.F. Warner's English team in 1898. If not for the long, uninterrupted careers of J.B. King and Percy Clark, and the availability of Lester and Patterson, outstanding batters who could also do double duty as change (relief) bowlers, many of these talented players would have had more opportunities to showcase their abilities at the international level.[50]

Two, however, would get the opportunity. Henry Sayen, Merion's young, tear-away, fast bowler, astonished cricket observers by bowling the first five Belmont batters for single digits in 1907, thereby claiming for himself a place on the Gentlemen of Philadelphia side for their tour of England the following year as King's "understudy."[51]

In the twilight years of the city's cricket, Henry Pearce, also from Merion, enjoyed a brief moment of fame in going 7–57, five clean bowled, against the powerful Australian team that visited Philadelphia in 1913.[52]

All these individuals, the great and almost great, would, however, be far eclipsed by the towering figure in the history of Philadelphia cricket: John Barton King.

Born a year after the MCC visit of 1872, this son of a Philadelphia dry goods dealer didn't seem destined for cricket at all until his close friend and future cricket teammate, Eddie Cregar, "weaned" him from his "overwhelming desire to become a baseball pitcher" and persuaded King to join the recently organized Tioga cricket club in the late 1880s.[53]

Initially a not particularly impressive performer as a member of that club's junior team, King, then known more for his batting, first gave evidence of his bowling talent with a 6–7 spell against the Philadelphia club juniors in 1889, the local press noting that here was a fifteen-year-old whose cricket abilities were "deserving of mention."[54]

Doing double duty as opener (leadoff batter) and captain of his Central High School cricket team as well as a starter for the Tioga senior side to which he had been promoted, King was soon earmarked as "one of the coming cricketers of the city" after an impressive 8–39 bowling performance against the powerful Belmont club in 1890. His bowling against Germantown the following year was "remarkably straight," leading observers to demand that this young talent "should be bowled both oftener and longer."[55]

King's bowling seems to have reached such a point of maturity and effectiveness by 1892 that the now eighteen-year-old was reeling off a string of eye-catching bowling performances over that summer, with spells of 5–73 against Germantown, 6–17 against Merion and bowling George Patterson, the city's premier batter, for ducks (a score of 0) on two occasions.[56]

The prognostications of "really big things" for the teenager were beginning to come to reality and demands that he should now be playing for the city's representative teams were satisfied with his selection to the United States side in its annual match against Canada that year. He didn't disappoint. On this, his debut in international cricket, King claimed three first innings wickets (put outs) for a miserly six runs in just four overs (four spells of, at that time, five pitches each), 2–15 in his six, second innings, overs.[57]

It was the inauguration of what would be a stellar, historic career at high-level cricket that would see King an automatic selection, over the next twenty years, for every representative Philadelphia side with the exception of several away matches against Canada.

King was a fast bowler, very fast. His lanky 6'1", 178-pound frame was ideal for the strenuous demands of this type of bowling (since the bowler in cricket can take a run up when he throws, the fastest bowlers often take long, sprinting run ups, followed by powerful, all-out releases), allowing him to consistently send down deliveries that were "first class, dangerous, well-varied, well-pitched, clean and resolute." Complementing these physical attributes were his long, powerful, fingers, so strong that King could, without moving his wrist, it was claimed, "send a new cricket ball to the second story window with a snip of two fingers and a thumb."[58]

His success, reputation and legacy would rest upon one signature pitch in particular: his deadly and lethal "angler," a very fast ball that sharply broke into a (right-handed) batter over the last yard. King himself claims to have learned to throw this delivery largely "by accident," though the ability to throw a "curve ball" in cricket was nothing new, having been utilized by several earlier Philadelphia bowlers as King himself acknowledged. Young America cricketer William Noble was throwing a ball that curved "while in the air" as early as 1885, and his successors Charles Palmer and Cope Morton could also bowl "a big curve." The Canadians were so amazed with the "curve" bowling of Germantown's Henry Brown during his destructive 6–12 spell in the U.S.-Canada match of 1888 that they believed they were witnessing "a great revolution in bowling."[59]

Philadelphia, in fact, seemed to nurture, both before and after King, a veritable school of fast curve bowling, Australian Herbert Hordern noting, during his cricket-playing tenure in the city as a University of Pennsylvania dental student, "nearly every bowler in America [meaning Philadelphia] is able to make the ball curve." It was a weapon in Philadelphia's cricket arsenal whose over-reliance didn't always work to its advantage. This "fast slinging" and "tear away, erratic" bowling that Philadelphia bowlers preferred to the neglect of slower, more deceptive, bowling would, on more than one occasion, put them at great disadvantage in conditions that did not favor their preferred type of bowling.[60]

The bowling of all these predecessors, no matter how successful, wouldn't, however, be as effective nor destructive as King's "angler," which was produced through a combination of ball speed, height of delivery, and wrist action rather than a swerve generated by ball polish typical of most modern swing (curve) bowlers. King claimed he could curve a ball best when it was new but could do it with a ball in any condition. This particular delivery of King's had to be released very high, almost over his left shoulder, and with a "sharp downward flick of the wrist," which seemed to provide the horizontal spin necessary for the inward curve, as explained by F.M. Gilbert in his contemporary article describing the physics behind a curving cricket ball ("one of the easiest spins for a right-hand bowler" he claimed, "with a high delivery"). These deliveries of King's weren't "floaters" and, to gain the required level of air resistance, "could not be bowled except with a very fast ball."[61]

These requirements account for the reports of King's unorthodox, even "freakish," run up and release. For his fastest ball he "took a longer run up from a point wide on the leg side [left side of the batter]." Then, as he sprinted in, King "raised his bowling arm high in the air" at the moment of release, throwing up his other arm "like Sousa conducting" in "a dreadful manner" that was "a most awe inspiring spectacle" before releasing the ball with such speed he seemed to be "simply a human cannon."[62]

Bowled under ideal conditions which, for King, was with a strong breeze blowing in from the off (batter's right) side, this "Wild Man from Borneo," also dubbed the "Hell Bender" by contemporary observers and opponents, was a "decidedly nasty one," a delivery "good for a wicket every time," and one from which King "knows he has bowled a man even before his ball strikes the ground."[63]

There were certainly other expert practitioners of curve bowling at that time, such as England's George Hirst, but even foreign cricket observers conceded "nobody is so good as the Philadelphia amateur" and few could deliver the near unplayable ball like the one King sent down to Bernard Bosanquet in Philadelphia's match against an MCC side in 1905. This remarkable ball "swerved from the off, pitched [bounced] just outside the off stump [the pole of the wicket farthest from the batter] and hit the leg stump [pole closest to the batter]. It must have bowled," an observer noted "any batsman in the world." E.R. Wilson, with Bosanquet's English team in 1901, and C.J. Burnup, with the Kent side that visited Philadelphia in 1903, certainly weren't the only batters so fooled by the movement of King's deliveries that they were both bowled without even playing a stroke (swinging at the ball).[64]

King's signature delivery, seldom seen or encountered by the rest of the cricket world, must have been particularly lethal against first-class (professional level) batters who faced King for the first time, and his record as a strike bowler (meaning by this the ability to get out one or both of a team's first two batters for single digits) against top-level cricketers was impressive.

A sampling: R.A. Bennett 0 (Philadelphia vs Hampshire, 1897), R.H. Howitt 0 (Philadelphia vs Nottingham, 1897), A. Peatfield 0 (Philadelphia vs Glamorgan, 1903), C.H. Eyre 0 (Philadelphia vs MCC, 1903), W.V. Jepson 0 (Philadelphia vs Hampshire, 1908), L.G. Wright 0 (Philadelphia vs Derbyshire 1908), W.L. Murdoch 1 (Philadelphia vs Sussex, 1897), L.J. Moon 1 (Philadelphia vs Middlesex, 1908), R.H. Turner 1 (Philadelphia vs Nottingham, 1908), C.H. Marsham 2 (Philadelphia vs Kent, 1908), Willie (not his more famous brother Walter) Quaife 3 (Philadelphia vs Warwickshire, 1897), C.E. de Trafford 4 (Philadelphia vs Lord Hawke's team, 1894), E.G. Wynyard 4 (Philadelphia vs MCC, 1907), Olympic gold medalist J.W. Douglas 5 (Philadelphia vs MCC 1907).

Against Australian international openers King claimed the wickets of: Charlie Kelleway 1 (Philadelphia vs Australians 1912), T.J. Mathews 3 (Philadelphia vs Australians 1912), and J. Darling 8 (Philadelphia vs Australians 1896).

The "angler" often came to the batter as a full toss (fly ball) and its effectiveness was diminished without an array of complementary pitches which King also developed. He was the only bowler, it was claimed, who could, without changing his grip, also swerve the ball to the off (away from a right-handed batter), even though King claimed this delivery was "of very little use except as a change." It must, however, have been an excellent "set-up" delivery for his frequently used, and deadly, in-swinging yorker (a ball that bounces at the batter's feet) along with a deceptive slow ball. To his teammate on Philadelphia's England tour in 1908, Herbert Hordern, King was "several very good bowlers in one man." To English cricket critics he was "a real schemer" in his uncanny ability to keep batters off balance and guessing with his arsenal of deliveries. Summed up by one English critic, this American cricketer "never seemed to lose his pace and his slow ball, coupled with a constant variety of length [ball placement] made his bowling very puzzling and effective."[65]

Correctly anticipating catches from an inside edge (ball ticking the edge of the bat closest to the batter), to his fast in-swinging balls, King placed his field in what would come to be conventionally known as "fast leg theory." As again described by Hordern, King had "short square leg in about three yards from the batsman; fine leg four or five yards back, mid-on close in, and a man like a silly mid-on about six feet away [fielders placed close in front of and to the left of the batter, behind the batter's left side, and close in to his right side, there being no foul territory in cricket]." This field placement, "peculiar" as it seemed to Hordern, was tactically effective enough to allow the Australian, himself usually playing at the short square leg position, to take, he claimed, sixteen catches off King's bowling during Philadelphia's 1908 England tour.[66]

Taken as a whole, the bowling of this Philadelphian, when at its best, must have put even the most talented cricket batters under intense pressure, severely testing their abilities and skills, as described in the sequence of pitches that led to the downfall of Australian George Giffen, a player "head and shoulders above all his colleagues" as a batter, when he faced King in 1893: "First ball just missed leg stump; second and third played with the greatest difficulty; fourth beat him; appeal for catch on the fifth; last went off bat shoulder to slip ["foul tick" caught by a fielder playing a short distance behind the batter]."[67]

Over the course of his playing career at high-level cricket, King would build a reputation that advanced from being the finest cricket player in America, to being a certain selection for the All-England team, and to being an unquestioned member of that era's All-World team.[68]

Can these claims be supported? Just exactly how good was this American bowler? The difficulty with making an accurate evaluation of King's true stature comes from the limited number of international and first-class matches he played. The 415 wickets he took (batters he got out), which included nine hat tricks (getting out three straight batters on three straight pitches), in just 65 first-class matches, is impressive enough, but this was spread out over a twenty-year period. On only four occasions, and nine total matches, did King's Philadelphia teams play against fully international strength competition: Ranji's England side in 1899 (a nearly All-England strength batting team with the likes of Ranji, Archie McLaren, Gilbert Jessop, etc., in the lineup), and the Australian sides of 1893, 1896 and 1912, the last being a less than full-strength Australian side.[69]

King's figures against Ranji's team were unimpressive (1–102 and 3–90). But his performances against the Australian sides were certainly noteworthy (5–78 in 1893, 5–43 in 1896 and 5–22 in 1912) and compare almost as favorably to the best performances by England's top bowlers against these same Australian teams (Tom Richardson 5–49 in 1893; 6–39 in 1896, and Frank Woolley's 5–20 in 1912).

Against non-representative first-class (professional level) teams many of King's performances are simply jaw dropping, with numerous multi-wicket hauls, the most notable being his 7–13 against Sussex (1897), 9–25 against Warner's English team (1897), 7–28 against Derbyshire (1908),

Seven. Flowering of Late 19th-Century Philadelphia Cricket   99

8–39 against Oxford University (1903), 4–19 against the MCC (1908) and 9–62 against Lancashire (1903), the last being, in Lester's estimation, "the best bowling ever done by an American in England."[70]

If King had limited opportunities playing against the best teams of his era, he would face most of its top batters and here his performances are even more impressive. He bowled Ranji first ball (first pitch) in Philadelphia's match against Sussex; bowled Stanley Jackson for 4 against Yorkshire; bowled Lionel Palairet for a duck against Somerset, bowled Bobby Abel for 6 against Surrey, all during Philadelphia's 1897 England tour, along with William Gunn for 10 against Nottingham on Philadelphia's 1903 England tour.

In the estimation of C.B. Frye (himself one of England's finest batters of that period, whose wicket King also picked up, for a single run, in an exhibition match against Sussex during Philadelphia's 1903 England tour). the first three mentioned were the finest English cricket batters of the era and King would, on the few occasions when he played against them, quickly, comprehensively, and cheaply, master them all.[71]

Bloodless statistics, however, tell only so much. When these figures are complemented by the personal testimony of the batters who faced King an even more compelling impression emerges of the Philadelphian.

Pelham Warner, who probably faced King more times than any other overseas player, was certainly in a position to personally justify the American's inclusion in his All World Eleven from the fact that this captain of England's national cricket team, who played against the best bowlers of his era, had fallen to King no fewer than five times for the paltry scores of 8, 3, 4, 13 and 17 between 1897 and 1903. Herbert Hordern had a long and close enough observation of King as his teammate on Philadelphia's England tour in 1908 to proclaim, without reservation, that this Philadelphia bowler was "worth a place on any team in the world." Syd Gregory, captain of Australia's national cricket team, would probably find few who wouldn't agree with his proclamation that King was the "greatest bowler in the world" after the American had bowled him for a duck with a "screamer" that went between his legs during Australia's visit to Philadelphia in 1912.[72]

Gregory would certainly get no arguments from his Australian teammates, who had been so thoroughly dominated by King's bowling during their visit to Philadelphia that, by tour's end, they could in all truthfulness state that this American was the one bowler in the world they "dreaded more than Barnes" (Syd Barnes, standout English bowler of that era).[73]

Against sub-first class opponents King was a man among boys, overwhelming hapless weekender teams with such ludicrous returns as 10–20 against a Manhattan, New York, side (all clean bowled), 7–1 against a K.I.B.A. side in 1895, and 6–16 against a Cleveland cricket team in 1899.[74]

Many demonstrably inferior opponents were often intentionally spared King's fury, such as the weak Sherwood team in 1900, the Bermuda team that visited Philadelphia in 1905, and a representative New York side in 1906, all matches in which King, mercifully, just batted but did not bowl for his team.[75]

Overlooked in most conversations of King's cricket abilities is the fact that he was also a not untalented batter, though this facet of his game developed much more slowly. From an inauspicious pair (failing to score a single run in his two times at bat) batting bottom of the order against a visiting Irish team in 1892, King progressively improved his batting abilities, steadily moving up the batting order on both his Belmont club (which he joined in 1895) and representative Philadelphia sides, and eventually securing his place as the established opener (leadoff hitter) in almost all important matches.[76]

Without question his greatest performance with the bat was against Surrey during Philadelphia's 1903 England tour, King coming up short, by just two runs, from making a century (98 runs in his first innings, batting for over two and a quarter hours; 113 runs in his second innings, batting for over two and a half hours, an onslaught that included eighteen fours—ground balls batted out of the ground) in each of his two times at bat. This feat was accomplished against a much higher caliber opponent, and thus much more impressive, than his 344 runs against a Merion "B" team in 1906 (to this day the highest individual score in North American cricket) or his 315 runs against Germantown in 1905.[77]

At the peak of his career King had progressed from being, in Warner's estimation, just America's finest all-round cricket player to being a genuine world-class all-rounder (a player who can hold a starting place as either a batter or bowler, comparable to a MLB player who, year in and year out, bats .295 and hits a dozen home runs as a batter and wins fifteen games as a pitcher), equal, perhaps, to some of the greatest in the game, as evidenced by the fact that on more than one occasion the Philadelphian excelled as both batter and bowler in the same match.[78]

His 7–13 spell when bowling against Sussex in 1897 also came with a well-played 58 runs when batting. A bowling spell of 8–39 against Oxford University in 1903 saw him also hit up a useful 47 runs that same match, while his 5–22 against the Australians in 1912 came along with a well-hit 45 runs. On more than one occasion his match performances became veritable ironman exhibitions, an extended opening batting stand immediately followed by a devastating spell with the ball. Kent was victimized twice this way in a single season, King opening with 47 runs and then blitzing the English county side with a 5–58 spell in 1903. He then followed this up with an opening 41 runs and 7–39 bowling onslaught against the same opponent when in Philadelphia that fall. Hampshire got much the same treatment in 1908, King opening with a half century (scoring fifty or more runs in a single time at bat) followed by a 5–110 bowling performance. So did Canada on two occasions. King, in the U.S.-Canada match of 1902, followed a 7–28 bowling assault with an opening 56 while in the 1912 match his opening 43-run stand came with a destructive 5–15 bowling spell. Things could be even worse for inferior sides, the Baltimore cricket club being bludgeoned by King's opening 168 followed by an 8–35 bowling blitz.[79]

By the end of his career, King had accumulated 39 centuries against all levels of competition and won the Childs Cup (awarded annually to the city's top-performing cricket player since 1880) nine times for bowling and seven times for batting, winning both awards the same season four times.[80]

And what of the man himself, the person behind the facts and figures? Fame seems to have rested lightly on this sports super-star, partially, no doubt, due to the circumstances of playing his cricket in America and partly to the nature of the man. The personality that comes through in Lester's pen portrait (see Appendix) reveals an athlete supremely confident of his abilities but not arrogant or overbearing, with no evidence of the moody, brooding temperament so often found with fast bowlers.

If cricket, as often claimed, is "eminently a social game," King fully immersed himself in this world. He was a great socializer, loved to give long, engaging, talks and was well known for his "storehouse of racy humor." By all accounts, this American cricketer was "a great personality," dubbed by one critic as "the Bob Hope of cricketers." With a career unmarred by controversies he was, whether acknowledged or not, the closest Philadelphia would have as an ambassador of its cricket, an individual who "has every requisite that personifies a star artist."[81]

Bowling in cricket is always done in pairs and a minimum of two players on the fielding team must bowl in any given match. The effectiveness of even the most talented bowler, consequently, is halved without the support of a reliable and effective bowling partner.

Throughout the prime of King's career, he and Philadelphia cricket were fortunate to have this complementary bowling threat with Percy Clark.

Clark was also a product of the Germantown junior system, though he began playing with the Young America club during its final years. Not a prodigious bowling talent like King, Clark, from the time of his international debut against the visiting Australians in 1896 to the final days of the city's cricket, would be on every overseas representative Philadelphia side except for the 1908 England tour (he was unavailable).[82]

His stock-in-trade was a fast out-swinger (a pitch that curves away from a right-handed batter), a ball that "appeared to be on the batsmen's legs and finished up on the off stump and, in addition, got up from the pitch very abruptly." Though never as consistent a wicket taking threat as his more famous bowling partner, Clark, with his ability "to make the ball curve from leg in a most remarkable and surprising manner," along with a slower ball and a pitch that seems to have been a cutter (a spinning ball that dips when it bounces), must have doubled King's effectiveness with this contrasting bowling style. King himself readily acknowledged the fact, noting "my effectiveness was to a large extent conditioned on what was coming down from the other end."[83]

Only four months older than King, Clark would spend almost his entire career in King's shadow, but it would be a longer international career ending at the age of forty-seven against the visiting Incogniti English team in 1920. Like King, Clark was also a useful and reliable batter, especially late in his career, and if this American bowling duo would never reach the stature of an Anderson and Broad or Ambrose and Walsh (two future record setting English and West Indies bowling duos), they could stake the rare claim in cricket history of being one of the very few fast bowing duos that were also both genuine all-rounders.

All the advances displayed by Philadelphia with its cricket during these years didn't, however, seem to overly impress the broader cricket world. Success on the international stage remained the true test for any aspiring cricket-playing nation, and the leading cricket countries were still reluctant to offer Philadelphia a place on this stage despite the Gentlemen of Philadelphia's noteworthy performances on their English tours in 1884 and 1889. Philadelphia's old adversaries, the Irish, had made a second trip to the city in 1888 but no English team had visited since 1886, while the Australians continued to snub the Americans, reportedly turning down numerous invitations to visit the United States during the decade.

The city's pleas to the wider cricket world were finally answered in 1891 when, after three years of repeated and concerted attempts, Germantown was able to persuade Lord Hawke to bring a team of English amateurs to Philadelphia that fall.[84]

Under the circumstances of the time, it was a logical arrangement. Lord Hawke—an "autocratic, opinionated, utterly self-confident" captain of one of England's strongest cricket clubs and a "bluff and abrasive Yorkshireman—was, like his close friend Lord Harris, a staunch imperialist and firm believer in cricket's role as a conduit of Anglo-Saxon values. It was a role that this "Odysseus of cricket" would play to the hilt, personally leading English cricket sides on numerous tours throughout the British empire; Philadelphia would be one of his first destinations.[85]

Seven. Flowering of Late 19th-Century Philadelphia Cricket

Many things seemed to foretell that there would be "never so much interest" in this particular cricket match: the first major match played at Germantown's new ground; an opponent led by a member of the English peerage; opposed by a youthful team of talented American cricketers. "From all sides the people came pouring in," the *Public Ledger* reported, fully 22,000 "by actual count" in attendance on the first day, an estimated 50,000 total for both matches. "No baseball game," it was claimed, "ever caused the commotion that this game of cricket did in the Quaker city," and for the first, but certainly not the last, time cricket would find the front pages of the city's daily papers.[86]

The outcome couldn't have been better scripted for the occasion, and when George Patterson hit the final, winning run, to bring the Gentleman of Philadelphia a surprisingly comfortable eight-wicket win (the Philadelphians beat the English score with eight of their batters still to be put out) "the crowd went fairly wild" in their belief that "the Americans had won the greatest cricket match ever seen in this country."[87]

Such was the exhilaration and emotional outpouring generated by the whole affair that it reverberated far beyond the city's immediate cricket community. Within barely a week of the match "a packed house" was "laughing themselves hoarse" at the quickly produced burlesque of the match, staged at the city's Carncross Theater, a "button busting farce" that critics hailed "as funny as they make 'em," with its hilarious and irreverent scene of Lord Hawke getting into a fistfight with an umpire. All this certainly seemed to represent something far more than passing popular adulation. It indicated an implied acknowledgment of cricket's permanent social presence within the broader Philadelphia community.[88]

The Hawke match, in short, represented nothing less than the fulfillment of three decades of effort, dedication, and persistence that the Philadelphia cricket community had expended to build its sporting world, and a confirmation of everything it stood for and aspired to. It would be the one, single, event—if one had to be found—that would catapult Philadelphia cricket into a decade of what would be its greatest achievements ... and greatest disappointments.

Eight

Ambivalence of Destiny

There were good reasons why the Philadelphia cricket community could interpret its win over Lord Hawke's team as the "high water mark" for its game. With some of the finest cricket facilities in the world now available for its cricketers, increasing participation, along with an impressive international win, everything, for the Philadelphia cricket community, seemed to "betoken a gratifying advance in American cricket."[1]

If the prospects for cricket in Philadelphia seemed to be expanding, the parameters for this future were, however, also narrowing. Philadelphia's rejection of the All-America cricket team proposal and its walk-over in the national cricket championship left little doubt that the city would, and could, now only be orientated trans-nationally. Philadelphia would never abandon the abiding belief that its game was a game for all Americans, even daring to make the preposterous claim, at the height of the euphoria generated by the Hawke match, that "before many years cricket will become the national sport of this country," an assertion scoffed at by ex-cricketer Harry Wright, now the manager of the Philadelphia Athletics professional baseball club.[2]

The reality was that Philadelphia, with its cricket, would be America's virtual portal to the world of late 19th-century international team sports and its sole representative in this expanding sports world. It was a role Philadelphia cricket authorities fully welcomed and, from the time of the Hawke visit to the end of the last decade of the 19th century, the city would host a visiting overseas team every year, establishing a decade-long tradition in Philadelphia of the annual fall international cricket match, one of the more anticipated highlights in the city's social calendar. These international encounters would not only gauge Philadelphia's worthiness in the world of international cricket but also test the very viability of the game's standing and endurance in the city, a challenge that would take Philadelphia cricket, over that decade, to seemingly inexplicable swings of dizzying successes and abysmal failures.

The city's cricketers got a foretaste of the challenges ahead when the giddy euphoria of the Hawke success was quickly deflated by the Irish team that visited Philadelphia the following year. No Philadelphia team had ever lost to its old adversaries, neither at home nor abroad, and when the city's representative team, a side expected to "win easily," lost the first of the two matches with the Irish team, it hit the city's cricket community as "something of a shock." King (5–45) and Wood (29 runs, the team's high score), both debuting for the Gentlemen of Philadelphia, didn't disappoint, but the rest of their teammates, most of whom had made significant contributions in the win over Lord Hawke's side, stumbled badly. The last five batters in Philadelphia's second innings, together, failed to score a single run, while, in the field, the local side "muffed and fumbled" catch after catch.[3]

Philadelphia's best cricket players, for all their talent and experience, just didn't seem to have, as critics pointed out, that illusive, yet critical, element of "pluck," and there could be no real consolation, the *American Cricketer* editorialized, to the reality "that the taste of defeat is not pleasant." This also would have been felt keenly, since this same Irish side, a week earlier, had lost its match in Boston—the first and only time that city would defeat a visiting overseas cricket team.[4]

Discouraging as this result was, the Philadelphians seemed to have no reservations, the following fall, about inviting the much more powerful Australians, on their way home from England in 1893, to play in the city. Why the Australians, after an eleven-year absence, had agreed to a stop-over in Philadelphia is something of a mystery. This had been a troubled side that didn't perform up to expectations during its tour of England that summer, a visit that had been "anything but pleasant" for these cricketers from Down Under. So perhaps a welcome change of opponents was needed, though the $3000 guaranteed by Philadelphia cricket authorities may have made the decision to come much easier, and soon after arrangements were finalized, a live kangaroo was on display in the Wanamaker department store to stoke public interest.[5]

The Australians' boat arrived late, and, not wanting to upset their well-planned match arrangements, Philadelphia cricket authorities, by some "lively hustling," rushed the visitors directly from their ship to the Belmont cricket grounds via a luxurious railcar Pennsylvania Railroad vice president and Belmont club director John P. Green had personally commandeered. There, the sea-legged Australians immediately came under a barrage of batting the likes of which they had never met in their four months of playing in England. From the first to the last ball of their innings (time at bat) the Philadelphia batters "pounded the Australian bowlers in all directions," bowlers who found the "Philadelphia batsmen were as hard to puzzle as the historic Philadelphia lawyer."[6]

Frank Bohlen led the assault, with a series high 118 runs in a remarkable innings that included fourteen boundaries (balls hit out of the ground) during the first day's play, almost matched by another twelve boundaries from teammate William Noble, the Philadelphia batters, at one stage, scoring at a rate of ninety runs per hour.[7]

Australian captain John Blackham's hope that a good night's sleep would invigorate his team's resistance did not materialize and the Philadelphia run total continued to climb unchecked the following day: past 300, past 400, past 500, the last Philadelphia wicket finally falling (batter put out) at the massive final total of 525 runs.[8]

It certainly wasn't, as ecstatic Philadelphia cricket supporters proclaimed, the "greatest innings in the history of the world," but it was, as *Sporting Life* correctly titled in its report, "A Record Breaker," and the wire services were soon notifying newspapers throughout the land that this Philadelphia team had scored more runs against the Australians than had the best English cricket teams that entire summer. It would be, in fact, the highest run total a Philadelphia team would ever make against an international opponent, far more than the Australians could overcome, who, stifled by King's five first innings wickets, went down to a decisive innings and 68 run loss.[9]

If the English cricket community, after the Hawke defeat, was forced to acknowledge Philadelphia was a not-to-be-slighted cricket entity, the Australians, with the manhandling of their national cricket team, certainly could not. "We have known for a long time that many things in America are on a big scale." the *Australasian* mused on receiving news of the result, "But we never dreamt that cricket was on that list.... Beaten by an innings and 168! By eleven of Philadelphia too!"[10]

This seemingly momentous step forward for Philadelphia cricket was, however, soon followed by two steps backwards with the return visit of Lord Hawke the following year, the Yorkshire cricket club captain, "craving for revenge," it was claimed, over his team's loss three years earlier.[11]

Supportive and obliging as visiting English teams had always been to the cause of American cricket, they never liked to lose to their understudies, Daft himself declaring his team of professionals would "rather lose a thousand pounds in gate money than lose one match" in America. Hawke, even with an amateur side, seemed fully motivated by this incentive. The English side, reportedly "fifty per cent better in batting" than the team Hawke brought to Philadelphia in 1891, proceeded to easily defeat its hosts in both matches. The second loss, by an innings and forty runs, brought down a torrent of criticism on the Philadelphia players. "Rarely," the *Public Ledger* decried, "has a Philadelphia team in an important international match fixture given as poor an exhibition of batting." The

Philadelphia Inquirer piled on, declaring the Philadelphia cricketers "play like a lot of college students having their first hack at a professional baseball club."[12]

Observers were totally perplexed at this seemingly A-not-equals-A equation for Philadelphia cricket teams; how the same players, playing under the same conditions and in the same location, could, at one time, play almost good enough to "meet England on equal terms" while, at other times, play so atrocious that it seemed they "had only trained for marbles."[13]

As had been the case after the discouraging experiences against professional sides a decade earlier, the Philadelphia cricket authorities retrenched, resorting to more competitively comparable opposition, which they found during the fall of 1895, arranging a visit by Frank Mitchell's English collegiate team, an arrangement with a new twist.

Since all members of Mitchell's side were present or former members of the Oxford/Cambridge cricket teams, an additional third match was arranged against a team of University of Pennsylvania "past and present" players, a logical fixture and one highly complementary to the American university's cricket program with so many of its graduates staffing city cricket clubs.

Lester rated Mitchell's Oxbridge side as the second weakest of the overseas teams to play in Philadelphia during the decade, an assessment recognized by city cricket observers and one that was fully confirmed during the intercollegiate match. The university side completed a 100 run win over the English collegians, a "brilliant victory for the university," also noteworthy as the one and only time in the city's cricket history that a representative Philadelphia team would win after having to follow on.[14]

Of their two matches against the English side the Gentlemen of Philadelphia lost (but should have won) the first match, but thoroughly outplayed their opponents in the second, amassing 404 runs in their single innings to win by a convincing innings and 39 runs. Philadelphia had its first, and what would turn out to be its only, outright series win against an overseas English or Australian side.

The series was also an occasion for exhibiting and reaffirming cricket's supporting ethos. These two sides, the scions of proper Philadelphia vs the elite of the English universities, though competitive on the field, represented a single, shared, social world of high society at play. Here was not a contest of stellar performances, with its "interesting mixture of sporadic batting, pretty fielding, and good and indifferent bowling," but a sporting occasion that, more than any cricket series in the city's history since the 1872 MCC visit, would so exemplify, both on and off the field, what Philadelphia admired and valued in its cricket. Mitchell himself, in a post-tour letter of appreciation to his hosts, confided that the occasion had been "one of the most pleasant and successful international series" he had ever played in. Little surprise that the Cambridge-educated Mitchell's collegiate rival, Oxford, itself expressed a desire (not fulfilled) to pay a visit of its own to Philadelphia the following year.[15]

The more cutthroat side of international cricket, however, returned to Philadelphia the following year when the Australians agreed to revisit the city for a rematch with the Americans. This was a more powerful Australian side than the 1893 squad, "a popular, highly regarded, and disciplined side," on its way home that fall from a successful England tour. Lester would rate it the strongest overseas side to visit Philadelphia that decade, the hosts themselves well aware that "the Gentlemen of Philadelphia are up against a stronger team than they ever faced before."[16]

It's hard not to suspect this Australian side, like its predecessor in 1882, would have bothered to make a return trip to Philadelphia after such a short hiatus without the motive of "sweet revenge" for its 1893 failings, which it thoroughly accomplished in the first match, beating the Philadelphians by a comfortable 123 runs. Future Australian team captain Joe Darling himself highlighted the Australian attack by landing two mammoth hits onto the roof of the Germantown clubhouse, their points of impact honored by their awed hosts with paint markings that would, it was proclaimed, "stay forever."[17]

More intense feelings were involved in the second match at the Belmont grounds, the Australians "straining every nerve," it was claimed, to efface the embarrassment they had experienced on these very grounds three years earlier, proceeding to run up 422 runs in their only innings on their way to inflicting an innings and 71 thrashing on the home team, a bigger margin of victory than the Philadelphians had achieved in 1893.[18]

This was unsentimental, bare-fisted, cricket the Australians were playing, a sporting world whose demands were evidently beyond the cricket capabilities of the Philadelphians both technically and psychologically. Frank Bohlen, the star of the 1893 series, was so unnerved by the hostility of the home crowds because of his fielding lapses that he refused to even play in the final match. Such high pressure demands had long been the norm in professional baseball and "the cricketers here" a less than sympathetic reporter from the New York *Sun* admonished, "will soon have to learn to submit to this."[19]

Having satisfactorily re-established their competitive superiority over their American opponents, the Australians could have packed their bags and left for home, but to ensure a decisive series result, they had asked, and been granted, three matches with the Philadelphians, allowing the home team to regroup and manufacture another totally unexpected surprise for the cricket world.

At the last minute Philadelphia selectors inserted the young, untested, Germantown bowler Percy Clark into the Philadelphia lineup who, in tandem with his thirty-nine-year-old brother Edward, completely ambushed the Australians with a one-two punch of devastating swing bowling. Percy finished 5–49 in the Australians first innings, his brother 6–24 in the second, a destructive spell of "curve bowling" during which "no less than five batsmen were caught at short slip, one at extra slip, and two at point, off deliveries swerving from leg [caught by fielders all playing shallow to the batters right]."[20]

So comprehensive was Philadelphia's win in this, the third and final, match (by an innings and 60 runs, a greater margin than in their memorable 1893 win) that the Australians had to deflect suspicions they had thrown the game. George Giffen insisted the Philadelphians had beaten his team "fair and square," but doubts weren't completely dispelled by teammate Ernst Jones' off-the-cuff remark that losing the game "won't hurt us any and it will do you people lots of good."[21]

Rather than wallowing in post-series speculations the Philadelphians, instead, quickly seized on this success over such a high quality opponent as entitlement to another English tour, this one with much more ambitious aspirations. The 1884 and 1889 Philadelphia teams had arranged their schedule against purely amateur English sides. On this visit, planned for the summer of 1897, the Gentlemen of Philadelphia would take on the first-class county sides at full strength, with their best amateur and professional players. Everyone knew this was a major step up for the Philadelphians and a decision, it was claimed, not made "without due deliberation" with not all parties in favor. Frank Mitchell forewarned the Philadelphians that "they would not have any chance whatsoever" against professional bowling, while the Australians "strongly advised" the Americans to take on the English county sides at full strength.[22]

Impressed enough by their opponent's performance at Belmont in 1893, the Australians had actually urged the Philadelphians, even at that time, to "go to England next year and give them [English] a dose of the same medicine." Plans had, in fact, been made for an English tour in 1894 only to be abandoned through a downturn in the national economy and unavailability of some key players, a "considerable disappointment on the part of local cricketers."[23]

In the end the advice of the Australians prevailed, team captain George Patterson himself evidently changing his mind from five years earlier, when he had advised the next Philadelphia team visiting England to schedule at least some strictly amateur teams rather than only full-strength county sides "as the results would be only too discouraging."[24]

The Philadelphia tour of England in 1897, an extended two-month trek that matched the Americans against fifteen of the strongest full-strength English county clubs would be the single most significant event in the history of the city's cricket. It would be the severest test yet as to the viability of their sporting world; whether these weekend Halifax Cup amateurs, drawn from a talent pool of not much more than 250 players, playing on the declared motive of "always trying to win but never for the winning," could, by sheer strength of character and emotional commitment, succeed or even sustain themselves in a sporting world whose intensifying competition and increasing specialization was everywhere challenging the sustainability of Philadelphia cricket's sporting ethos.[25]

As it played out, the Philadelphia tour was, for the most part, a repetition, on an extended scale, of the well-confirmed pattern of past representative Philadelphia sides: the isolated, spectacular, and breathtaking success intermixed with a few competent performances amid numerous, sometimes abysmal, failures.

The spectacular came the Gentlemen of Philadelphia's way in their fourth match of the tour against Sussex and, as in most of these instances, came about largely through King's heroics. There may have been a hint something special was coming in this match as soon as King, having just bowled the Sussex opener, and Australian transplant, Billy Murdoch for three runs, sent down his first pitch to the next batter, the legendary Prince Ranji. It would be the most famous pitch in the history of American cricket, best described by the victimized batter himself: "The first ball came along wide of the wicket. I let it alone. Just when it was too late for me to prevent it, the ball made a swerve in the air and coming across bowled me as I made a wild, but ineffective, chop."[26]

It was a ball, the match umpire claimed, that "would have taken out the stumps [a pitch hitting the batter's wicket, the "strikeout" in cricket] of any batsman in the world," no doubt one of King's signature "Hell Benders," and Ranji, "the most brilliant figure during cricket's most brilliant period," who had, the year before, broken W.G. Grace's record for most runs in a season, was out in cricket's most humiliating fashion: a first ball duck (a score of 0). The immediate response of King's teammates isn't recorded, but in the post-match ecstasy, they were all clamorously, if only wishfully, awarding their star player "brown stone fronts and country seats in Chestnut Hill."[27]

King himself, who had been "damned with faint praise" for his unexceptional bowling up to that point in the tour, was just beginning, ripping through the rest of the Sussex lineup to finish with what would be, at least statistically, the finest bowling performance of his entire career against first-class opposition, 7–13. The Philadelphians had, in barely a hundred pitches, bundled out a powerful Sussex batting side in their first innings for a scant 46 total runs (roughly comparable to a side holding an NBA team to under thirty total points in a half), eventually finishing the match with a comprehensive eight-wicket win. It was Philadelphia's first success in England that summer and would be "by far and away the most sensational achievement of the Philadelphians throughout the whole tour."[28]

It would also be the first of only two matches that the Philadelphians would win that summer, the second coming several weeks later against Warwickshire. This second win was a solid, but not spectacular, victory by five wickets, the Philadelphians "rising to the occasion in brilliant style," with a rare, full team, effort all but one batter reaching double figures in Philadelphia's first innings, with King also taking twelve wickets (got out twelve of the opponent's twenty batters), clean bowling six of the last seven Warwickshire batters in the second innings.[29]

For the balance of the tour, however, the Philadelphians would be able to show in their favor nothing more than a number of favorable draws.

The most praiseworthy of these efforts came against Nottinghamshire, the Philadelphians' 421 first innings total standing as the highest ever by a representative Philadelphia side against first-class English opposition. Their hereto underperforming team captain George Patterson here struck form, accumulating 162 runs over five hours of patient, faultless batting. Along with Arthur Wood's even hundred runs in that same match, these would, however, be the only two centuries that Philadelphia batters would put up over the entire tour.[30]

The Philadelphians' draw against Yorkshire, a strong side captained by their old adversary Lord Hawke, also did them no discredit. The match wasn't played at Yorkshire's regular ground at Trent Bridge but the shabby Bramall Lane ground, a dirty, neglected facility where "a fieldsman risked smutty trousers if he reclined on the turf" and where, the Americans found, "the dressing rooms remind you of cells in a third rate prison."[31]

The local crowds here were also less than hospitable. No doubt incensed by Patterson's snail-like pace that took him an hour and a half to make just three runs, the Yorkshire crowd "hooted the visitors whenever they came near the boundary [stands]." But King certainly must have briefly and emphatically silenced them when he got out their opener Stanley Jackson a batter that, it was asserted, "never was a bowler brought before the public of whom he was afraid," this star English player seeing his wicket shattered by the Philadelphian with only four runs to his credit.[32]

The Philadelphians had, in fact, put this, England's champion cricket club, by the end of the first day's play, in an unfavorable position until Lord

Hawke who, it was claimed, "does not like afternoon batting," pressured the umpire into declaring the weather unsuitable to continue play and, consequently, the match was declared a draw ... just as bright sunlight was breaking through.[33]

The Gentlemen of Philadelphia were also in "a very satisfactory position" against Somerset before rain washed out the game, though not before King had claimed the scalp of another of the era's batting legends, Lionel Palairet, whom King "speedily bowled" for another first innings duck. Though unfinished, Somerset star bowler Sammy Woods would remember the match as one the best he ever played in.[34]

Win, lose, or draw, the Philadelphians always seemed to play well against Surrey. They did so in their two previous England tours, and did so this time as well. Their batting was uniform and balanced, all but one of the Americans reaching double figures. But they couldn't match the play of this powerful English side, and though "the Philadelphians gave an exhibition of which any county might have been proud" and "played a plucky, stern-chase game," the visitors could not avoid a 154 run loss.[35]

And then there were the abysmal, all-too-frequent performances that seemed to show the Philadelphians were in a sporting world where they didn't belong. "From first to last the Americans were outplayed" in their match against Cambridge University, N.F. Duce, whom the Philadelphians had neutralized when he was with Mitchell's Oxbridge side two years earlier, along with Gilbert Jessop, always the bane of Philadelphia bowling, "made the [Philadelphia] bowling look stupid," both standout English batters making centuries to send the visitors to a 168 run loss.[36]

The Americans were also virtually helpless to stop Kent from amassing 454 runs—the most ever made against a Philadelphia side in international competition—and fell to an innings and nine run loss. Against Gloucestershire, Jessop bludgeoned the Philadelphians for another century and, with W.G. Grace making his first century of the season, that county pinned an even worse loss on the visitors. Patterson tried to stem the avalanche of runs with his two half centuries in the match but "the rest [of the Philadelphia batters] did practically nothing."[37]

Lester, with some fine batting, tried single-handedly to carry his side against the MCC but couldn't save his team from suffering another "severe defeat," the visitors going down to a 227 run loss. Here, as would happen so often on the tour, the rest of the Philadelphia batters did "nothing to disturb the calm of the spectators."[38]

Even more discouraging, if not unsettling, was that many of these embarrassing losses came at the hands of English sides far below full strength. A few, like Gloucestershire and Sussex, honored the Philadelphians by fielding their starting elevens, but for the most part the visitors found themselves playing against teams "far short of the strength which had been hoped for."³⁹

Yorkshire reckoned they didn't need their top bowlers George Hirst and Schofield Haigh against the Americans. Hampshire was without F.E. Lacey and their captain E.G. Wynyard while Warwickshire didn't bother to include Willie Quaife or H.W. Bainbridge. Nottinghamshire rested star batters William Gunn and Arthur Shrewsbury while Surrey gave Tom Richardson and D.L. Jephson the day off against the Philadelphians. Such moves, along with Lancashire's enrollment of fifty-year-old A.N. Hornby in their side's game against the Philadelphians and Nottinghamshire's enlistment of fifty-year-old Alfred Shaw in theirs, made known to "the public very clearly what estimate they [English clubs] had formed of the merits of the Philadelphia team."⁴⁰

With the sub-par abilities of their overseas visitors becoming more evident as the tour progressed, what public interest there was in the Philadelphians, not unexpectedly, sharply declined. There had been some hopeful speculation these America cricketers, like the Australians, would "do something phenomenal" and, initially, there was some ambivalence with the English public whether to "rush out" to see the Philadelphians or give them "the cold shoulder."⁴¹

The Philadelphians got the benefit of the doubt in some of their early matches, "flattered" that six thousand spectators were in the stands for their match against Lancashire, three thousand at Yorkshire while the Americans "proved a considerable attraction" in their match with Middlesex.⁴²

With their performances not coming up to public expectations, however, the Philadelphians eventually became little more than objects of curiosity. Small crowds were the norm for most of the later matches, by which time the sporting public were resigned to the reality that without the excitement and appeal of the Australians that summer "the most will have to be made of the Philadelphians." By tour's end the English assessment of the visitors was largely dismissive, it being "idle to pretend that the tour [of the Philadelphians] aroused any special interest among the cricket public."⁴³

Not unexpectedly, financial returns from the tour were also negligible. Oxford had lost $250 by bringing in the Philadelphians, a return probably in line with most of the county sides whose gate receipts, in most cases, "did not pay the printing and advertising" expenses incurred for their Philadelphia matches. The Gentlemen of Philadelphia had modified their financial "give away" arrangements of previous English tours, this time only contributing to English charity that share of the gate receipts left after a deduction for expenses. But even then, few English charities and even fewer of the Philadelphians who had contributed to their team's guarantee fund, probably saw any money.[44]

It could not have been easy to put a positive spin on a team that had optimistically expected to win "five or six" games and then finish with a poor 2-9-4 record, though Milton Work, the Philadelphia team manager, did the best he could in his tour assessment that appeared in *Harper's Weekly*. Blame was placed on unfamiliar playing conditions, poor conditioning, and, in an attempt at redemption, even an out-of-context quote that had Lord Harris declaring that "the Philadelphia team has done wonderfully well."[45]

Other English critics were not even this charitable, finding these American cricketers deficient in almost all qualities necessary for high-level cricket. Patterson, Lester and Bohlen were competent enough batters, but with the rest of the team, "there was a general lack of life in the batting." The Philadelphians seemed to just bat in a survivalist mode, telegraphing to their opponents, "Here I am. Now try and bowl me out if you can," and could manufacture "none of the great stands which wear out the bowling and do so much towards the success of a side."[46]

As to the bowling, King was "far and away the best man on the side," the Philadelphian being only one of three bowlers that English cricket season to take a wicket (get a batter out) in every match and, not surprisingly, by tour's end he was receiving offers (all declined) to play for several county teams. As for the rest of the Philadelphia bowlers, "none of them [were] of a caliber," English critics concluded, "likely to get anything like a strong side out."[47]

"Nor was the fielding of the team," something in which the baseball experienced Philadelphians had always taken pride, according to critics, "at all up to the best traditions of American cricket." Through most of the tour the Philadelphia fielding just "lacked smartness and accuracy" and, at its worst, "was often slow and almost slovenly."[48]

In the estimation of some critics the cricket abilities of fully half this American team was "scarcely first class" and three members in particular—Lynford Biddle, H.L. Clark, and Fred Bates—"did nothing to justify their selection" for the team.[49]

This was a cricket team that had clearly "over estimated [its] own abilities" in trying to compete at this level of competition, with most observers concluding that it had been an out-and-out "mistake" for the English counties to have even included these Americans in their schedules.[50]

It couldn't have been anything else than deeply disillusioning for a side that, on the confidence of its recent successes at home over English and Australian sides, believing it could "look for the time when America can meet England on equal terms" was, in reality, a team assessed by English cricket critics as no better than the weakest of their county sides.[51]

The English tour of 1897 had severely exposed the deficiencies in the sporting principles on which Philadelphia had built its cricket. It's structural anchorage in "pure amateurism," its moral anchorage in the "spirit of the game," were shown to be increasingly incompatible with the drift in world sports towards winning and contrary to all sporting conditions necessary to win. A continued belief in their ethos had effectively locked Philadelphia cricket into a state of perpetual apprenticeship to English cricket, always "learning" but never significantly progressing, "consoling ourselves" as the *American Cricket Annual* summarized the entire experience, "with the thought that while whippings galore were in store for us, we would gain a good insight of English first-class cricket."[52]

The English cricket community was always happy to lay out the welcome mat for these Philadelphians, a side that always "plays the game for the game's sake," optimistic, cheerful cricketers whom, their English opponents claimed, "the more we beat them the more they like us." All the Philadelphia visits would pass without any controversies or incidents (at least not publicly) that frequently marred England/Australia cricket encounters and would always contribute to "strengthening the pleasant relations which have always existed between the cricketers of England and America." To the cricket world, the Philadelphians were always a side to be respected and admired. They were not, however, and seemed far from becoming, a cricket team that their opponents and the English cricket public really wanted: a team, like the Australians, to be feared.[53]

Yet in under two months these same Philadelphia cricketers would once again confound all the dismissive summations of their abilities, this time in their matches against the English side that agreed to visit Philadelphia that fall, this team led by another sporting imperialist, future English team captain Pelham Warner.[54]

Like his cricket-playing predecessors Lords Harris and Hawke, Warner was also "a traveling salesman for cricket," but of this cricket triumvirate he "was by far the most imperially minded" who would, over his cricket career, take sides as far afield as South Africa, the West Indies and Australia. That Philadelphia would be his second overseas destination evidenced the hopes the cricket world still seemed to hold for America's place in this expanding sports network.[55]

Warner's team would meet a Philadelphia side in transition during its two-match series. Patterson had announced, at the end of the English tour, his retirement from international cricket and would never again play for the Gentlemen of Philadelphia. Frank Bohlen would now only be available sporadically because of demands on his legal career. After the first match Lester would leave for his studies at Harvard and not return to cricket for four full years.[56]

Philadelphia's hopes were now largely on the shoulders of King and the Clark brothers, and their star bowler delivered in spectacular fashion in the first match. Coming to bat in fading late-afternoon light at the end of the first day's play, Warner's side saw before it that illusive, unpredictable, but very real, sporting avatar: Philadelphia the Cricket Astonisher. In the span of a handful of deliveries, King and E.W. Clark cut down the first four English batters without allowing a single run. Warner himself was caught off Clark while H.B. Chinnery, H.H. Marriott, and F.M. Stocks were all bowled by King, the last seeing one of his stumps (each individual pole of the three-pole wicket is a "stump") broken in half by the impact of King's pitch.[57]

King continued his rampage the following day, taking the rest of the English wickets, all clean bowled, including that of Philadelphia's long-time tormentor, the heavy hitting Gilbert Jessop (bowled for seven runs). King finished the innings with a remarkable return of 9–25. In the span of four months, this Philadelphia bowler had his second once-in-a-lifetime bowling performance and the home team, after its long, frustrating English summer, would have a solid win over a passably good English side by four wickets.[58]

Like Lord Hawke, like the Australians, Warner's first brush with Philadelphia cricket had left bruised reputations and, also like Hawke and the Australians, Warner returned to Philadelphia in short order, redeeming himself by winning both matches against the Gentlemen of Philadelphia with another team he brought to America the following fall. More stellar bowling performances by King (including a 6–32 "sensational performance" in the second match that included a fifteen-pitch spurt in which he took five wickets while allowing only five total runs) couldn't save his team from losing both matches. But they were so closely contested it must have still left a clear perception in the eyes of the cricket world that there was still plenty of fight in Philadelphia cricket.[59]

At least until the arrival of Prince Ranji's English side of 1899. Coming to Philadelphia in a last-minute change of plans after its expected trip to India fell through, Ranji's team of English amateurs that came to Philadelphia that fall was, as Lester correctly pointed out, the strongest English batting side to ever visit North America. It was a "little below test [international all-star] quality," with the likes of Ranji, Archie McLaren, and Gilbert Jessop.[60]

The Philadelphians knew full well their bowlers stood little chance of containing such a star-studded batting side and, amid laments from a crowd wondering, "shall we ever get them out," the English team methodically rolled up over 350 runs in each of their two matches. Philadelphia's cautious confidence that their own batters could at least put up decent totals against the English team's sub-standard bowlers completely evaporated when the American batters fell to the opposing bowlers one after another like "a lot of ninepins to be bowled over," the Gentlemen of Philadelphia failing to reach so much as 160 runs in any of their four innings.[61]

The city's representative cricket sides were certainly no strangers to defeats, but the two lopsided losses to this English side shook the Philadelphia cricket community to its very core, a single series in which a visiting team had managed to "destroy the cricketing reputation of a continent." The attitude of the English players themselves descended to one of almost dismissive condescension, the visitors finding their American opponents so unchallenging "none of them cared very much what happened" once the outcome was no longer in doubt. It was an attitude that the English players made no effort to conceal, confiding to one reporter, "We would have enjoyed the matches much more if your chaps had pushed us a bit."[62]

The Philadelphians' complete and comprehensive "failure" against Ranji's side threw the city's cricket community into some deep soul searching. Faced with the unpalatable reality that "we are bantams" among the top cricket nations, the Philadelphians were forced to reevaluate the state of their game. At the beginning of the decade, the city's cricket had arguably been at a higher level than, and with at least as promising prospects as, the other emerging cricket countries of South Africa, West Indies and New Zealand. But now, after ten years, the city seemed to be falling badly behind the rest of the cricket world.[63]

Warner himself had advised the Philadelphians to take a break from international competition to "let the cricket out there settle itself." It may have not been on this advice directly, but a pause to regroup and reassess was, perhaps reluctantly, adopted by Philadelphia cricket authorities and, for the first time in ten years, no overseas team would come to Philadelphia in 1900.[64]

NINE

"A Civilization of Its Own": The World of Late 19th-Century Philadelphia Cricket

To its most dedicated supporters, and in its perceived and desired social mission, Philadelphia cricket was without boundaries, a sporting ethos for all Americans. In the eyes of George Newhall, this entailed, for the city's cricket community, a unique responsibility wherein it must "settle upon the city of Penn to show that the game ought to be everywhere in America."[1]

In reality, however, Philadelphia cricket was an institution strictly defined and limited by locality and social class, a world that, though part of America's broader late 19th-century sporting landscape, was also a world apart, an acknowledged fact that "Philadelphia cricket is altogether a thing unto itself."[2]

At the heart of this sporting world was the unique social establishment, the cricket club. The antebellum and immediate postwar Philadelphia cricket clubs were, like other cricket clubs across the country, single purpose, male-exclusive, associations offering its members active participation in a single, self-contained, sporting experience. From the time of their inception, however, most, if not all, of the city's early cricket clubs enrolled a significant number of non-playing members, whose input and interests inevitably moved these clubs to satisfying more diversified social interests. The Belmont club became the first to officially allow female members in 1879, a policy soon followed by most of the city's other large, propertied clubs. In doing so, these clubs began to progressively assume identification as "a community service and not a profit-making enterprise," like schools, social clubs, and churches, contributing to the general quality of life for its members and the surrounding community. By the late 19th century, the city's larger cricket clubs had evolved into year-round centers of social gathering and entertainment, with dances, banquets, and other non-athletic activities during the off season.[3]

Cricket remained the *raison d'être* of club existence, but even here this purpose expanded and evolved, these clubs soon accommodating new, emerging sports of the era in response to the changing trends of the times and tastes of their expanding membership. Tennis made its initial appearance onto the American sports scene through the country's cricket clubs. The *American Cricketer* was carrying tennis reports from the time of its inaugural issue in 1877 and would, for a period, function as the official organ of the country's National Tennis Association. Soon there followed golf, football, and soccer, all of which were first nurtured or supported within the city through its larger cricket clubs.[4]

More than three hundred documented cricket clubs were active in Philadelphia over the half century between the Civil and First World Wars, clubs of various sizes, strengths, and organizational identity.[5]

At the apex remained the clubs participating in the Halifax Cup competition, whose membership varied over the years but continued to be dominated by the "Big Five" clubs of Philadelphia, Germantown, Merion, Young America, and Belmont. These most affluent, propertied clubs had the most members, owned or leased their grounds, and sported impressive clubhouses. They were also the clubs that monopolized the best players, had the best playing facilities, could afford professional coaches/grounds men, and had the means to make extended out-of-city trips.

Just below the Halifax Cup clubs was a tier of Halifax wannabes, organizations with less pretentious facilities and slightly weaker teams, such as the Belfield and Moorestown cricket clubs. Lower down the competitive scale were clubs that, though competitive, had no realistic expectations of Halifax Cup status, such as the Melrose, Linden, North End, St. Davids, Yeadon, and Jenkintown clubs, a tier that also included a number of west New Jersey cricket clubs just across the Delaware River such as Haddonfield and Gibbsboro. A number of clubs had company or workingmen's affiliations such as the Pennsylvania Railroad and K.I.B.A. clubs, while other, less formal teams were organized along vocational lines, such as reporter, government office, bank, and even jewelry store clubs.[6]

From first to last, the Philadelphia cricket clubs, of whatever status, remained true and dedicated to the purpose of their sport as "eminently a social game," to be played and enjoyed by all members of all athletic abilities. Every Halifax Cup and many second-tier cricket clubs had both first and second "elevens" (the official number of players on a cricket team), the former able to also field, at various times, second, third, and even fourth "elevens." All of the Halifax Cup and some of the second-tier clubs had junior teams while all the Halifax Cup clubs had veterans' teams.[7]

Within the larger clubs, cricket activity was highly organized and regulated. Under the arrangements at the Germantown club in 1889, the first and second elevens had their practice on Tuesday and Thursday from 4:30 to 6:00 p.m., their practice games on Monday, Wednesday, and Friday at the same time. The junior sides had their practice on Tuesday and Thursday from 2:00 to 4:30 p.m. It was an arrangement probably followed by the other major cricket clubs, with Merion and Belmont going even further, offering their members winter practice with indoor sheds or wooden pitches placed over the snow.[8]

All this cricket had to assume some competitive format and over the decades a plethora of leagues and competitions came and went throughout the city.

The premier cricket competitions remained the Halifax Cup, named after the trophy won by the Philadelphia team during its visit to Halifax, Nova Scotia, in 1874. The winner of the annual competition, inaugurated in 1880 and restricted to the larger, propertied clubs, would remain, to the end, the recognized cricket champion of the city, with rivalries between the stronger clubs, such as Germantown and Belmont, "second only" to international matches in public interest and participant intensity.[9]

In recognition of the cumulative cricket accomplishments of their organizations, the Halifax Cup clubs introduced, in 1888, the Club Record Cup, awarded annually to the Halifax Cup club that had the best combined record of its first, second, and junior teams. The competition was reformatted at the turn of the century with separate competitions set up for the second elevens, the Philadelphia Cup, and juniors, the Radnor Cup, to which was added the Hirst Cup awarded to the city's best junior second eleven.[10]

The city's less prestigious clubs, barred from the Halifax Cup, formed a number of separate leagues among themselves. The Philadelphia Cricket Association, organized in 1891, was joined that year by the Quaker State league, the former revamping into the Minor League competition in 1900. By 1905, there were no fewer than six cricket leagues and competitions active in Philadelphia.[11]

Because of its noticeably hierarchical arrangement, with the affluent, upper class, Halifax Cup clubs dominating the city's cricket, Philadelphia cricket has often been put forward as "Exhibit A" by those scholars who contend cricket failed as an American sport because the country's upper class confined the game to its social tier—that the "elites literally took cricket from the public sphere and confined it to their own social circles."[12]

A close and detailed examination of the historical realities of Philadelphia cricket will reveal, however, the difficulties of maintaining this interpretation.

Cricket was certainly the "favored sport of the upper tandem" in Philadelphia over the last half the 19th and first decade of the 20th centuries, the one location where "no other branch of sport is so popular with Philadelphia's 400," the city's often interrelated movers and shakers.[13]

A closer look at Philadelphia's cricket "elite" soon reveals, however, that these supporters were overwhelmingly centered within the city's upwardly mobile, college educated, professional and business class (especially lawyers and doctors) rather than the "capitalist" or "old wealth" class. As Jable, following Baltzell, has pointed out, the city's athletic clubs were near the bottom tier in prestige among Philadelphia's social organizations, far below the status of the Philadelphia or Rittenhouse Clubs, the city's most prestigious social organizations.[14]

Several wealthy patrons were long associated with the game, such as railroad magnate Thomas McKean ("decidedly *the* cricket patron in America") and Henry Pratt McKean, both longtime financial underwriters of the Germantown cricket club, who, over the years, paid the salaries of that club's professionals, leased the club its grounds at Nicetown, and paid for its grandstand. The Philadelphia cricket club was heavily patronized by land developer and railroad magnate Howard Houston, who lent the club his property at its new location in Wissahickon.[15]

On the whole, however, the city's highest tier "capitalist" class wasn't nearly as deeply involved with Philadelphia cricket as its professional classes. A "patriarch's match" that included University of Pennsylvania provost William Pepper, "sugar king" Charles C. Harrison, and judge H. Reed in 1888 was one of the rare instances of actual participant involvement in the game by the city's highest "elites."[16]

More detailed information about those who actually supported Philadelphia cricket in the 1880s can be gleaned from the list of subscribers to the guarantee fund that underwrote the Gentlemen of Philadelphia's tour to England in 1884.[17]

Not unexpectedly, a number of the city's prominent and influential cricket players, both past and present, are listed: Frank Brewster, Charles Collis, Maskell Ewing, John P. Green, Jones Wister, and George and Charles Newhall. These are joined by a diverse array of prominent businessmen such as shipping magnate C.A. Griscom, Fidelity Trust company president Rudolph Ellis, financier Lincoln Godfrey and Germantown Trust company president Edward Mellor. Four railroad executives, A.J. Cassett, Henry H. Kingston, F.J. Kimball and Frank Thomas, also contributed along with architect Charles F. McKim. These are joined by a varied, but less notable, number of contributors, such as Civil War heroes Henry D. Landis and William Redwood Wright along with William Potter, who would unsuccessfully run for Philadelphia mayor in 1907. Many of these individuals, however, were self-made men or highly paid functionaries and few were the scions of Philadelphia's "old wealth" elites. As a general statement, those Philadelphia "elites" involved with cricket could be best described as the equivalent to what has become conventionally known as the "upwardly mobile" stratum of society, native-born Americans who during periods in their lives may not be wealthy or influential but had such background and traits that they *would* be wealthy and influential sometime in their lives.[18]

And even then, those directly involved with the city's cricket at that time were themselves aware of, and sensitive to, the charges of "elitism" which they strongly countered by insisting their game wasn't for "people of wealth" but a game for all classes where "rich and poor ... play together." City cricket authorities repeatedly pointed out that whereas inherited wealth and privilege gave a number of English cricketers the opportunity to play the game free of financial concerns, the cricketers of Philadelphia were "no gentlemen of leisure" but individuals who balanced sports and the pressing demands of careers.[19]

Those associated with the Halifax Cup clubs always claimed that "every encouragement was given to these [small] clubs by the older organizations" and, as members of the United States Cricket Association, these top tier clubs were under the direct obligation to "consider means by which cricket may be made more popular in the United States." With only fourteen of the city's hundreds of cricket clubs ever participating in the Halifax Cup competition, never more than six at any time, it was, logistically, simply impossible for this, or any, small number of "elite" clubs to come anywhere close to controlling "access" to the game, even if this was their intention.[20]

Philadelphia's "elite" cricket clubs may have had little control over *who* would play cricket in their city but they did have some control over *whom* they would play, and in this, and only in this limited sense, can the city's "elites" be said to have been the "gatekeepers" of the game.

This was largely the legacy of proper Philadelphia's self-appointed role as the guardians of cricket's moral standards and purity of purpose. Since before the Civil War proper Philadelphians had sheltered the cricket they played from the objectionable influences of smaller, predominantly English, working-class clubs. Experience repeatedly confirmed that this social stratum couldn't be entrusted to uphold the integrity of the game and, consequently, had to be kept at arms-length, a relationship that didn't significantly alter over the second half of the century. In justification of this relationship the elite (Halifax Cup) clubs had only to point to the routine reports of player misconduct, umpire abuses, and flagrant disregard of the game's code of conduct among the smaller Philadelphia clubs during this period.[21]

As a result, competitive contacts between the Halifax Cup and the city's smaller, less prestigious cricket clubs were held to a minimum. Not surprisingly, the Associated Cricket Clubs of Philadelphia, organized by the Halifax Cup clubs in 1895 for the purpose of equitably distributing the increasing number of international matches between themselves, never allowed smaller clubs into its membership. Nor would any non–Halifax Cup cricketer ever play for the Gentlemen of Philadelphia despite a declared intention from the Halifax Cup clubs to loosen this restriction.[22]

But even then, the competitive segregation between the "haves" and "have nots" of Philadelphia cricket was far from absolute.

Their competition having been largely concluded by the end of July, the Halifax Cup clubs relaxed their restrictions on competitive contacts with non–Halifax Cup clubs during late July and during the vacation month of August. Beginning in the 1880s, Halifax Cup players would regroup into "amalgamated" teams, with players from the different Halifax Cup clubs coming together to play on temporary, ad hoc sides (King briefly left his own Tioga club to play for Germantown and Arthur Wood played for the Pennsylvania Railroad club under this arrangement) that were free to play any club in the city during the late summer.[23]

By the 1890s, these "amalgamated" sides were largely superseded by "summer elevens." Under this arrangement Halifax Cup clubs would continue to play under their own club names while allowing players on the second eleven, and even club pros, to play along with the club's first eleven. These combined teams were also permitted to play against any other clubs in the city, even allowing these smaller clubs to play on the normally restricted Halifax Cup club grounds.[24]

By playing the smaller and less socially prestigious clubs, the Halifax Cup clubs could not only claim to be fulfilling their stated objective of "helping" these smaller clubs but also reinforce their moral leadership by exhibiting their competitive superiority over these minor clubs.[25]

In almost all occasions where Halifax Cup sides, even those weakened by the absence of their best players on vacation, opposed non–Halifax Cup teams, the latter were completely outplayed. The Halifax Cup teams routinely beat clubs in the Quaker State league while Belmont's summer team, in 1892, easily defeated the North End club, probably the city's strongest non–Halifax Cup club. Four years earlier the same Belmont club overwhelmed the small Montrose club 295–45, but this wasn't nearly as bad the Merion 2nd team's annihilation, in 1899, of the Radnor 2nd team 405–9. Even a less than full strength Germantown side had no trouble beating a team of small-club All-Stars in 1891.[26]

As it was, the Halifax Cup clubs seemed perfectly willing to maintain competitive contacts with the much more numerous but less prestigious minor cricket clubs throughout the city, but they made it clear they would only do so *on their terms*. Philadelphia's cricket "elites" didn't so much evidence an intent to "control access" to cricket as much as they did an intent to control something far more important: the moral integrity of their game.

At the opposite end of the competitive spectrum from, though historically prior to, the Halifax Cup competition was the cricket played in Philadelphia schools.

Sports and the fervor of youth go hand in hand, and it's been noted how antebellum cricket in Philadelphia was overwhelmingly a game of young men, played largely in a non-institutional setting of loosely organized clubs. This cricket fervor of the 1850s inevitably also found its way into the traditional institutional centers of youth, the city's schools. In an era without compulsory attendance and a deep suspicion of the value or appropriateness of athletics in educational institutions, sports in antebellum Philadelphia schools was on a small, unofficial scale and almost always limited to in-house activity, such as the inter-class games played by Central High Schools students in 1859. Only rarely were matches played against outside clubs, such as those arranged by the Episcopal Academy in 1861, and even rarer were inter-school contests like the one between the Episcopal Academy and John Wylie Faire's Classical School that same year.[27]

In line with all school sports played around the country prior to the 1880s, cricket, when it was played, was organized almost entirely as a student initiative, with no institutional recognition, little administrative support or even encouragement, and no financial assistance. Nor did school sports in any way function during that period as a "feeder" system for more advanced-level sporting institutions such as colleges or organized clubs. The development direction was, in fact, just the opposite, with many students who organized school cricket teams having initially learned their cricket as junior members of the city's organized cricket clubs. Consequently, the few inter-institutional matches that were arranged were not between other schools but outside clubs or even colleges. Germantown Academy's match against the University of Pennsylvania in 1880 was its first recorded against an outside opponent, while Central High School's first recorded extra-institutional match was against the Tioga club juniors in 1886.[28]

School sports in Philadelphia got a boost with the formation of the Interacademic Athletic Association in 1887, organized among the city's private institutions from mostly Protestant denominations, which made it possible for cricket teams at these schools to orientate their competition more towards other schools, such as Episcopal Academy's matches against Haverford Grammar school in 1889 and Martin's School in 1891.[29]

It wasn't until 1893, however, when the Interacademic Association put cricket "on an equal footing with other sports," including the game in the calculation of that association's all-round champion, awarded to the school with the best combined record of all the association's recognized sports for that year, did the number of inter-school cricket matches began to noticeably increase. Germantown Academy, for one, saw its cricket schedule grow from a single school match in 1890 to four by 1897.[30]

Many of these Interacademic schools, such as William Penn Charter, Germantown Academy, and Friends Select School, were the preferred educational institutions for proper Philadelphians and cricket's increased presence at these schools was an opportunity for cricket supporters to demonstrate how the game's traditions and values reinforced these institution's stated mission "to provide a more or less primary group social world within which the younger generation is socialized." The sentiments expressed in an 1895 editorial from the Westtown school student newspaper in all likelihood were shared by most Interacademic Association schools towards the game, declaring, "The very atmosphere which surrounds a cricket match, the vocabulary of the spectators and all the associated ideas, do seem to be more refined and elevating."[31]

School cricket in Philadelphia reached its zenith in the decade before the First World War boosted by the formation, in 1901, of the Interscholastic Athletic Association organized primarily among the city's public schools, though several private schools also belonged to the organization. Along with the traditional cricket-playing private schools of Germantown Academy, William Penn Charter, Friends Select School, Haverford Grammar School, Delancey School, Protestant Episcopal Academy (and, for a short period, Westtown School), at least eight public schools also fielded cricket teams, at various times, as members of the association: Central High School, Germantown High School, Radnor High School (which reportedly, for a short period, dropped baseball for cricket in 1904), West Philadelphia High School, Northeast Manual Training School (today Northeast High School), Frankford High School, Central Manual Training School and Williamson Training School.

Inter-school cricket proliferated during these years. The eight cricket matches that Germantown Academy played in 1904 (the "peak" year, according to Lester, for Philadelphia school cricket) increased to thirteen in 1909 and to fourteen in 1910, at which point the *American Cricketer* could proudly declare school cricket in Philadelphia to be "on a better foundation than ever."[32]

A further incentive to all this activity came with the inauguration, in 1908, of the Merion Cup, annually awarded to the city's school cricket champion, an incentive that may have brought out fully fifty students to join the Westtown school cricket team the following year.[33]

Better facilities and greater alumni/administrative support gave the competitive edge, for the most part, to the more affluent private schools in the city's cricket competition. Some schools, such as Friends Select, could afford their own professional coach (Lester himself, for a short period, coached the Haverford Grammar school team) as well as provide such amenities as indoor practice facilities.[34]

Not unexpectedly, the private schools generally dominated the association's cricket competitions (Germantown Academy had won, by 1908, the Interscholastic cricket championship three years in a row), with contests between private and public school teams often one-sided. Penn Charter beat Northeast Manual 76-12 in 1910, and Frankford High School 121-3 in 1913, though these weren't as bad as Germantown Academy's 258-4 drubbing of Central Manual school in 1908.[35]

This wasn't, however, a necessarily pre-determined outcome. The non-denominational Drexel Institute school won the Interscholastic title, undefeated, in 1904. In 1914, Northeast Manual became the first public school to win the Interscholastic cricket championship after producing, four years earlier, the talented J. Howard Savage, Jr. Savage's batting skills materially helped his Germantown cricket club teammates during their England tour in 1911.[36]

With many graduates of these schools continuing their cricket at the University of Pennsylvania and Haverford College, these two institutions of higher learning reciprocated the favor by doing what they could to encourage the game at the school level.

The Haverford 3rd team played matches against Williamson Trade School in 1912 and West Philadelphia High School in 1913. Earlier, in 1902, 1907, and 1909, the college organized matches between its varsity squad and a team of interscholastic cricket All-Stars. The University of Pennsylvania also did its part, the university cricket team playing a game against Central High School in 1900 and also arranging its own matches against interscholastic All-Star teams in 1912 and 1913.[37]

Serving a largely identical, if more advanced, social role than the city's schools, Philadelphia's prominent institution of higher education, the University of Pennsylvania, would, historically, largely replicate the evolutionary path of school cricket: progressive integration of an independent activity of youthful fervor into a more organized and formal institutional purpose.

Students at the university had also been caught up with the cricket mania of the 1850s, and ad hoc inter-class cricket games were appearing as early as 1857. Fully reflecting the youthful character of sports during that period, here also was a scenario of students establishing cricket at the college rather than the college establishing cricket. Cricket activity at the university would be, for years, inaugurated and arranged entirely on student initiative totally independent of, and at times in opposition, to university authorities.[38]

The consequences of a university having, during this period, no athletic facilities, no coaches, and no athletic budget were predictable. Interclass games were the norm, an identifiable university cricket team first competing with an outside opponent in 1862, a loss to the Pennsylvania cricket club.[39]

On those occasions when university students did engage outside clubs, which was infrequent until the late 1870s, they were almost always defeated, sometimes badly—falling, for example, to the novice Merion cricket club, Young America club 2nd team, the Delphian, the Philadelphia cricket club, and a Nassau (Princeton University) side, all in the 1860s.[40]

The university cricketers, in their loss to Haverford College in 1864, the inauguration of what would be a long and storied sports rivalry, had found themselves facing an opponent "stronger, more athletic," a scenario repeated in their bad loss to the Harvard cricket team in 1873, the Philadelphia collegians managing a paltry eight and seventeen runs in its two innings.[41]

Two developments, one within the university, one outside it, dramatically boosted cricket's presence at the institution in the late 1870s. The university, during these years, was moving "from its local and little known status to a recognized position among the greater educational institutions" and as a result of this its early "instinctive hostility to athletics" gave way to a formal recognition of student sports activity. An officially recognized Athletic Committee was created that included C. Stuart Patterson, George's father, whose influence most likely brought about an officially recognized (though initially unfunded) university cricket team in 1877.[42]

With the proliferation of junior teams within the Halifax Cup club by the early 1880s, university cricketers also began to take full advantage of being an educational institution that was "situated in the town that is the center of support of American cricket," relying more on the city's cricket resources rather than the university's for assistance and development.[43]

As more and more talented cricket club–trained students enrolled at the university (J. B. Thayer, Jr., from Merion, Milton Work and David Stoever from Belmont, William Noble from Germantown, among others), the university sides of the 1880s would be some of its best, the 1885 team "a very powerful one," able to beat a fairly strong representative Philadelphia side that year. Eligibility standards of that period, which allowed graduate students to continue playing for varsity sides, also made it possible for individuals like Milton Work to play for the varsity side a full six years: first as an undergraduate, then as a student at the university's law school.[44]

The structure of the university's cricket also began to take on a more recognizably modern form. Inter-class games declined, as did the graduates' matches with Haverford College, while matches against city clubs were replaced with an increasing number of annual matches with other college sides.[45]

This last development, in fact, came about largely through the efforts of university cricket team captain John B. Thayer, Jr., who seems to have been the driving force behind the formation, in 1881, of the Intercollegiate Cricket Association, which brought the cricket teams of Columbia, Princeton, Trinity College (in Hartford, Connecticut) and Harvard, together with that of the University of Pennsylvania, to play an officially recognized collegiate cricket championship. The first three institutions dropped out of the competition after the first year and until Cornell's admission in 1904, the intercollegiate cricket championship was a modest competition among Penn, Harvard, and Haverford College, the last joining the competition in 1883.[46]

With a plethora of talented players, the university dominated the early years of the competition, winning the championship eight of the first ten years, leaving little room to dispute the university's claim that its cricket teams were "head and shoulders above our sister colleges in playing this manly game." Five of the university's cricket squad were on the United States side that beat Canada in 1888, and four were on the Gentlemen of Philadelphia side that toured England the following year.[47]

The resurgence of Haverford College cricket, along with continuing handicaps of having no cricket ground of its own (plans, in 1894, to have one laid out at the university's new athletic facility, Franklin Field, never materialized) nor any designated cricket coach until 1899 (and then only a part time one), contributed to some lackluster years at the university in the 1890s, until two developments brought about a strong rebound in the university's cricket fortunes at the turn of the century.[48]

Most notably, the university was now becoming the beneficiary of the expanding cricket activity in area schools, which were fashioning themselves into something more akin to the modern "feeder" system, channeling students who had begun their cricket at schools, not just clubs, onto the university teams. By 1897, the university cricket team had in its lineup former captains of the Central High School, Friends Select School, as well as the St. Paul's School, cricket teams. Within a few years, it had in its sides students who had also played cricket at Germantown Academy, Drexel Institute, and Haverford Grammar School.[49]

The university's growing international reputation was also bringing in experienced cricket players from abroad, many attracted to the university's highly regarded dental school, which seemed to be the program of choice for students from the cricket-playing countries of Australia and

New Zealand. The Australian dental student Robert McDonald was playing for the university cricket team as early as 1890, a prelude to his later career in first-class cricket. By 1904, six of the seventeen members of the university cricket team were from Australia, enough to arrange, that year, a scrimmage between the team's American and Australian members.[50]

The upshot of all this was that university cricket enjoyed a "distinct revival" during the early years of the 20th century, with the university fielding some of its strongest teams since the 1880s, able to beat, by 1905, the full-strength Germantown and Belmont clubs.[51]

The presence of this talent, at a time when international cricket tours were proliferating, brought the university side and its supporters to the decision, in 1907, to send its varsity side on its own England tour. The idea had been floated as early as 1901 and the university team had experienced a taste of international competition with a tour to Canada in 1906.[52]

A significant, perhaps decisive, factor in making this decision was the arrival at the university that year of the Australian dental student Herbert Hordern, one of the earliest and most proficient practitioners of the recently developed "googlie" bowling (a ball that bounces with a clockwise spin when the batter's expecting a counter-clockwise bounce; one of cricket's most difficult, but deadly, pitches). With this assembled cricket talent; the financial assistance of friends, alumni, and players; and an unexpectedly generous $5000 contribution from the university's athletic association (which had, up to this time, never extended any more than $300 to its cricket team), the university side would complete, over the summer of 1907, "one of the greatest tours in the history of American cricket" that included a slate of sixteen matches mostly against English public school sides, traditionally the prime breeding grounds for top English cricket players.[53]

As a team of undergraduate- and graduate-level members (Hordern himself was twenty-four at the time) that included two future Gentlemen of Philadelphia players, Charles Graham and Charles Winter, the collegians were essentially playing against high school age, but more experienced and better trained, English school sides. Yet this did no discredit to the university's final record of 8-2-6, the best ever achieved by a Philadelphia cricket team playing in England and a record that included a number of impressive wins.[54]

After losing to Harrow, where the university's F.W. Baker "brought the crowd to its feet" with "a brilliant diving catch," and being "robbed" of a win over Shrewsbury school, the university side notched "a ridiculously easy victory" over Charterhouse school. In short order the varsity side "easily defeated" Winchester, considered one of the strongest

English public school sides at that time, while subsequent opponent Tonbridge school "was easily mastered."[55]

Though unappreciated at the time, what was probably the university's most impressive performance came in its favorable draw against Repton school, "as fine a side," it would later be claimed, "as had ever done duty for a public school." On that team were five future first-class cricketers, Harry Altham, A.E. Cardew, G.C. Campbell, R. Sale and A.T. Sharp, but the Pennsylvania bowlers, in this match, sent them all back to the pavilion (dugout) with scores, respectively, of 0, 0, 1, 10, and 11.[56]

Consistent, steady batting, all up and down the order (eight players finished the tour with batting averages above 20), contributed to the university's success, though not nearly as much as Hordern's deadly bowling, the future Australian international cricketer finishing the tour with an impressive 8.39 average (gave up 8.39 runs for every batter he got out, roughly equivalent to a baseball ERA of .85).[57]

These accomplishments earned every member of the team the athletic association's coveted "P" (hereto only awarded annually to the top two bowlers and batters of the university cricket team), and even before the team had left for home, it received a cable from university provost Charles Harrison: "The university follows your progress with pride and admiration." In little over a year after this achievement, enrollment on the university cricket team soared to forty-five, the most ever.[58]

Like the University of Pennsylvania, the Quaker educational institution of Haverford College was also the beneficiary of being in the right place at the right time for the appearance and development of its cricket, though the hold the game would have on this small college would run deeper and more resiliently than its much larger cricket-playing institution.

Tradition has claimed cricket was "introduced" to students at the college in the 1830s by its English gardener William Carvill. Lester himself has pointed out some discrepancies in this chronology but Carvill, who lived in Philadelphia up to the time of his death in 1887, always made this claim himself, which was confirmed by at least one alumnus who attended the school at that time.[59]

If cricket was introduced to Haverford students in those years, it was, as was the case with Wister's circle in the 1840s, more of a passing fad and the game soon disappeared, being "unknown" to Haverford students in the 1840s and early 1850s, considerably undermining the college's future claim as "the cradle of cricket" in America.[60]

More deserving of credit for the "second era" of cricket at the college is the unnamed English tutor at the nearby school run by Englishman James Gilborne Lyons, who reportedly re-introduced the game to

Haverford students in 1855 or 1856, and from that time on, cricket would retain a firm and permanent place at the college.[61]

Why cricket should endure to the extent that it did at this particular location was due to number of social and institutional factors. As a small, self-contained community of like-minded individuals from similar socio-economic backgrounds, the student body could readily adapt and integrate an activity of strong appeal to a point of intense, self-reinforcing peer identification and allegiance. Add to this administrators, faculty, and alumni who not only valued cricket for its "quiet, less militant" character but also reinforced its presence through direct involvement with the college teams. Thus the conditions were ideal for ensuring Haverford would be a "tight little cricket college." Such a sporting "goldilocks" zone nourished cricket at a number of other socially similar small, self-contained American educational institutions in the 19th-century schools such as St. Paul's school in New Hampshire and Racine College in Wisconsin. But not immersed in an extensive, supportive, cricket community as Haverford was in the Philadelphia area, these institutions wouldn't be able, over time, to maintain their cricket.[62]

Fully reflective of other educational institutions of the era, cricket at Haverford existed, in its earliest years, entirely on the initiative, support, and organization of the students themselves. Student reminiscences from these years portray a raw, rustic, unsophisticated game, played in primitive conditions, when players "practiced themselves to proficiency in snow, slush, mud, ice or unmowed grass" and where the "ability of a fielder to hunt in the long grass and plunge into the creek after a ball" was expected of everyone involved.[63]

Inter-class games prevailed, the college team not playing its first outside opponent, the Media club, until 1862. Only twenty total matches against outside opponents were played up to 1881, and never more than two per school year over that period. Over a two-year span from 1869 to 1871, the faculty specifically forbade the college team, which at this time played under the title "The Dorian Cricket Club," from playing any outside opponents and never allowed the cricket team to play matches away from the school.[64]

The game took a decided downturn at the college in the 1880s. Without a coach, or the assistance of graduate students, the college, in matches with its larger cross-town rival, was saddled with the competitive handicap whereby "Haverford with her hundred shall be compelled to play Pennsylvania with her thousands." Haverford cricketers often played against clubs that had professionals in their sides and faced a travel prohibition that prevented the college from entering the newly formed Intercollegiate Cricket Association; thus, the outlook for its cricket at the time was bleak. Its season of 1881 was the "worst ever," a competitive state that didn't improve the following year with a string of bad losses against the university, a single win in 1887, and none in 1888.[65]

The state of affairs at the college by now had "reached a crisis in cricket." The college newspaper in 1887 had even made the hereto unthinkable declaration that "cricket has ceased to have any claim to be considered the college game," followed by the even more heretical suggestion that it was now time for baseball to take its place.[66]

The reaction to these statements was swift and forceful. "Shall the gentlemanly game, the Haverford game par excellence," an alumnus wrote to the paper, "give place to the vulgar game of baseball, the abomination of desolation? Shall science be supplanted by brute force?" The counterattack was backed up with an outright warning that should cricket be dropped as a school sport, the alumni association would immediately end all future financial support for college athletics, its main source of revenue.[67]

The agitation aroused by the crisis had its desired effect. New playing facilities would be built and, in 1888, college president Isaac

The Intercollegiate Cricket Championship cup on display at the Haverford College library around 1885. Inaugurated in 1881, the competition was one of the country's first intercollegiate sporting competitions, continuing unbroken until 1924 (courtesy Library Company of Philadelphia).

Sharpless, a strong cricket supporter, took the game-changing step of hiring the school's first cricket coach, the standout English professional bowler Arthur Woodcock.[68]

The Englishman turned out to be "just the man we need," not only molding raw college students into accomplished cricket players but also boosting the college's competitiveness by captaining and playing alongside the college students in their matches against non-collegiate teams.[69]

A turnaround was under way and it came quickly. Of the ten matches the college played in 1889, only one was lost. With the added benefit of a new and improved indoor "shed" erected in 1893 to offer winter practice (which had become mandatory for all team members the year before), the college team won eleven of thirteen matches that year. Now a member of the Intercollegiate Cricket Association (the administration had, several years earlier, lifted its ban on off-campus travel), Haverford would win the championship four of the next five years.[70]

Also reestablished was the college's competitive dominance over the University of Pennsylvania, handily beating its old rivals three of four years between 1890 and 1893, the other being a tie. Year in and year out, these wins over its local opponent were always regarded as an accomplishment that "cancels at all" any number of losses to other teams.[71]

The crisis of the 1880s had passed, the baseball threat had been turned back, and at least for the foreseeable future cricket at Haverford seemed

Colin Cooper's period painting of an international match at the Germantown Cricket Club in 1892. This depiction captures the style, status, and social elegance of Philadelphia cricket at its zenith (Library Company of Philadelphia).

secure in its traditional claim that it "will always continue to be THE college game."[72]

The good times for Haverford cricket got even better with the enrollment, in 1892, of a recently arrived young Englishman, John Lester. His batting average of over 100 the following collegiate season gave early and impressive evidence of his future status as one of Philadelphia's greatest cricketers.[73]

Lester's presence most likely influenced the momentous decision, made during his senior year in 1896, to send a college team on its own England tour, becoming the first foreign collegiate cricket team to visit that country. Enthusiastically supported by the college's administrators, friends, and alumni, especially longtime arch-alumnus Henry Cope, who personally covered a large proportion of the tour expenses, the team members' modest expectations "not to make themselves ridiculous" were more than satisfactorily rewarded with a tour record of 4-4-7, which resolved any doubts as to where the Haverford cricket team "really stand[s] in relation to England's best cricket-playing schools."[74]

The English themselves were captivated by their overseas visitors, most schools, like Harrow, thrilled by "the novelty of the fixture" against these American collegians, while *Cricket* magazine declared, after the college's 1904 tour, that these visits from an American college had ushered in a "new era in the history of English cricket." With Lester finishing this inaugural tour with an almost eighty-run batting average, and the Haverford team registering the first American win over the MCC, headquarters of English cricket, the college side returned home having left a "very favorable impression" with its English hosts.[75]

The celebrated excursion, in the estimation of the college administration and alumni, now fully confirmed that "Haverford and cricket are inseparable." As a result of this tour, an understanding was also reached to send a college team abroad every four years, and, in 1900, the college cricket team made its second trip to England. This side had no player of Lester's ability and returned home with a mediocre 3-4-7 record, but continued exposure to international-caliber competition would soon begin to pay long-term dividends.[76]

Signs of this had begun to appear in the college's win over the university in 1898, the Haverford team limiting its rival to just twelve total runs in the first innings, Pennsylvania's lowest score in this long-running cricket rivalry. Fully four-fifths of the student body were, by this time, playing on the various college teams, and by 1901, Haverford was turning out so many accomplished cricket players that they could be found on virtually all of the city's top clubs: twenty-one on Merion (a club so dependent on Haverford graduates that it vetoed a motion that year to admit the college to the Halifax Cup competition), seven on the Moorestown cricket club, five on Radnor, four on Germantown, two on the Philadelphia club and one each on the Belmont and Haddonfield clubs.[77]

The thirteen matches played by the college in 1903 would be its most ever, and would include wins over all the Halifax Cup clubs, the highlight being the 244 runs the Haverford team put up against the Philadelphia cricket club in just an hour and a half of batting.[78]

By general consensus, the Haverford side that left for its quadrennial English tour in 1904 was "the strongest ever," due in no small part to the presence of the second standout cricketer that would come from the college: C. Christopher Morris. The cricket talent of this graduate of Friends Select school, who had tagged along with the Haverford team to England in 1900 as a "sub freshman" substitute player, had been so evident in his undergraduate days that he, a college junior, would be selected for the Gentlemen of Philadelphia side on its English tour of 1903.[79]

With this extensive international experience under his belt, Morris, a cricketer who always seemed to have something of a "subconscious understanding of the game," would captain his Haverford side, in 1904, to a commendable 5-2-8 record. It would be the most successful Haverford team to visit England and could count among its triumphs another symbolic win over the MCC, the collegians honored to find in the opposing lineup MCC member Arthur Conan Doyle of Sherlock Holmes fame.[80]

By any standards—competitive success, institutional popularity or even international prestige (from its international tours Haverford had accumulated so much fame that English observers made the flattering equation of the college to Harvard and Yale)—cricket at Haverford, by the early 20th century, was at its high watermark.[81]

Clubs, schools, and colleges were the day-to-day flesh and blood of Philadelphia cricket, manifestations of the broad and pervasive hold of the game on the city, or at least the most influential segments of the city. Outsiders were bemused, curious, and outright perplexed why cricket continued to thrive in this specific American location, a game that others in the rest of the country had long abandoned, if they had ever played it at all.

As a blanket explanation, contemporaries explained this phenomenon as an expression, a reflection, of the peculiar character of Philadelphia society itself. Whereas New York, the metropolis to which Philadelphia was invariably compared in almost every facet of urban life, was a city of faceless, ceaseless, bustle and drive that obliterated social ties and deified change, Philadelphia was, to both locals and outsiders alike, a "slow" city whose vitality was more measured, and one that valued and preserved social ties. It was a city of extended families and neighborhoods that displayed distinct social identities, such as the Germantown area itself, which long claimed to have "an individuality of its own, with a society and interests of its own."[82]

Author Henry James, during his visit to Philadelphia in 1906, was impressed with this American city's "inherent habits of sociability, gayety, gallantry," characteristics he hadn't found in other urban areas. Decades earlier, native Philadelphian Sally Wister had pinpointed one unique social trait of her city, noting that whereas "the interests of that respectable city [Philadelphia] are neither so various, perhaps, as those of some other towns the same size, but it is surprising to see when an idea penetrates the community how completely it pervades it."[83]

Unsatisfactory as such anecdotal explanations may seem by strict sociological standards, cricket thrived in Philadelphia, according to contemporary observers inside and outside the city, because the city simply had a "civilization of its own," and this sport just seemed to dovetail perfectly with the city's social mindset. To author and University of Pennsylvania graduate Edwin Morris, there was just "something about this cricket that seemed so calm, so Philadelphian," while the *New York Tribune*, in 1879, couldn't help noticing that in Philadelphia, "everybody, according to the habit of that enormous, friendly, village knows everybody else and everybody knows cricket." Asked for an explanation of the success of the city's representative cricket teams, Dan Newhall was perfectly truthful in pointing out that he and his teammates participated in cricket just as much to deepen and maintain social bonds as they did to maintain their business and family connections.[84]

Philadelphia was, as Michael McCarthy has documented, a city certainly infested with all the social problems of other late 19th-century American urban areas: poverty, ethnic/racial tensions, and, above all, government corruption. But proper Philadelphians would ensure that none of these social issues that surrounded them would intrude into this sporting world they had created.

If newspapers have always been the most reliable barometers of all local interests, this world of late 19th-century Philadelphia cricket was revealed to its fullest extent through the city's dailies. Sports coverage by Philadelphia's major papers grew exponentially over the last two decades of the century, and coverage of the city's cricket happenings followed *pari passu*. Most of the dailies had dedicated cricket reporters by the 1890s, providing detailed and extensive coverage of important domestic matches, developments in the game, and regular listings of club standings, statistics, etc.

International matches drew the greatest journalistic attention. The first day of these occasions were frequently illustrated front-page news, regularly accompanied by multi-column, sometimes even full page, ball-by-ball analyses, spiced up with the occasional cartoon. As prime occasions for proper Philadelphia society to not only see but be seen, every international match covered by the papers included lengthy rosters of those movers and shakers who were in attendance.[85]

The reporting style also progressed from the staid, straight-laced reports of the 1870s and 1880s to the colorful, irreverent and mock-serious yellow journalism of the 1890s that both amused and irritated overseas cricket teams and players. Lord Hawke himself had to acknowledge that for all the mocking jabs the local press directed at his peer standing, these Philadelphia cricket reports had "a quaint American phraseology ... a freshness in dealing with cricket that is racy and quotable."[86]

Extensive as the local press coverage was for cricket, Philadelphia cricket authorities believed the doings of the game needed its own outlet and on June 28, 1877, Dan Newhall, Henry Cope and Henry Brown brought out the inaugural issue of the *American Cricketer* magazine. Despite their noble intentions, the founders of this "interesting little paper" misjudged their market and over the first dozen years of its existence, the magazine never fully emerged from financial difficulties. It was in financial straits by 1884 and only the assistance of local clubs saved it from discontinuation in 1885. By 1887, it was still only taking in $975 in subscription fees.[87]

Editorial neglect also plagued the publication. In the early 1890s, it was largely just reproducing match reports from the daily papers and never bothered, or couldn't afford, to send its own reporter to cover any of the Gentlemen of Philadelphia teams on their five tours to England. Inclusion of kindred sports, tennis at first and later golf and soccer, seems to have provided the paper with greater financial security by the turn of the century, enabling it to not only endure as the most extensive record of Philadelphia cricket but also as the most tireless and conscientious advocate of the game.[88]

The depth, intensity and sincerity of Philadelphia's passion for its cricket should never be doubted, just as it would also be incorrect to assume it was only here that a passion for the game existed among Americans, even this late in the century.

John G. French, the standout antebellum bowler from Utica, New York, was still umpiring cricket games in his area in 1878 while Daniel Baker, the American from Newark who had so strongly advocated popularizing the game with his countrymen at the first meeting of the National Cricket Convention in 1857, was still officiating cricket matches in his hometown in 1882. Few antebellum American cricketers probably evidenced more enduring passion for cricket, however, than the standout antebellum cricketer Isaac Jackson, who was still umpiring, fully half a century on, for the Amsterdam cricket club he had played for in 1856.[89]

Yet there could be little questioning that Philadelphia stood alone as the one place in America that exemplified the claim that there "was just something about cricket which seems to attach itself more firmly to the affections than most other games."[90]

Acquaintances of Spencer Meade were astonished how this bowler, in his youth, could be found playing, every day, from three until dark. Always at the top of Philadelphia cricket club captain John Mason's New Year resolutions was his intention of becoming the country's best cricket player, while life's top three priorities for John P. Green were his family, the Pennsylvania Railroad, and his Belmont cricket club. These value priorities were fully demonstrated in 1889 when this director of the Belmont club frantically rushed to his club grounds and single-handedly tried to block a developer from cutting an unauthorized road through the club property. A no less deep and intense attachment to the game comes through in the confession of an unnamed Philadelphia cricketer in 1898: "After the last ball has been bowled in the autumn I exist.... I don't live."[91]

This love of the game was a fully transportable commodity, which numerous Philadelphians transported far beyond their city to the far corners of the country and even beyond.

Jones Wister formed a cricket club in Harrisburg almost as soon as he had relocated to that city in the 1870s. Farther west, C.S. Newhall was instrumental in forming the Toledo, Ohio, cricket club in 1894 and eventually helped to organize the nearby Cleveland cricket club six years later, even serving as captain.[92]

Ex–Young America and Merion club players W.W. Eisenbray and E.H. Lycett lent their services to reviving the St. Louis cricket club in 1874 while another former Young America player, J.J. Keyes, was a prominent member of the Grand Rapids, Michigan, cricket club when it was organized in 1876. Two more ex–Young America cricketers were instrumental in establishing the Duluth, Minnesota, cricket club in 1886.[93]

Other members of Philadelphia's cricket diaspora took their game to Kansas City in 1885 and as far west as Oregon, where they were active in organizing the cricket activity at Portland's Multnomah Athletic Club in 1891 as well the cricket club in Astoria, Oregon, in 1895.[94]

A Haverford graduate was even able to bring the game into the purview of Teddy Roosevelt while tutoring the president's sons in 1903. The president, it is said, quickly "developed into an enthusiast" for the game and was even led to join, at least on a pro forma basis, the nearby Huntington Manor cricket club.[95]

Even on their travels abroad, Philadelphia cricket teams would find themselves crossing paths with old acquaintances, sometimes even among the opposition. In its match against the MCC during its 1904 England

Nine. "A Civilization of Its Own"

tour, the Haverford college team found MCC member Frank Bohlen in the opposing lineup while the University of Pennsylvania side that toured Canada in 1910 discovered that its Toronto Cricket Club opponents had enrolled ex-Merion cricketer H.A. Haines, now residing in Canada, on their side.[96]

By far the most impressive long-haul Philadelphia cricketer was the standout antebellum player Charles Vernou. Making the military his career after his Civil War service, eventually rising to the rank of captain, this former Young America member became a veritable Johnny Appleseed of cricket, taking his cricket interest everywhere he was stationed. In 1880, he was playing single wicket (a sort of cricket "one-on-one") with youngsters in Leavenworth, Kansas, and a few years later would organize a cricket team featuring his garrison colleagues at San Antonio. He was playing cricket in Cleveland in 1887 and at his post in Detroit in 1890. Such far-flung cricket travels must have provided a treasure trove of entertaining tales and stories for his old cricket companions when he returned to Philadelphia in 1904 to take part in Germantown's 50th anniversary celebrations that year.[97]

"Such men the land breeds."[98]

TEN

Visions of Viability: The England Tour of 1903

As badly as the Ranji debacle had shaken Philadelphia's confidence in the international competitiveness of its cricket, a more serious consequence seems to have been the damage it inflicted on the city's already insecure standing among the wider cricket world.

Philadelphia's failure to arrange an international match in 1900 was an ominous omen of an increasing reluctance by quality overseas teams to visit the city. Efforts to bring the Derbyshire County club over that year came to nothing, nor did overtures to W.G. Grace himself to bring over a team in 1902 receive positive response.[1]

The Australians continued to show no serious interest in these American cricketers. The side that toured England in 1899 did at least put the Philadelphia invitation to a vote (the new players wanted to come; the veteran majority did not), while the 1902 team effectively reneged on its agreement to come to Philadelphia, preferring to play in South Africa on its way home that year, even though the decision probably brought the Australians less than the $3000 that the Philadelphians had guaranteed them.[2]

Eventually Philadelphia cricket authorities were able to persuade Middlesex county cricket player Bernard Bosanquet to bring over an English team in 1901, though the side was without the top players he had promised. Consequently, the weakened side did "nothing to inspire a great feeling of fear among local cricketers" and the Gentlemen of Philadelphia probably took little pride in easily beating the English side by 223 runs in its first match.[3]

If the cricket world was becoming increasingly reluctant to send quality sides to Philadelphia, the Associated Cricket Clubs of the city felt it necessary to again knock on the door of English cricket and, late in 1902, the decision was made to send the fourth Gentlemen of Philadelphia side to England the following summer. George Patterson had retired from international cricket and couldn't be persuaded to change his mind.

But the side selected still included eight veteran players from the 1897 tour, among them King, Lester, Bohlen and Clark, along with newcomers C.C. Morris (still an undergraduate at Haverford College), the talented young Germantown batter Nelson Graves, and Merion's Fred Sharpless, all of whom, it was hoped, would show up better against the anticipated caliber of opposition than did the untested players of the 1897 squad. Scheduling another slate of matches against full-strength English county sides, the Gentlemen of Philadelphia would again, with six more years of cricket development and experience under their belts, be requesting another audition for admission to the highest levels of international cricket.[4]

And this audition would be a challenging one for the Americans. They would be coming to England in the wake of Australia's visit the year before, a tour of "nerve-jangling excitement," one of the most memorable cricket series between England and Australia, during which the greatest batters of the two countries had been on display, exciting and thrilling the English pubic and raising the standard of sporting expectations for all future visiting cricket teams to even greater heights.[5]

If the curiosity aroused by the Philadelphians in 1897 had long passed, memories of their shortcomings had not, and expectations of these visitors were low. "They expect to improve their modest record of six years ago," an unnamed English observer bluntly proclaimed, "but are not strong enough to cause our players any uneasiness."[6]

The Philadelphians could again expect that they would play against teams divested of their best player (Nottinghamshire would field an "experimental" side against them while the Lancashire side they would play was "hardly better than a second eleven") and would be watched by small crowds. Old Trafford, the Lancashire home ground, like numerous other venues, was "practically deserted" at the start of that county's Philadelphia match.[7]

If Philadelphia had hopes of graduating beyond its status of cricket apprentice, no longer participating just "to learn," it would, as Lester pointed out in his preview of the tour published in *Outing* late in 1902, need to address the deficiencies in all three facets of the game that had crippled the 1897 team: "unaccountably poor fielding," batting that was "weak and uncertain," and an overall "need for uniformity and consistency" in its play.[8]

As the *American Cricketer* saw it, all these weaknesses had been shorn up with this 1903 squad. The entire team, it was confidently predicted, would "surely acquit itself well in the fielding" and there was full confidence "almost every member is likely to make runs." Above all, this was a team that could be counted on, if nothing else, to "play bright [aggressive, exciting] cricket." Only with the bowling did the publication express the "greatest anxiety," uncertain who, outside of King and Clark, could threaten the best English batters.[9]

As the tour unfolded, it would become increasingly clear that Philadelphia cricket authorities, not for the first time, had completely misjudged, for both better and worse, the very real strengths and weaknesses of their team.

Long accustomed to the view that baseball-familiar American cricketers were always one-up on their foreign opponents in the area of fielding, supporters were, from the start of the tour, surprised and disappointed with the Philadelphians' substandard performances in this area. Their first match of the tour, against Cambridge University, was lost because of at least "ten muffs" (others claimed it was at least a dozen), negating Lester's 96-run and Bohlen's 62-run performances. With such a lackluster debut on the English cricket scene, "[i]t cannot be said," the *Manchester Guardian* snorted, "the Philadelphians have made a good impression."[10]

In their loss to Somerset as well the Americans' "catching was greatly at fault," the visitors putting down no fewer than eleven catches, placing the bottom-order batters of Nelson Graves and Percy Clark (the latter at least having the satisfaction, as King did six years earlier, of bowling that county's star batter, Lionel Palairet, for single digits) in the hopeless position of trying to bat their team out of a massive first-innings deficit.[11]

The Philadelphians, who made the "very expensive mistake" of dropping P.F. Warner when he had scored just eight runs, very likely deprived themselves of a symbolically significant win over the MCC, as Warner then went on to make the decisive thirty runs for his side to win a close, low scoring, match.[12]

The English critics who may have been impressed how these Philadelphian cricketers would "never give up pursuing a ball which is hit towards the boundary" were also appalled at how "ridiculously slow" some of them were in the field. Even the *American Cricketer* had to retract its earlier optimism and admit, by mid-tour, that "our fielding has been a disappointment."[13]

That publication's confidence in the strength of the Philadelphia batting was also not entirely fulfilled. Lester was again, as he had been in 1897, the main engine of the team's run making as was evident from the 96 runs he put up against Cambridge in his side's very first match. The team's heavy dependence on the Merion player was evident enough in Philadelphia's match against Worcestershire, his absence from the team because of injury giving the Philadelphians little "chance of coming out of the match with much credit" and they duly lost the game by 215 runs.[14]

Frank Bohlen, with a half century in that same match, would be the other veteran to score reliably during the tour while of the new players in the side, Nelson Graves acquitted himself admirably as the only member of the team to make two centuries, and coming up five runs short of a third, over that summer.[15]

With the rest of the side, however, the batting was simply "unreliable." C.C. Morris did put up the team's highest score of the tour, his 164 runs giving the Philadelphians the rare luxury of being able to declare (a cricket side that, batting first, builds up a big score can, at any time, stop batting, "declare," and let the other team come up, somewhat akin to softball/baseball's "mercy rule") against Nottinghamshire eventually sending the English side to its first loss of the season. But that single score would be nearly half of the total runs he would make over the rest of the tour. There would be better times ahead for the twenty-year-old.[16]

As would become all too apparent from the very first match against Cambridge University, when the "tail [bottom of the order] did nothing," Philadelphia's poor performing lower order batters would be a tour long weakness. In only two matches, their win against Kent, when seven Philadelphia batters each scored over thirty runs, and the win over Surrey, when nine reached double figures, did the Gentlemen of Philadelphia exhibit anything like uniform and balanced batting.[17]

All too often the lower order just couldn't offer any support. Most indicative was Philadelphia's loss to the MCC, the last eight American batters together contributing a paltry seventeen runs, "scarcely international cricket form." Six members of the team would end the tour with single-digit averages and everyone on the team, save Lester, would fail to score in at least one innings. Newcomer Harold Haines was out for a duck seven times, nearly half of all his times at bat. As Lester noted half a century after the fact, this supposedly stronger batting side was not, statistically at least, the equal of the 1897 team.[18]

The Philadelphians' overall approach to their batting certainly didn't win many admirers among the English public. Even after factoring in the very wet English summer that year, and their unfamiliarity with opposing bowlers, the Americans couldn't deliver on their expected "bright cricket." Their scoring was often slow, even "painfully slow," in their match against Surrey. One member of the team in particular, Fred Sharpless, was singled out for criticism, the Merion player arousing the "indignation" of English spectators for his slow scoring, up for half an hour before making his first run against Kent, and taking two and a half hours to put up just thirty runs against Surrey.[19]

As had been the case with almost all their international contests in the past, as would be the case in almost all in the future, for these 1903 Philadelphians, the "secret of their success" would again be squarely centered in their bowling. The anxiety Philadelphia supporters may have expressed over this facet of their game, especially in the support available for King and Clark, quickly evaporated as the tour progressed. Lester proved to be a more than capable change (relief) bowler and would actually finish the tour with a better bowling average than Percy Clark. His stellar 11-33 bowling performance against Gloucestershire would be the best of his career and allowed the Philadelphians to turn a modest 155-run total into an innings and 26-run win, "the most decisive victory ever won by an American team in first-class cricket in England." So completely had this English county side been outplayed that even local critics concluded it "thoroughly deserved defeat."[20]

Eddie Cregar, King's Belmont teammate, also provided useful backup, stepping in against Warwickshire after King had been incapacitated with a pulled muscle, heroically trying to stave off defeat with what would be his career best bowling, 8-35.[21]

Once again, it was King and his increasingly effective partner Percy Clark who carried the Gentlemen of Philadelphia during that English summer. Both "bowled like demons" throughout the tour and, working in tandem as a one-two punch, they "carried everything before them" in Philadelphia's win over Kent (King 5-58, Clark 4-57) and also delivered a two-barreled attack in the Americans' win over Leicestershire (King 5-88, Clark 4-50). Both bowlers would, statistically, make great strides forward by tours end, King lowering his bowling average nine full runs per wicket (per batter put out) from the 1897 tour, Clark an impressive eleven-run-per-wicket improvement. The latter would also register an international career best 8-91 in a valiant effort to single-handedly save his side, playing without the injured King, from its loss to Worcestershire.[22]

Whenever King was in top form, the Philadelphians knew they always had a realistic chance of beating any county side they played. He was "phenomenal" against Oxford University (8-39), overwhelmed Glamorganshire (7-38), and made a fight of it for his side against the MCC (7-55).[23]

An unfortunate Lancashire side, however, would get a taste of King's bowling at its most "super human" during the tour and the county would suffer a severe penalty for fielding against the Philadelphians a side with only four starters.

With five first innings wickets already in his pocket for just 46 runs, and a strong wind behind him, ideal for his angler, King unleashed a furious second innings assault on the Red Rose batters. To a spellbound *Manchester Guardian* reporter, King's "pace was at times absolutely terrific, its pitch never becoming erratic and nearly every ball was on the wicket." In a whirlwind three over (18 pitch) blitz King took five wickets while conceding a miserly six runs, among the victims Lancashire's number six batter

John Sharp whose "off wicket [sic] disappeared as by some unseen force the instant after a whirl of King's arm." The *Guardian* reporter, witnessing this American bowler in full flight, could only conclude "his capacity for hitting the wickets is absolutely unrivaled. Even Richardson [England's star fast bowler at that time] in his deadliest hardly equaled it."[24]

By innings end, King had taken nine wickets for 62 runs, eight clean bowled and had been on the hat trick three times, carrying his team to a comprehensive nine wicket win. "No fast bowler at all comparable to King has been seen at Old Trafford this season," the *Guardian* reporter continued in his tone of amazement, unavoidably pondering "whether McLaren and Tyldesley [two of Lancashire's absent batting stars] or any other batsmen could have resisted King for very long yesterday."[25]

Little wonder that after this, and other stellar performances over the course of the tour, King would receive offers, as he had in 1897, to join a number of county sides, in this case both Lancashire and Sussex.[26]

On the whole, this Gentlemen of Philadelphia side would at least show more steadiness and resiliency than its predecessor six years earlier. The team would still find difficulties on the persistently wet English pitches and struggle against unfamiliar bowling. The Americans were "given a valuable lesson in leg bowling" with Len Braund's and Lionel Canfield's deadly leg breaks (pitches thrown with a spin that bounce away from a right-handed batter) against Somerset and would be repeatedly deceived by Bosanquet's googlies against Warner's XI. There would be, however, no disastrous collapses nor innings losses on this tour, and when everyone was healthy and was able to play on a rare dry wicket, the Philadelphians could be a formidable side indeed, as become fully evident in their last matches of the tour.[27]

Even with a modest 4-6-2 record by the end of July, this Philadelphia side had won twice as many matches as its 1897 predecessor and on that accomplishment alone could have returned home satisfied. But over their last three first-class matches, the Gentlemen of Philadelphia, now hardened by two months of non-stop playing, would finish the tour in a flourish and confirm *Cricket's* post-tour assessment that this side was indeed the "strongest American team that every left these shores."[28]

Paced by Nelson Graves' 95 runs (that included 15 boundaries) and King's 7-38 bowling onslaught, Glamorgan barely survived into the second day against the Philadelphians, the Welsh side crashing to a ten-wicket loss (the Philadelphians beat their opponent's score without any of their second innings batters put out). Following this, Lester's "faultless" 126 runs and Percy Clark's 4-50 sent Leicestershire to a crushing 101-run defeat, setting up Philadelphia's final match against a long-familiar adversary: Surrey.[29]

Lester would remember this contest as the "most satisfying first class match I ever played in" and for several reasons. Featuring a full-strength Surrey side, a decent-sized crowd (a welcome change from most other matches where the American's presence had "made little difference in attendance") and good weather, the match would be a tense, high-scoring, and hard-fought affair throughout.[30]

If spectators were not treated to a close finish, they would at least witness an exciting one, with the final two Surrey batters—star player Tom Hayward and legendary fast bowler Tom Richardson in his final season of first-class cricket—doggedly trying to survive the Philadelphia bowling, play out the final hour, and salvage a draw. With time winding down, and Philadelphia's hopes for a signature win dwindling as the final ten minutes approached, King sent down a fiery ball that got past, and crashed into, Richardson's wicket, securing for his team a 110-run win. Throughout the match the Philadelphians had "played up to their very best form" and proved that "on a hard, dry, wicket the visitors are the equal of the best county elevens in England."[31]

Even the always critical London *Times* had to acknowledge this was a win that the Gentlemen of Philadelphia "thoroughly deserved in every respect."[32]

With the Surrey win (and a final favorable draw against Scotland), the Philadelphians would finish the tour with a 7–6–3 record, having beaten the county sides of Gloucester, Nottingham, Kent, Lancashire, Leicester, Surrey, and a first class–aspiring Glamorgan and thus achieving a quantitative leap forward from the results of their 1897 visit.[33]

Still no cricket "conquerors" comparable to Australia, the Gentlemen of Philadelphia had, nevertheless, completed this English tour with a noticeably better record than the West Indies—a rising cricket power—had achieved in England three years earlier and had played stronger opposition than the rapidly rising South African team did in its 1901 England tour. Assessed by observers on the commencement of their tour as weaker than the latter, the Philadelphians, by mid-tour, were being favorably compared with some Australian sides that had visited England.[34]

To the Philadelphia cricket community itself, the results were satisfying confirmation of the belief in the validity of its sporting ethos which had now been buttressed by the "proof of power": face to face, on the field, success against the sporting ethos of competition and specialization, confirmation that "cricketers taken from the amateur ranks of those playing in Philadelphia have shown all that cricket as played in Philadelphia is on a par with cricket as played in the English counties." The *New York Times*, jumping on this modest bandwagon of success, brashly carried this observation to its logical conclusion, proclaiming, in a post tour editorial, that the accomplishments of these Philadelphia cricketers had set a viable pathway and precedent "to secure for this country permanent cricket supremacy in the cricket world."[35]

As reports of the success of his fellow cricketers began to come in over the summer, George Patterson, back home in Philadelphia, must have followed them with increasing exhilaration and not a little self-satisfaction (and perhaps regret at his decision not to join the team) in the confirmation of his prognostication six years earlier. Interviewed by an English reporter at the conclusion of his team's disappointing 1897 tour, Patterson had sheepishly conceded "we have much to learn" in the business of playing top-tier cricket ... immediately followed by the bold and now realized prediction "and we are going to learn it."[36]

Eleven

Twilight of Internationalism and the Drift from Nativism

With the moderate success of the Gentlemen of Philadelphia's 1903 English tour, the Philadelphia cricket community was confident that it had now secured a permanent place in high-level international cricket and that, as a result of the tour, "our cricket will certainly be held in much greater respect now than ever before" throughout the cricket world. The city's old hope, so often frustrated with the wild swings in its international fortunes, again revived—it was "just a matter of time" before Philadelphia could reach competitive parity with bellwether cricket power England itself.[1]

Nor did two losses to the Kent county club that visited Philadelphia that fall following the England tour seem to dampen this optimism. The Kent side, the first English county side to ever travel abroad (though by no means the first that wanted to come to Philadelphia), was a much stronger side than the one Philadelphia had beaten in England several months earlier. The two matches were close and hard fought, reassuring the city's cricket community that the results "do not in any way detract from the high position Philadelphia won this summer."[2]

The verdict of England observers on the state of, and prospects for, cricket in America was more ambivalent. The MCC showed enough respect for the Philadelphians to solicit their opinion on the issue of widening the wicket (expanding the strike zone) in 1903, a gesture it didn't extend to New Zealand or the West Indies. But the London *Times*, which had declared Philadelphia's England tour "from first to last a decided success" didn't seem to consider the American visit worthy of any mention in its review of the 1903 cricket season. While acknowledging the noticeable advances Philadelphia had exhibited with its cricket, English cricket observers considered any expectations of competitive parity still to be far in the future, and that "possibly the time may never come when America is strong enough to challenge England at cricket."[3]

Eleven. Twilight of Internationalism 149

English cricket authorities certainly didn't seem to extend any special considerations to the Philadelphians in its international scheduling over the next few years. Following Australia, English cricket seemed to become increasingly reluctant to send quality teams to America. Philadelphia's success in the motherland of cricket was evidently not impressive enough to attract any foreign cricket teams to Philadelphia in 1904 and the composition of the MCC team that visited in 1905 showed visible and ominous indications of lowered expectations from its American hosts. This English side, made up exclusively of Oxbridge undergraduates, wasn't a strong one and Philadelphia wasn't overly taxed in winning one of the two scheduled matches. Financially, at least, this was a much better arrangement for the hosts who did not have to absorb the expenses, as in the past, of lavishly spending international overseas players, but the precedent of holding the match in the summer, rather than in the fall, resulted in disappointing attendance and Philadelphia cricket authorities vowed such arrangements "won't be repeated."[4]

More worrisome was the suspicion that this English side was in Philadelphia not so much to test or gauge Philadelphia's competitiveness as it was just as a favor to keep the city on the international cricket calendar, something that now seemed to be more and more challenging for Philadelphia cricket authorities. Philadelphia would get no overseas cricket team to visit the city in 1906 and could persuade only the MCC to pay a visit the following year. This was a stronger side than the one that visited two years earlier and though rain prevented the completion of the two matches, the contests didn't give any evidence the standard of Philadelphia cricket had appreciably advanced. No one could have known it at the time, but this MCC side would be the last fully first-class English cricket team to ever visit Philadelphia.[5]

The awareness that their city was now fading from the world cricket stage must have motivated Philadelphia cricket authorities to take up the MCC's suggestion to send another representative team to England and, over the summer of 1908, the Gentlemen of Philadelphia would make their third—and final—first-class England tour.[6]

It was a team of largely long serving, noticeably aging, veterans: Lester, Bohlen, Wood, Cregar, King (all now over thirty), fully ten having been on previous Gentlemen of Philadelphia sides in England. Mixed in were some talented younger players, such as Frank White and Frank Green, both from the Germantown club, and the standout Australian dental student, Herbert Hordern, making a second trip to England following his tour with the University of Pennsylvania side the year before.[7]

The Gentlemen of Philadelphia would find their reception from neither the English public nor the English cricket community up to the expectations to which they may have felt entitled after the results of five years earlier. With no Australians nor the emerging cricket attraction South Africa visiting that year, the *Times* outright dismissed the visiting Americans as poorer quality competitive substitutes.[8]

County sides that had welcomed the Philadelphians on previous tours this time around declined to give them matches, so that the visitors found themselves playing a slew of less challenging opponents such as the Royal Artillery, South Wales, and Ulster. As in previous tours, the Philadelphians found themselves facing less than full strength sides (Surrey, which had shown the Philadelphians enough respect in 1903 to field a full-strength side this time around, put into the field "practically a second eleven") and few spectators (barely 500 on hand for their match against Nottingham).[9]

The tour would largely play out as the doings of a fading cricket aspirant, exhibiting the great things American cricket could have been but never would be. The hereto old-line, reliable Philadelphia batters were now aging. Lester and Bohlen, the two longtime mainstays of their batting, both had poor tours. Newcomer Frank White compensated with some fine service, but it must have been a point of serious concern that the player who ended the tour with the team's best batting average was 47-year-old Arthur Wood. The fielding was again slipshod, to English observers "at times brilliant in the extreme, at others far below the average of our ordinary county teams." Against Nottingham in particular the Philadelphia fielding could not "be characterized as anything but slovenly."[10]

Once again, it was their bowling that carried the Philadelphians to what success they found that summer. Even more so than in previous English visits, the visitors rode the wake of King's heroics which, during this tour, would reach unprecedented heights of achievement.

If, in the estimation of English cricket observers, King had progressed from being "a good bowler ... but not a great one" in 1897, to "a really great bowler" in 1903, he would be, by the end of the 1908 tour, pressing hard on borderline legendary. Now a few months short of 35, King had brilliantly adapted his bowling style to the declining physical abilities of his age, relying less upon his deadly speed and swerve and more on location and change of pace. "He has modified speed and developed cunning. He can still bowl a very fast ball," as the *American Cricketer* explained it, "but he keeps in in reserve. It comes out suddenly and unexpectedly. Often it is a yorker [a pitch that bounces at the batters feed] delivered at once to a new batsman, frequently with disastrous results."[11]

The *Fortnightly Review* now saw this Philadelphia bowler as "a real schemer, and his attack does not depend solely upon the success of his

The famous George Beldam action photograph of King bowling in full flight, taken ca. 1908, that exquisitely captures the force, power, and dynamic of America's greatest cricket player (courtesy University of Pennsylvania Press).

wonderfully fine swing ball." No longer just a bowler with tear-away speed, King had now matured into "a pace bowler with many tricks up his sleeve," a bowler who may now be a bit slower but one who was still "as individual in style and persevering as ever."[12]

Though much slower in his development in this capacity, King, shown here in a stylized photo-op, was also an outstanding batter (author's collection).

In match after match, King's bowling offset his side's often lackluster batting performances: 7–39 against South Wales, "invincible" with his 7–28 against Ireland, "almost unplayable" in his 5–43 against a full strength Worcestershire side and 6–12 against a hapless Durham team. "Varying his pace with great skill" in his 7–28 onslaught against Derbyshire, "and repeatedly deceiving the batsmen in the flight of the ball, he had the Derbyshire team at his mercy."[13]

Perhaps his finest performance of the tour came in a loss to Nottingham, the county batters falling to King "like chaff before the wind," the Philadelphian going 7–76 and 7–54 over the duration of the match, one observer concluding it was "doubtful if J.B. King has ever bowled better in his career."[14]

By the end of the tour, King had taken fully half of all the Philadelphia wickets and would finish squarely on top of the English first-class bowling averages with in unprecedented 11.01 average (roughly equivalent to a season ending MLB pitching ERA of 1.25). It was a bowling record that would stand for half a century and wouldn't be surpassed until 1958 by Derbyshire bowler H.L. Jackson who finished that season with a 10.99 average.[15]

True, as critics pointed out, King put up these numbers often playing against less than full-strength English sides. But every record-setting cricket player would accumulate some accolades against less than top-tier opposition over their careers (W.G. Grace, England's record-setting batter, amassed a sizable portion of his career totals against sub-standard bowling). And, true, King, over the tour, didn't play a full English season. But, if instead of the 339 overs he bowled that summer for his 87 wickets, while allowing 958 runs, King had bowled the 623 overs of Schofield Haigh of Yorkshire (the runner-up in bowling averages that season), there can be no doubt the Philadelphian would have taken much more than that Englishman's 105 total wickets for much fewer than his 1,380 runs.[16]

Judged strictly by the numbers, the Gentlemen of Philadelphia completed the 1908 English tour with an almost identical record as five years earlier, 7–6–2. They had the satisfaction of winning their "most important fixture" finally beating the MCC, the symbol of English cricket, and had shown isolated flashes of competitive brilliance, such as their win over Durham, in which the Philadelphians "outplayed them [the Durham team members] at all points of the game."[17]

None of these accomplishments, however, could obscure the fact that only four of these wins were against first-class sides, and among the losses was an embarrassing innings and 37-run defeat to Hampshire and a disastrous collapse for only 37 total second innings runs against Kent, the lowest total ever made by a representative Philadelphia side. It all clearly indicated a backsliding in the city's international competitiveness and the *American Cricketer* couldn't hide the truth that, as a result of this English visit, it was "doubtful the tour has enhanced the reputation of Philadelphia cricket."[18]

During the banquet he held for the Philadelphia side, Lord Harris, still England's number-one cheerleader for U.S. cricket, could continue to publicly express hope that these American cricketers would "improve up to the highest rank of cricket," but after decades of futility in this effort, he must have been well aware that this hope had all but faded into unreality.[19]

With this Philadelphia side, like the two previous that had showcased their cricket wares to first-class English cricket, "their matches made no appeal to the public," and for much the same reasons. These Americans were the perennial "nice guys" of world cricket, always warmly welcomed for "playing a thoroughly sporting game right up to the hilt"—a friendly, obliging, unobtrusive side but still not a side that could strike fear around the cricket world. If, from the very beginnings of international cricket competition, the dominant spirit of the English sporting public had been "we would rather be beaten by phenomenal players than triumph over inferior ones," Philadelphia cricket, as an international sporting attraction, was doomed.[20]

What remaining hopes the Philadelphia cricket community may still have entertained that this tour could revitalize the city's declining role in world cricket would prove chimerical after 1908. Philadelphia as a setting for cricket rapidly descended into international marginality, a sporting destination attractive to fewer and more inferior overseas teams, with shrinking competitive horizons and dwindling public interest.

Philadelphia's persistent, yet futile, efforts to attract quality visiting teams was evident enough the following fall, with a visit by a "lamentably weak" Irish team. Most were college students, little better than a "juvenile side," which the Gentlemen of Philadelphia steamrolled in their two matches, winning each by an innings. King bowled every Irish batter during one innings, eliciting for this star player now entering the twilight of his career a much deserved standing ovation from the crowd.[21]

For once in their long involvement in international cricket the Philadelphians could claim to have won a laugher over an international side. But with the departure of this Irish side, the city wouldn't see another overseas team for over three years.

Philadelphia's cricket horizons were irreversibly contracting. There was always the familiar stand-by, Canada, and the U.S.-Canada cricket match which, since its revival in 1879, had been faithfully held each year with only two interruptions. Though officially a fixture arranged by the listless United States Cricket Association, the series had, since the early 1880s, come under full and complete organizational control of Philadelphia, where the American leg of the series was always played save for one year, and the "United States" team composed of, year after year, mostly Philadelphia players.[22]

When Philadelphia began to turn its attention to higher quality international competition in the 1880s, the series declined in importance and never resumed its antebellum status as a marquee event on the American sports calendar. The Dominion continued to be a popular, easily accessible, destination for travel-eager Philadelphia cricket teams, both club and college, into the early 20th century. But these contests steadily deteriorated from tests of competitive strength into joyful excursions for social enjoyment.[23]

This was also largely the situation with the inferior international substitutes of Bermuda and the Caribbean islands, to which Philadelphia began to increasingly look. An informal Philadelphia side had first visited Bermuda in 1891, but the city's cricket community first took notice of the little island as a competitive opponent when a Bermuda team visited Philadelphia in 1905. With its international standing in decline at that time, and Bermuda's on the rise, Philadelphia found with these islanders a nearby, convenient, and competitively comparable opponent, and up to the outbreak of the First World War, no fewer than six Philadelphia teams would visit Bermuda. Like their forays north of the border, Philadelphia's trips to the mid–Atlantic for their cricket, however, couldn't be construed as anything other than a forced and reluctant acceptance that Philadelphia was now a second-class citizen in world cricket.[24]

What could have been a promising new competitive market for the city's cricket, the Caribbean, was never to be. An invitation to play in Trinidad in 1899, eleven years after an American side first played in the West Indies, had been declined. Jamaica's invitation in 1909 was accepted, but Philadelphia's first visit to that island would be its last. These two centers of cricket activity—Philadelphia and the West Indies, so close and, at that time, so competitively equal—would never become the cricket rivals everything seemed to indicate they should have been for the sole reason that these two cricket cultures were, by now, fast moving in opposite directions, the one into decline, the other into ascendancy.[25]

Even in its decline, the broader Philadelphia cricket community continued to look to England as its destination of choice, and if prospects were fading for the city's representative teams, the Germantown club kept them alive with its own single club tour to England in 1911. The decision was certainly "quite a departure" for Philadelphia cricket and would subsequently inspire the Philadelphia club to undertake a tour of its own the next year followed by the Merion club in 1914.[26]

These excursions, no doubt, did succeed in providing the younger players in these clubs with some much needed incentives to stay with the game. In the case of Germantown, its "youthful team" did acquire some invaluable and soon to be tested international experience. The Merion side that toured just at the outbreak of the First World War (necessitating an abandonment of five scheduled matches) was the most successful in upholding Philadelphia's fading cricket luster. It was certainly "a good side," *Cricket* concluded, and "the team played up to the hilt" for its 4–2–3 record, which included a hastily arranged match with the Essex county club—one and only English county side, up to this time, that had refused to give any of the seven previous visiting Philadelphia teams a match.[27]

On the whole, however, these single club tours were, by now, irrefutable evidence of Philadelphia's all but permanent withdrawal from representative cricket. The city's best cricket teams, which a decade earlier were playing full-strength county sides on almost equal footing, were now struggling to beat the likes of Stoke Poges, The Mote, Free Foresters, Reigate Priory and Mitcham Green. The Germantown team, during its England tour, even suffered the embarrassment of seeing 63-year-old W.G. Grace, playing for the Blackheath club, take seven of their wickets.[28]

All this wasn't lost on the Philadelphia public. Having reached a peak at the end of the century, attendance at international matches in Philadelphia noticeably declined from that point on. Appearance at these events was no longer *de rigueur* for the city's "smart set," the dwindling American attendance displaced by the many local English immigrant mill workers "who had always populated the 'English corner'" during the city's international matches, something they had been doing regularly since the MCC tour of 1872, often numbering in the thousands and rarely cheering for the home team.[29]

It wasn't a straight-line decline. The crowds that turned out for the 1907 MCC matches were reportedly the largest in ten years, but the trend was undeniable and by 1910 H.H. Cornish, editor of the *American Cricketer*, had to confess that for Philadelphia cricket the "time of the big crowds is past."[30]

Just at the point when it seemed Philadelphia had all but retired from the stage of international cricket, a former overseas adversary reappeared in the city in the fall of 1912. Why cricketers from Down Under, after a sixteen-year absence, had decided to make a stop in Philadelphia on their way home from England is puzzling. This was a troubled side, weakened by defections of some of its best players over pay disputes with Australian cricket authorities so acrimonious that English observers sneered, "Their petty squabbling at home brought into too bold relief that good money rather than good cricket is the primary object of their chronic invasions." This Australian side was "an unsophisticated lot"—undisciplined, loose, and deemed one of "the worst behaved ever assembled" of Australian cricket sides sent abroad (though no reports of misconduct came to light during their time in Philadelphia).

As was the case with the 1893 Australians, perhaps a detour to America, away from the intense and hostile English scrutiny, was just what the team needed.[31]

When the Australians had last been to Philadelphia in 1896, they had encountered King as a young 22-year-old perfecting his art. Now they met a tested, experienced, and savvy 38-year-old veteran at the height of his abilities and awareness. In the first of the two scheduled matches the American star not only propelled the Gentlemen of Philadelphia to a first innings lead with a 5–40 bowling spell, but he also snatched victory for the home team (after another notorious second innings batting collapse that so chronically plagued Philadelphia teams) by bowling the last Australian batter with the visitors within three runs of winning. It would be Philadelphia's closest match ever against a first-class opponent.[32]

King would follow this up with an even more impressive showing in the first innings of the second match. Here he was "absolutely at his best, his curve was working finely, carrying the ball strongly to leg from the pitch and he varied it with his slow curving or straight ball, with an occasional break from leg." Against such skillful bowling the Australians "fell down to the bowling of Bart King in such an easy style," the Philadelphian finishing the innings with a 5–22 bowling blitz, the visitors all out for a scant 101 total runs (comparable to holding an NBA team to 60 points). Meanwhile, Percy Clark was doing damage at the other end, going 3–34, the *American Cricketer* proclaiming "the two veterans bowled as they have seldom done and their performance deserves to rank among the brightest annals of Philadelphia cricket." Yet another second innings batting failure squandered Philadelphia's commanding position and the Australians, who had come to the city in the "fairly confident belief that the Americans would have no hope against them" had to thank their stars to escape with a split in the series.[33]

The Australians left, however, with an inkling that here just may be, in North America, an untapped cricket market that they had overlooked. Or so it seemed to Australian sports entrepreneur R.B. Benjamin, who contrived to arrange another Australian team to visit the United States and Canada the following summer. This was going to be a much more powerful side that would include standout batters Warren Bardsley and Charles McCartney, both of whom now seemed to sense they had missed something by refusing to come to Philadelphia with their teammates the year before.[34]

For this full-fledged summer tour, the Australians would travel from Vancouver, Canada, across North America and have a stop in Bermuda, an excursion that Benjamin, with his partner Edgar Mayne, actually seemed to believe could boost cricket to a status of becoming the "national game" in North America.[35]

If the Australians had misread the future of American cricket in the 1880s, they horribly misread it now in the early 20th century, and the chameleonic Benjamin would be as embarrassed in his expectation that the tour would put cricket "on par with baseball" in North America as he would be five years later with his preposterous claim that baseball would soon replace cricket in England and Australia.[36]

Their asking fee was steep, $3000 per fixture, and after being "turned down by dozens of clubs" around the United States and Canada, the Australians had to reduce their asking price "to get games at any price." They found much more willing takers in the $1000–1500 range, including the cricket association in Edmonton, Canada, which persuaded its evidently over-awed city council to pick up the visitor's $1200 tab.[37]

The English cricket world, on the other hand, looked askance at the whole escapade, seeing it as little more than a thinly veiled caper by the Australian cricketers "to get a little easy money," which, in fact, it was. The entire venture was soon seen for what it really was: rank exhibitionism, with the powerful Australian side leisurely making its way across Canada and winning with ridiculous ease, like an NBA All-Star team casually annihilating one Division II and III college team after another.[38]

Things continued this way during the American leg of the tour. The Australians' win over an eighteen-man Pittsburg team was so overwhelming that the result wouldn't have been any different, it was claimed, "if there had been 80" players on the host team. The match against Schenectady was so one-sided that it "had no real importance"; the New York team lost so badly that the game was dismissed as "little better than a farce."[39]

Philadelphia, where tour organizer Benjamin, because of his demeaning remarks about the city's cricket the year before, did "not find favor in certain Philadelphia circles," fared little better. King had retired at the end of the previous season, and without the sheet anchor of their cricket, the Philadelphia sides were easy pickings. In the three scheduled matches, the Australians tore through the Philadelphians like "a cyclone," administering, in the first two matches, the worse defeats that city cricket teams would suffer in international competition, and claiming a hugely favorable draw in the third. So effortlessly did the Australians win all their matches that local observers simply dismissed these contests as "just practice" for the visitors.[40]

If Philadelphia cricket was on its deathbed as an international presence, these Australians appeared to be its gravediggers. Yet even now, in its near terminal state of existence, Philadelphia cricket rose in one final, totally unexpected burst of glory.

After visiting Bermuda, the Australians were passing through

Philadelphia and Canada on their way home. They agreed to play a final, unscheduled match against the Germantown club as a "sort of farewell exhibition" on behalf of their beaten-down hosts.[41]

It must have struck observers as suicidal for a single, non-representative, Philadelphia cricket club to take on what was effectively a team of the best cricket players in Australia. But the Germantown side, fortified by the experience gained by its players during a tour of England two years earlier, inserted into their lineup two young bowlers, J.H. Savage and Frank Green, whom the Australians had not seen before. This move completely surprised the visitors, with each bowler snapping up four first innings wickets. The members of the powerful Australian batting side, which had put up over 500 runs against a representative Philadelphia side earlier that summer, found themselves all out, against this Germantown side, for a mere 144 runs.[42]

On the Germantown side was also the cagey veteran Percy Clark who, on this one occasion, emerged from the shadow of J.B. King, with whom he had done so many years of steady yeoman service, and batted his side to a first innings lead with a determined 82 runs. "Although Clark has made weightier individual efforts," the *American Cricketer* proclaimed, "it is questionable if ever he has played an innings of more value."[43]

Clark immediately followed this with a stellar 6–38 bowling spell in Australia's second innings, knocking out the talent-loaded side for an even more meager 126 second innings total. All the Germantown bowlers must have had their trademark swing bowling working to perfection that day. Fifteen hits came to the Germantown fielders, almost all to the close fielders, and fourteen were caught—ten by one fielder alone, William O'Neil—and many in spectacular fashion. That facet of the game which had long been such a crippling handicap to Philadelphia cricket, its fielding, was, at this one point in time, as one participant in the match would recall, "The best fielding I ever saw on the cricket field."[44]

Still, needing only 81 runs to win, the Germantown players well knew their experienced, determined opponents "had full belief in themselves" to pull the match out, and the specter that had so long haunted Philadelphia cricket in its international play, unaccountable and horrendous late-game batting collapses, seemed to reappear when the home side quickly lost its first four wickets (first four batters put out) for only a handful of runs. But William Newhall, George's son and the only offspring of the famous cricket-playing brothers to progress to international-level play, dug in and, batting with "dogged will," carried his Germantown side to a remarkable four-wicket win. This "fine achievement" of the home team would saddle the heretofore invincible Australians with their one and only loss during their lengthy 53-match tour.[45]

It would also be the last first-class cricket match Philadelphia would ever play. But it would be a finale at least worthy to ensure that the story of the city's place in international cricket would endure, to be told and retold, over and over, around the hot stove league of world cricket lore.

As is usually the case with all noticeable social changes, especially those disruptive to normal expectations, this decline in the competitive standard of the city's cricket had, years earlier, incited a search for remedies, and the one most convenient remedy suggested now was the same as in the past: bring in professionals.

The *Philadelphia Times* had called loudly for an end to the cricket community's long-standing "absurd policy" of allowing only amateurs on representative Philadelphia teams following the Ranji debacle in 1899, a call that grew louder during the selection of the Gentlemen of Philadelphia side to tour England in 1903. Even Lord Harris was puzzled why these Americans stubbornly persisted in handicapping their cricket with the "old amateurism" that refused to allow any assistance from professional players, an antiquated sporting scheme jettisoned by English cricket decades ago for the vastly more competitive "new amateurism" of professionals playing along with, but under the direction of, amateur players.[46]

1. King; 2. Bates; 3. Jordan; 4. Brown; 5. Scattergood; 6. Bohlen; 7. Morris; 8. Clark; 9. Lester; 10. Cregar; 11. Sharpless; 12. Graves; 13. Haines; 14. LeRoy.
Photo by Rolfe.
PHILADELPHIANS' ENGLISH TEAM.

The Gentlemen of Philadelphia team that toured England in 1903, the most successful non–Australian cricket team to visit England at the time (*Spalding's Official Cricket Guide*).

Eleven. Twilight of Internationalism

If nothing else, the policy repeatedly made it impossible for Philadelphia to field its best teams. Career demands prevented some of the city's best players from traveling with the Gentlemen of Philadelphia side that toured England in 1889 and forced the outright cancellation of a planned English tour in 1894. Having taken so much time away from their careers to tour England in 1897, Bohlen and Lester couldn't spare any more time to play against Warner's team that fall in Philadelphia. Nor could George Patterson, though the press pleaded that he "should sacrifice something and help us out."[47]

The total dedication demanded from the increasingly specialized world of top-level sports was becoming more glaringly incompatible with the world of Philadelphia cricket as a part-time occupation. The local papers, years earlier, had even become accustomed to publishing lists of the city's top cricket players who would be unavailable to play, or play only "occasionally," because of career commitments.[48]

Even when available, the city's best cricketers sometimes found pressing career demands followed them right onto the playing field. Bohlen was forced to leave right in the middle of the Oxbridge match in 1895 "for some legal business." Reynolds Brown had to abandon his teammates in England in 1903 and return home to tend to pressing business matters, as did Arthur Wood, returning home and missing his team's last match against Kent in 1908. Off-field matters were evidently so pressing for William Lowry that he was "inexcusably absent" from even the all-important match against Australia in 1882. Due to off-field demands, Newbold Etting was tardy for his team's match against Warner's side in 1897 and even King, for personal reasons, was an hour late for the start of Philadelphia's match against Ranji's team in 1899.[49]

Perhaps it took an outsider to impress upon the Philadelphians that their uncompromising insistence on the amateur purity of their cricket was not only increasingly out of step with the competitive requirements of the new order of world sports, but was also breeding, among these Philadelphia players, a mentality of acceptable, self-satisfied mediocrity. As the *New York Tribune* saw it as early as 1885, "American elevens have gone far enough to show that if they really wanted to do so they could play cricket, but they have been content to prove this much and stop."[50]

Philadelphia cricket authorities had heard all this before and were no more swayed to change their stance now than in the past. They had built their sporting world on the amateur ethos, unapologetically and unequivocally a world of the non-specialist. It was the sporting life they believed in and were willing to stand or fall by on the field of play. "It would be better for this country," as the *Philadelphia Inquirer* saw the matter in an editorial of 1896, "to continue to play cricket for sport and to play a little worse cricket than to improve the game by hiring men to devote their whole time to it."[51]

Philadelphia's insistence (or, more correctly, the insistence of the controlling Halifax Cup clubs) on the amateur purity of its cricket went hand in hand with its nativist policy; that cricket in the city was always to be, first and foremost, in the interest of Americans. While city cricket authorities would stand firm in the first, they began, however, to waver in the second over the years leading up to the First World War.

The American-dominated Halifax Cup clubs had always been greatly outnumbered by the many smaller, mainly immigrant English, clubs that populated the city and this disparity began to noticeably alter the organizational balance of the game. The city's more English-identified clubs such as the Albion, Alfred the Great, Tennyson, Robin Hood, etc., came together to form their own league, the St. George, in 1904, the league increasing from eight clubs in 1906 to ten two years later and playing fully ninety matches that year.[52]

Some of the larger, more ethnically diverse, non–Halifax Cup clubs in Philadelphia and west New Jersey also came together around this time to form the Interstate Cricket League. By 1909, the league was "more flourishing than ever," increasing, by 1913, to fifteen clubs, with two divisions, and playing ninety-eight total matches that season.[53]

With the number of Halifax Cup clubs remaining unchanged, what this meant was that while the total numbers of Philadelphians playing cricket may have been steady, or even increasing, proportionately fewer and fewer of these players were native Americans.

This wasn't necessarily seen as a concern for the Halifax Cup clubs so long as they retained the competitive superiority they so long enjoyed over the city's numerous non–Halifax Cup teams, whom they continued to hold at arms-length, seldom engaging them in head-to-head competition. This competitive segregation became increasingly harder to maintain, or even justify, however, with the growing number and strength of the non–Halifax Cup clubs and, beginning in 1909, an annual match between representative sides of the Halifax Cup and Interstate league clubs was agreed to. Initially the Halifax Cup clubs reasserted their competitive dominance winning all three matches that year, including the finale by the lopsided score of 316–33. The competitive gap, however, rapidly closed over the next few years and by 1911 and again in 1915, Interstate sides won two of the three matches against the Halifax Cup teams.[54]

This was the extent, however, that the Halifax Cup clubs were willing to go in relaxing its arms-length relationship with the city's smaller cricket clubs. In light of the fact that representative Halifax Cup sides continued to enjoy success against representative immigrant English sides such as

Philadelphia's innings and 349-run annihilation of New York in 1900, the Halifax clubs saw no compelling reason to modify its long-standing policy of relying entirely upon born-and-bred Americans for its representative sides.[55]

Despite these intentions, Philadelphia cricket authorities couldn't prevent a slow infiltration, during these years, of non–Americans into the Halifax Cup clubs or even into its representative sides. So long as they met the approved, and rather lenient, qualification requirements, foreign residents had always been welcomed into the Halifax Cup sides. Belmont had long been the most welcoming. Arthur Wood had been playing for the club since the 1880s and was joined a few years later by the Scottish American Ralph Melville, while Englishman Eddie Leech would keep wicket (catch) to King's bowling for many years. Lester, since his graduation from Haverford College, had been the backbone of his Merion club. Only Germantown stood firm as the uncompromising bastion of nativism and only Americans "to the manner born" would play for that club.[56]

Enforcement of, or at least attitudes towards, these playing restrictions seems to have begun to give way in the early years of the century, with a number of talented cricket-playing "birds of passage" finding their way onto Halifax club sides. The Philadelphia club, long the most lax in enforcing the league's "American-first policy," seemed to be their preferred destination. The talented Bermuda cricketer Reginald "Reggie" Conyers evidently liked what he found in the city during his team's visit to Philadelphia in 1905 and decided to stay on and play for the Philadelphia club, where he was soon joined by his brother Greg.[57]

His Bermuda teammate, the globe-trotting Australian Bernie Kortlang, also decided to roost in the city for a while during his worldwide cricket travels by also joining the Philadelphia cricket club. Here they were also joined by the peripatetic Irish cricketer James John McDonogh, who would actually become the captain of the club side. Around that same time the Oxford graduate John Harvey Gordon would find his way into the Merion club.[58]

The appearance of non–American players of questionable loyalties, if not qualifications, on Halifax club sides didn't, however, arouse as much concern as their appearance on the representative Philadelphia sides from which they had long been barred. A mild protest arose over the inclusion of the English immigrant W.H. Walker, also a member of the Philadelphia club, on the Philadelphia side that played against the visiting Kent county team in 1903, not only because he had been in the country barely two years but also because his selection had allegedly denied a place to the long-serving Frankford cricket club player William Foulkrod. As a result, for the first time in over twenty years, a non–American was playing for the Gentlemen of Philadelphia.[59]

This breach of Philadelphia's impermeable, decades-old firewall of nativism with the city's representative sides didn't precipitate any inundation of non–American players, but it unofficially sanctioned their slow infiltration. The symbolic policy shift represented by the Walker selection was confirmed five years later when the Australian dental student Herbert Hordern, who had led his University of Pennsylvania team on its triumphant England tour of 1907, was selected for the Gentlemen of Philadelphia tour to that country a year later. Any objections to this decision was probably obviated with Percy Clark's unavailability for the tour, but here for the first time in Philadelphia cricket history a non–American who had no intentions of making the United States his home was on a Gentlemen of Philadelphia team that would represent the city abroad.[60]

Hordern's selection seems to have set something of a precedent, or perhaps more correctly, indicated a weakening resolve of city cricket authorities to uphold its American-only policy. Hordern was joined by Reggie Conyers and Bernie Kortland on the representative "Philadelphia" side that toured Jamaica in 1909, Kortland also joining the Philadelphia team that visited Bermuda—a team he had himself played for—the following year. With the importance of the U.S.-Canada matches in decline, and corresponding indifference in selection for these matches, James McDonogh found his way onto the "United States" team for the 1909 match while John Gordon was on the "American" team for the 1911 match. The Philadelphia club seemed to sense no violation of national preference in allowing Reggie Conyers to also join the team on its English tour of 1912, though the editor of *Cricket* certainly did, sarcastically quipping that it was "rather amusing that the Conyers who hail from Bermuda are accepted as genuine Americans."[61]

With the decades-old desideratum of permanent international presence all but now out of reach, and the will to maintain the nativist integrity of their cricket wavering, Philadelphia was left with only one pathway forward: the resurrection of the largely discounted hope that cricket could grow and expand beyond the confines of the city, that this sport could still somehow be "the game of games for America." Local euphoria that routinely came in the wake of every international success or overseas tour, it was always assumed, would somehow infect the rest of America with a passion for the game. "Before many years," supporters had over-optimistically predicted after Philadelphia's 1889 England tour, "cricket will become the national sport of the country."[62]

That such an occurrence would require nothing short of a revolution in the time-tested parameters of what Americans found exciting in their bat-and-ball sports didn't seem to cross the minds of Philadelphia cricket authorities, who blindly and stubbornly expected "it will not take

Americans long to perceive that an excitement prolonged over three days is more exciting than an excitement over in three hours."[63]

Great doers are needed for great plans to be achieved, and Philadelphia, in its acquired capacity as the country's leading cricket center in both popularity and accomplishment, always could take the role of national cricket leader. The Philadelphia cricket clubs that tried to revive a national cricket association in 1867 failed, but the city renewed the effort in 1878 with better success. From its inception, this new national cricket body—in membership, policies, and location—was effectively a single-city organization. Though tasked with "the advancement of cricket interests" nationally, its activities rarely extended beyond arranging the annual U.S.-Canada match and the short-lived national championship of 1891.[64]

By the mid–1880s it was common knowledge the association was "regarded more as a Philadelphia organization," a perception that hadn't changed by 1889 with only Philadelphia clubs in attendance at that year's annual meeting. Not unexpectedly, dissatisfaction arose over the city's primacy in the organization, a concern that initially expressed itself among individual clubs. The Pittsburg cricket club saw no benefit in belonging to the association and resigned in 1890, as did a club in Philadelphia's own backyard, Oxford, that same year.[65]

Dissatisfaction took a more extended form when cricket clubs in New York, Chicago, and even far-off California, began discussing, in 1891, plans for organizing, among themselves, a separate and presumably more inclusive national cricket association. This sense of inadequate leadership simmered throughout the decade and reemerged in 1903 with a movement among cricket clubs from the Eastern Seaboard to the Pacific slope to establish a formal Cricket Association of North America, the movers behind the scheme expressing so much confidence in their plans that they brashly invited outsider Philadelphia to join.[66]

Little could probably be said in defense of the poor stewardship Philadelphia exercised in its leadership of American cricket. The city quite simply failed to leverage its international prestige and competitive superiority to the benefit of the game beyond the Quaker city. But then, Philadelphia could point to these factors as the very reason for its neglect. Since the national championship mismatch of 1891, the city's cricket infrastructure was just so much bigger and better than that of other cricket organizations in the country. Any cricket association that wanted to include Philadelphia couldn't but be an organization of extreme unequals. Given the vast disproportions between Philadelphia cricket and cricket everywhere else in the land, no one could really fault the Philadelphians for putting their own cricket interest first. It was never that Philadelphia was unwilling to provide leadership to the nation's cricket but that there was, in its estimation, so little worth leading.[67]

Yet, the Philadelphia cricket community fully recognized that the progress of the city's cricket came with an obligation to extend its game "with the general public" beyond its immediate confines. Requests, even demands, for Philadelphia to send teams beyond the city's traditional competitive boundaries of New York, Baltimore and Boston were coming from as far away as Chicago by the early 1880s, and even distant California clubs as late as 1911, and the Philadelphians did oblige.[68]

The Germantown club had actually contemplated a national cricket tour as early as 1870, but a commitment to what the Philadelphia cricket community would refer to as "missionary cricket" began in earnest as a lead up to its England tour of 1884. That year, the Young America club played the cricket clubs in Pittsburg, Altoona and Harrisburg. This was followed, a year later, with a trip by a combined Philadelphia squad to Chicago and Pittsburg.[69]

Perhaps because of its greater number of members not born in Philadelphia, Belmont, of all the Halifax Cup clubs, always seemed the most willing to act upon its proselytizing obligations. The club would swing by Detroit during its Canada tour in 1887, returning for another visit, including a stop in Chicago, four years later. A year earlier the Belmont side had even obliged the small coal-mining club in Pottsville with a game. After a few years of non-travel, the club was on the road again, visiting Cleveland in 1899 and Pittsburg in 1910 (Pittsburg had also received a visit from the Haverford College team in 1909).[70]

By far the most extended excursion by any Philadelphia club was undertaken by the Frankford cricket club in 1911, this team "for the first time in history" venturing as far west as Seattle and Portland for some matches against these appreciative clubs.[71]

Philadelphia's other plans for raising the profile of its game, some with considerable promotional expectations, never came about or had little benefit. For some reason, the side Philadelphia had chosen to represent the United States in the 1904 St. Louis Olympics never made the trip, effectively killing the cricket competition that had been planned for the event. A cricket exhibition for President William Taft on the White House lawn in 1911 also never came off, while the exhibition game staged by Philadelphia cricketers at Montpelier, James Madison's ancestral estate in Virginia, that same year accomplished little more than titillation and edification of the estate's owner at that time, business magnate William Dupont, with a crass American imitation of English country house cricket.[72]

The Philadelphians must have been well aware that all their efforts to carry their cricket beyond the confines of their city would accomplish very little. The competitive gap between Philadelphia cricket and the rest of the country remained so vast (Belmont beat the Cleveland club it visited in 1899 by the laughable score of 419–75) to effectively preclude any expectations that the game would get a boost from any success by the locals. And even then, Philadelphians well knew that cricket's cause in the country would never be served by just giving games to teams which were staffed everywhere by resident Englishmen.[73]

For all the hopes and aspirations the Philadelphians may have held out for their cricket, prospects for their game among the greater American sporting public were, by the early 20th century, effectively no better than what they had been thirty years earlier. The Philadelphia *Times*, editorializing amid the euphoria of Philadelphia's 1884 English tour, could still only expect that it would be many, many years in the future before any Americans outside Philadelphia would take to cricket, "if at all."[74]

Twelve

Decline, Denial, and Dreams: The Passing of Philadelphia Cricket

With what must have seemed to be good reason the *American Cricketer* proclaimed, in 1905, that cricket in Philadelphia was "never ... in such a flourishing condition as it is today." The publication listed more than 375 total cricket matches that year, spread over all competitive levels and clubs throughout the greater metropolitan area, the most that would ever be played in a Philadelphia cricket season.[1]

Behind these raw numbers, however, *American Cricket* editor Sidney Young was confiding that same year to his English counterpart at *Cricket* that he was sensing an ominous change in the game's fashionable appeal and a corresponding waning of overall interest in the game.[2]

Indeed, worrisome signs had been appearing within the landscape of the city's cricket by the early years of the 20th century, indications that seemed to justify serious uneasiness over the health and vitality of the game.

The earliest signs appeared in that segment of Philadelphia cricket where it interfaced most directly and extensively with native-born Americans: the colleges. Since the second year of its existence, the Intercollegiate Cricket Championship had been a modest three-horse race among the University of Pennsylvania, Haverford College, and Harvard. After 1905, Harvard dropped out (reportedly because that university's decision to increase the residency requirement for athletes largely cut off its supply of Penn/Haverford cricket-playing graduates who were usually pursing a one-year master's degree).[3]

Harvard's place was filled by Cornell University, a chronically weak side whose participation at least avoided the "more or less joke" of having an intercollegiate championship between only two institutions until that university dropped out in 1913.[4]

Now down to just two contestants after that year, the University of Pennsylvania and Haverford sides did the best they could to lend legitimacy to the championship by resorting to playing each other, after 1913, multiple times each season.[5]

But even then, it was becoming increasingly difficult for these two institutions themselves to maintain cricket at anything like a viable, competitive manner in the years leading up to the First World War, though for different reasons.

Cricket at the University of Pennsylvania was, ironically, negatively impacted by the school's growing international status and reputation, a trend that, by attracting more foreign students from cricket-playing countries, wasn't only diminishing playing opportunities for local cricket-playing students but also ushering in an unwelcome dependence on foreign talent. The university baseball coach had also unwittingly accelerated this dependence by forbidding, beginning in 1904, any members of the institution's baseball team from also playing on its cricket team.[6]

The omnipresent Australian/New Zealand dental students on the university cricket team were now, by 1912, joined by foreign cricket-playing students from South Africa to an extent that, by the end of the First World War, the team had to resort to outright pleading for novice Americans to come out for the sport. Still without a ground of their own, forced to practice among the quads, and only assisted by temporary, itinerant coaches, the university cricket teams found themselves progressively dependent on foreign talent, like the standout West Indies student Francis L. Aris, who single-handedly sustained the team after the First World War.[7]

Cricket at the university, in short, was lapsing back into the antebellum scenario that the Philadelphia cricket community had been tirelessly working to overcome for half a century: novice American cricket players totally dependent on experienced foreign players.

At Haverford College, developments closer to home were ever so slightly beginning to weaken the school's iron-clad loyalty to the game. The increasing enrollment of students from outside the immediate Philadelphia area unfamiliar with cricket was a cause for concern for the student newspaper by 1909, with many of these cricket-ignorant students lobbying for greater support for baseball, which, after many years as a peripheral activity at the college, gained recognition as an official college sport in 1915.[8]

Support for cricket among alumni, faculty, and administrators, however, remained solid, making possible the renewal of the college cricket team's quadrennial tour to England in 1910 and 1914, though neither of these teams was able to uphold the expectations of supporters. The team captain and last standout cricketer to come from the college,

Harold Furness, whom English critics had "stamped ... as a cricketer of the highest class," couldn't prevent his side from being "outclassed in nearly every game" in 1910, finishing with a poor 3–11–1 record. The college side posted barely improved results four years later, returning home with a 4–9–3 mark.[9]

The fact that the college had been seriously considered for admission to the Halifax Cup competition (vetoed, understandably, by a Merion club heavily dependent on Haverford alumni) also underscored the predicament of the "Big Four" clubs within Haverford's own competition: a stifling and worrisome insularity in their control and hold on the traditions of Philadelphia cricket.[10]

The Halifax Cup clubs were themselves well aware that their highly restrictive competition was, by the turn of the century, "too narrow," "monotonous," and—in the view of outsiders—"self-absorbed." A strong Frankford club was admitted in 1903, and the Moorestown club in 1906. But the latter held a place in the competition for only five years—not much longer than the Radnor club that it had replaced.[11]

Rather than admit the Baltimore club (an organization which was in decline at that time) or New York, something that had been proposed in 1902, the Halifax Cup clubs opted to instead remain "narrow" by having Germantown and Merion enter two teams in the competition in 1906, an awkward arrangement that was abandoned after a couple of years.[12]

The insecurity of the city's cricket even at the highest level fully hit home in 1913 with the disbandment of one of the "Big Four" clubs: Belmont.

The development didn't come as a complete surprise. The west Philadelphia organization always had one of the smallest membership rolls in the Halifax Competition and the lowest membership fees in addition to what seems to have been a lackluster management.[13]

The demise of the Belmont club, rumored as early as 1898, was averted at that time, but rising taxes and a heavy debt made the $148,000 purchase offer by the city (which had been eyeing the club property as a public playground for several years) too irresistable. With its acceptance, the club would at least pre-empt the newly formed professional Federal Baseball League, which had also been eyeing the location for its Philadelphia franchise, from turning its revered cricket ground into a baseball park.[14]

Well aware of the Belmont club's importance to their quality of life, neighbors made a last-ditch effort to stop the sale, petitioning Philadelphia's mayor to reconsider the purchase, but did not succeed. The transaction was completed in early 1913 and soon thereafter visitors to the location found "swings, giant slides, and merry-go-rounds litter what was once considered one of the best cricket fields in the country."[15]

Twelve. Decline, Denial, and Dreams

That the disbandment of one of Philadelphia's storied, top tier, old-line cricket clubs came just a year after the *American Cricketer* had confidently declared that "with all six Halifax Cup clubs well on the road to prosperity, it may be well for the cricket pessimists to hush their baleful prophesizing about the future of the game in Philadelphia" seemed to evidence a troubling state of ignorance, even denial, within the higher levels of the city's cricket community over the true state of its game.[16]

The local press, always the most reliable barometer of public interest and sentiment, more accurately indicated a downward trend. In the years leading up to the First World War, the dailies carried fewer and fewer cricket reports of diminishing content and detail. Disappearing, except for the international matches, were the extensive, multi-columned match reports of the 1890s which had been reported in great detail by cricket-knowledgeable reporters, progressively replaced by single-line notices now rarely accompanied by a box score and written by reporters with little more than a rudimentary knowledge of the game. The *Philadelphia Inquirer*, one of the city's most dedicated cricket-reporting papers, in 1910, gave the reason: the state of the game in the city was such that "no one seems to care for cricket news just now."[17]

Lester supplements this anecdotal evidence of the game's decline in a more quantitative manner with a graph of the city's reported cricket matches over a fifty-year period, which reveals a sharp and precipitous drop after 1905. Within a decade of that date the number of cricket fixtures had fallen by nearly half and within another decade, fewer cricket matches were being played in Philadelphia than in 1878.[18]

Such a sharp and rapid decline with any social or institutional activity is unmistakable evidence of a dramatic change in emotional attachment to that activity and, as such, demands an explanation.

The Philadelphia cricket community initially explained the decline as a loss of "sports space" to the newly emerging games of tennis and golf. Both of these sports had, in fact, been nurtured in the Halifax Cup clubs, tennis appearing as early as the inaugural issue of the *American Cricketer* in 1877 and golf soon occupying considerable space in the publication. Half-hearted resistance within these clubs couldn't halt the rising popularity of tennis (the Philadelphia club unsuccessfully tried to ban tennis from its grounds in 1888) while golf, "the insidious sport," was soon even attracting some of the city's top cricketers, among them King and Bohlen. This seemed evidence enough to lead Lester to the far-fetched conclusion that, by allowing these competing sports into its clubs, Philadelphia cricket "did not so much die as commit suicide."[19]

In the eyes of the city's cricket authorities, tennis, golf, and kindred sports were luring athletic-minded club members to a sporting experience far inferior to the traditions and values found in their game. In point of fact, however, participants in these upstart sports were displaying far greater emotional honesty by playing these games less for any extraneous value than their direct emotional appeal and, as such, stood as threatening alternatives to the bedrock foundation of cricket's sporting experience.

To its participants and supporters, cricket had always been a sport deeply rooted in *obligation*, a sporting experience that had always been a "matter of tradition and heritage" in which participants were expected to tolerate diminished excitement appeal for the sake of such perceived extraneous benefits as peer interaction and character development.[20]

The non–cricket-playing students at Haverford College clearly sensed this, noticing something "artificial" in the way that the college cricketers played the game as much to satisfy the expectations of the college cricket supporters, alumni, and administrators as they did for the pure enjoyment of the game. Even George Newhall, who, in 1884, had boldly and confidently proclaimed "there is nothing in the game unattractive to Americans," twenty-six years later retreated to an entirely survivalist tone, conceding that now, in 1910, "cricket ... is not interesting to watch nor its merits understood as in the writer's generation."[21]

In the years leading up to the First World War this sense of obligation, the bedrock foundation of Philadelphia cricket's sporting ethos, seems to have progressively weakened and then precipitously lost its force altogether. And without the immediate, unconditional, emotional appeal and excitement of other popular Americans sports to buttress this loss of obligation, cricket simply could no longer hold any compelling attraction for newcomers, squarely putting the game on a path of rapid and irreversible decline.

The Philadelphia cricket community had long been aware of this deficiency in its game, understanding that cricket, forced to stand strictly on the merits of its excitement appeal, was "at variance" with the American temperament, and the *New York Times* didn't have to remind the community that "after all, a Philadelphian is an American."[22]

George Newhall had long been aware that his fellow American cricketers "have shown a certain fretfulness and impatience under the restrictions and customs which prevail." Americans had always shown they wanted to play their cricket with "eagerness," "astuteness" and demanded, with their cricket, "to have the play sharp and spirited."[23]

Especially in batting, the engine that generates excitement in all bat-and-ball sports, Americans wanted aggressive and attacking cricket play even at the cost of orthodox style and technique. "When a man goes to bat," John P. Green had insisted, "it is not for the purpose of exemplifying theories but making runs." Purists may have objected to how these

Twelve. Decline, Denial, and Dreams

American cricketers "want to play or score off every ball" with their "slashing and slogging" style, but American players found intolerable the cautious but unexciting "making pokey" batting style preferred by English players, exemplified by a member of the Hargreaves family, who annoyed his American teammates in "allowing ball after ball to pass him by without making the slightest attempt to make runs." This was a playing style and mindset, an observer forewarned, that was guaranteed to be "a good way to kill what little interest there is manifested in cricket in this country."[24]

In order to align cricket with the excitement experience demanded by a broader segment of Americans, something baseball had so successfully achieved, it had long been known that this would require "a very material alternation" to some of the game's official rules and established traditions in order that cricket, in the United States, could become "a game based on Americans conditions and American requirements and not on English traditions and English methods."[25]

This, however, squarely required a willingness to deviate from, or outright challenge, the highest authority in the game, the MCC. Their restlessness and annoyance with what was perceived as the constraints of foreign regulations wouldn't push the Philadelphians to the point of demanding, as George Newhall did, that "if the MCC does not suit us, either we must go or the MCC must go." But a general consensus prevailed within the city's cricket community that "MCC rules should not stop the progress of this great game" in America. "Let us govern ourselves," the *American Cricketer* demanded. "Why take our cue from London?"[26]

Throughout the history of cricket in Philadelphia, its advocates would propose, experiment with, and directly adopt numerous modifications to cricket in its traditional form, always seeking to mold their sport into an experience that would synchronize, as far as realistically possible, with the bat-and-ball excitement experience preferred by Americans.

At the top of the list was the one feature that annoyed cricketers not only in Philadelphia but also throughout the land, "the languid pedestrianism of the overs [two batters are always up together in cricket, both of whom are bowled to, alternatively, in opposite directions after a prescribed number of pitches, like throwing from the pitcher's mound to a batter at home plate for several pitches and then throwing from home plate to a batter at the pitcher's mound. This change of bowling direction—called an "over"—requires the fielders to repeatedly shift their positions after each completed over]."[27]

Philadelphia cricketers would have fully agreed with the *Detroit Free Press* observation that "it's tedious work this over business" with the constant and time-consuming field shifting, and the Philadelphians, for decades, continually experimented with ways to optimize the number of overs in a game. Among the more radical ideas the Philadelphians tried was a change of bowling direction only at the fall of a wicket or after thirty minutes (a brief experiment for the Philadelphians in 1872), changing only at the fall of every five wickets or at the fall of every third wicket (an experiment by the Philadelphians in 1882).[28]

It was eventually found to be more satisfactory to simply increase the number of pitches per over which, during this period, was officially limited to four or five. In the expectation of infusing "more snap" into the game, the Philadelphians, beginning in 1885, increased the number of pitches per over to six, then to eight in 1890 ("hailed as a great success") and, after permitting it as an option in 1892, to fully ten balls per over in 1912, a modification even *Cricket* conceded was "an improvement to the game." The ten-ball over would remain a unique and special feature of Philadelphia cricket that would continue to be utilized into the 1920s.[29]

The other feature of the game contested by the Philadelphians was the LBW rule (acronym for Leg Before Wicket, where the batter is declared out for blocking, with his body, a pitch that would have hit his wicket and got him out) or, more specifically, the MCC's interpretation of the law, which gave the batter immunity from being out LBW so long as he blocked the ball outside the line of the off stump (roughly equivalent to a baseball umpire prohibited from calling strikes on the outside corner of the plate).

In what was almost certainly a concession to the increasing popularity of swing bowling among their players, the Philadelphians, in 1888, "virtually declared their independence from the MCC" by adopting their own "simplified" LBW rule whereby the batter would be out if he blocked any ball the umpire judged would have hit the wicket. It was a modification that seems to have been popular with the city's entire cricket community; as the *Public Ledger* proclaimed, there was "not one player of any standing on this side of the water who does not believe that the American [LBW] rule is a fairer and wiser one" than the official MCC interpretation.[30]

Other modifications Philadelphia either implemented or contemplated were efforts to impose greater rationality on participation, game length, and record keeping. In permitting a team to declare at any time, adopted in 1889, the Philadelphians were following the MCC, which had adopted that interpretation the same year. But in counting the not-out batter (the fielding team has to get out ten of its opponent's eleven batters, leaving the final batter up, not out), for statistical purposes, as a turn at bat, they didn't. The Philadelphians wouldn't adopt the radical idea, proposed in 1868, of using a four, rather than the official three, stump wicket (which

Twelve. Decline, Denial, and Dreams 175

would have contributed to more frequent outs in a game) or increasing the number of players from the standard eleven to thirteen (which would allow more participation, like softball's ten-player teams, rather than baseball's nine-player teams) but they did join the growing chorus of parties who, by the First World War, were advocating sports be allowed on Sundays. Always motivated to play their cricket in a spirit of "moving things along," the Philadelphians reduced the traditional thirty-minute lunch break (roughly cricket's equivalent to the "seventh inning stretch") to ten minutes and also reduced the official two-minute allowance for a batter to come up to a single minute.[31]

The influence of baseball on Philadelphia's ongoing deliberations about its cricket could hardly be avoided. Permitting double plays (not allowed in cricket) was proposed, but rejected, at the United States Cricket Association meeting in 1885, though the Merion club experimented with recording errors and earned/unearned runs (neither statistically recognized in official cricket to this day) in their match with New York's St. George club in 1874.[32]

Behind all these experiments was Philadelphia's earnest and unrelenting effort to integrate its cricket into America's own culturally conditioned demands for bat-and-ball excitement. Any insistence on simply keeping its game on the "old, worn out, beaten path of cricket customs" was subject to ongoing scrutiny or even outright rejection, like the short-lived "tea break" introduced during the MCC matches in 1905, a decision "severely criticized" and never repeated.[33]

Most of these modifications and experiments, whether adopted or contemplated, however, were little more than tinkering around the edges and didn't directly address cricket's greatest challenge for its acceptance by Americans: satisfactory length determination, critical not only because of the time involved (it took Merion and the Philadelphia club fully five days, played on a stop-and-resume basis, to complete one Halifax Cup match in 1911, a not uncommon occurrence with games in that competition) but also because of its direct impact on the level of game excitement.[34]

The difficulty that Philadelphia faced with its cricket can perhaps best be illustrated with an analogy with baseball. Let us imagine a baseball game that had to complete its 54 total outs in, say, a three-hour time limit, and that if the full nine innings couldn't be completed by that time, the game would end and be declared a "draw" regardless of the score.

Clearly, under such a length determination, baseball games would assume a radically different character and would certainly exhibit a greatly diminished level of excitement. The side that found itself trailing in the late innings would be motivated to stall (pitchers working slowly, etc.) and prevent a full nine innings from being completed in the three-hour time limit, thus allowing the losing team to claim a "draw" and avoid defeat. And if a game were high scoring, taking up so much time in the early innings that it was apparent a full nine innings couldn't be completed in the remaining time, all interest in the game among players and spectators would effectively evaporate.

The challenge for the Philadelphians, then, was how to avoid such a scenario with their cricket: how to infuse a baseball-like level of excitement while maintaining, as closely as possible, cricket's traditional playing structure. To this end, three major schemes were put forward over the course of the game's history in the city.

The first to be devised was the "Average System," originated and advocated by Dan Newhall with his Young America club in the late 1870s. In its basic form, a game under this scheme would be decided not by the team with the highest score but by an "average" determined by each team's total score divided by the number of wickets lost (batters put out). If team A, for example, batting first, scored 100 runs and all ten of its batters had been put out, the team would finish with an average of 10. If its opponent, team B, at the completion of the allocated time limit for the game had scored, say, 90 runs but only eight of its batters had been put out, it would finish with an "average" of 11.25 and would thus be declared the winner. Such a scheme, it was pointed out, would maintain cricket's traditional format while also guaranteeing a definite result by the end of play, thus eliminating unsatisfactory draws.[35]

After this plan's trial in 1875, Newhall formally proposed the plan at the inaugural United States Cricket Association meeting in 1878. Though not widely utilized, it was adopted by the Halifax Cup clubs in their matches in 1886 and was still being used by some Philadelphia clubs as late as 1909.[36]

The second, and more controversial, scheme was the "American Plan," devised and advocated by John B. Thayer Jr of the Merion club. Under this arrangement, teams, in their second innings, wouldn't each bat through their entire order as prescribed by traditional cricket, but switch after the fall of every third wicket (i.e., after every three outs) a la baseball.

After this plan's trial in the 1880s, Thayer introduced the plan at the United States Cricket Association meeting in 1890, a move that immediately aroused controversy in U.S. and overseas cricket circles. Henry Chadwick, still a strong supporter of American cricket, hailed the plan as "a revolution in the cricket field" and the scheme won the endorsement of George Wright, now playing for Boston's Longwood cricket club. George Patterson, however, condemned it as a "mongrel game" while Dan Newhall himself, in a letter to *Cricket*, attacked the scheme, declaring it "would not be the cricket I have loved so well," a sentiment seconded by the magazine's editor, seeing in the plan nothing less than an "emasculation" of traditional cricket.[37]

The city's cricket clubs, however, were given the option of adopting the scheme for their matches and college teams in particular, like the University of Pennsylvania, used it in a number of their matches with some success.[38]

The third scheme, which took its name from originator John Mason of the Philadelphia cricket club, required the two teams, after the completion of their first innings, to equally divide the remaining playing time during the second innings—i.e., if two hours of playing time remained after the first innings was completed, each team would, in its second innings, be allowed to bat no more than an hour each, thus ensuring a result. First used on a trial basis in 1910, the "Mason Plan" was, after some debate, also provisionally adopted by the Halifax Cup clubs the following year.[39]

Despite the optimistic expectations from their originators that these schemes would revitalize cricket and lead to more exciting and decisive games, these schemes showed flaws once put into practice, soon making it apparent that these expectations wouldn't be realized.

Dan Newhall may have been confident that his "Average System" would "save cricket from an unhealthy and dragging existence in this country," but he must have known, if he didn't acknowledge, that his scheme had the glaring drawback of allowing a team to win without actually beating the opponent's score, as indicated by the above example. And once the team batting second had, at any point during its innings, reached a higher "average" than its opponent, it could simply bat defensively, not needing to score any more runs and, assuming it did not lose any more wickets, could simply drag the game out to finishing time.[40]

John Thayer may have believed that, with his "American Plan," "the new game will preserve the essentials of the old, but it will be an American development of the old." But Arthur Wood quickly recognized the flaw in this "new game," ordering his team, when ahead, to bat slowly and defensively to prevent opponents from coming to bat, and, when behind, to bat aggressively and recklessly to get the lead in its allotted three outs. Both interest-killing strategies effectively refuted predictions by plan proponents that "Adopt the Thayer Plan and many a boy who now plays base ball will change to cricket."[41]

Nor were these deficiencies effectively remedied with the "Mason Plan." The *American Cricketer*, in pointing out the incentive for sides, when behind, to engage in reckless batting and, when ahead, to engage in all-out stalling, correctly concluded that in games played under this scheme, "the second innings quite frequently degenerated into a farce."[42]

For all their expressed desire that "this game should be suited to the character and natural feeling of the populace," two of these plans were little more than a reallocation of remaining playing time between the competing sides (with its three-outs-and-switch arrangement the "American Plan" had at least tried to inject some of baseball's "ebb and flow") while the third was little more than an artificial concoction to ensure a result at the expense of fairness. None of these schemes, ultimately, resolved the core issue confronting cricket of maintaining a satisfactory excitement level within a pre-determined time limitation.[43]

Never, it appears, was the Philadelphia cricket community, for all its innovative bent, inspired to take the so seemingly logical and self-evident step of determining its games on the basis of total pitches rather than total time, an innovation that, since its introduction in the last few decades, has propelled modern cricket to new heights of worldwide popularity.

More surprisingly, hints for such an innovation had long been under the very noses of the American cricket community. As early as 1858, the *Clipper* was advocating that, as a time saver, each batter be allowed no more than twelve pitches during practice games, a recommendation that *Turf, Field, and Farm* was still suggesting ten years later. It was an option known by the Philadelphians, as all batters in the veterans' match played as part of Germantown's 50th Anniversary celebration in 1904 were limited to fifteen total pitches—only a few more deliveries per batter than is allocated in some of the more popular modern limited pitch formats.[44]

Perhaps the deep and resilient undercurrent of traditionalism that pervaded the Halifax Cup clubs made impossible any such Copernican-type turn with their cricket, determining their matches on the basis of a predetermined number of pitches rather than a total time limit. In the eyes of Philadelphia's cricket elite, "real" cricket always remained the traditional, two full innings game, with anything deviating from this format stigmatized as little more than "happy-go-lucky" frolics. To George Patterson, all complaints about cricket's slowness and length could be easily remedied by the simplistic and experience-disproven suggestion of "beginning matches with greater punctuality and not wasting so much time."[45]

Eventually, a mindset of wearied resignation seems to have set in on Philadelphia cricket authorities. These Philadelphians had tried "remedy upon remedy" to invigorate their cricket, and all the many "attempts to shorten the game," the *Philadelphia Times* concluded, "have never been successful." Cricket in its traditional format, it seems, could only be a lengthy, slow-paced game that Americans had to accept, like it or not.

Twelve. Decline, Denial, and Dreams

The *American Cricketer* summed up the seemingly irresolvable dilemma by simply declaring, "We have no remedy to suggest and perhaps none is needed." Everywhere and at all times the "American element" was pushing, throbbing, yearning to burst forth in their cricket, but Philadelphia's cricket authorities were steadfastly determined that there would be no "American hustle" in their game. If the city's cricket "elites" could be faulted at all in their stewardship of the game, it wasn't because they wouldn't allow more Americans into their cricket but because they would not, or could not, allow in more *Americanization*. "Proper" Philadelphians, by a process of reinforcing self-persuasion, had come to hold an uncompromising allegiance to an excitement experience contrary to the demands and dictates of their own social nature as Americans.[46]

And there were certainly plenty more Americans to be had if they could have been reached. Cricket may have been more popular with Americans in Philadelphia than anywhere else in the country, but, even here, large segments of the city's populace remained uninvolved with the game. Most of Philadelphia's cricket activity was centered in only two geographic areas of the city: the 22nd Ward, whose "people used to be a mild, quiet, orderly, cricket-loving, well-behaved community," and the Kensington area, whose people were primarily English-immigrant workers. The game seems to have had virtually no presence within the city's large Catholic population, with only one Catholic educational institution, Villanova University, known to have a cricket team during this period.[47]

Cricket had reportedly been "the favorite game" in the city's significant Afro-American community during the game's heyday before the Civil War, with at least three African American cricket clubs active in the city during that time: the Olive, Diligents, and Metamora. After that period, however, only one of the city's many cricket clubs can be positively identified as African American.[48]

Most glaring of all was the minimal involvement of Philadelphia's female population in the game, effectively excluding fully half the city's populace.

Philadelphia women were known to be keen cricket spectators since the earliest years, attending matches with "pencil and scorebook in hand"; it became an established fact that the Philadelphia "cricket girl is a type entirely distinct." The presence of women in the game took a major step forward in 1879 when Belmont became the first Halifax Cup club to allow female members, a move soon followed by the city's other leading cricket clubs.[49]

With their presence in these clubs formally recognized, women were eventually encouraged to become not just spectators but active participants. But in this facet of the game Philadelphia, for once, lagged behind other cricket-playing areas of the country, even though the game, by the late 19th century, was gaining a reputation as a pastime particularly suited for women (possibly because of its leisurely and non-contact character).[50]

Girls at the Seabright Lawn Tennis and Cricket Club in New Jersey were playing the game as early as 1888, while the women at the Staten Island cricket club had formed a regular team in 1895, even extending a challenge to the women of Philadelphia for a match that same year.[51]

In Philadelphia, meanwhile, female involvement with the game had been largely informal and unorganized, like the impromptu girls' game at the Henry Houston estate and the light-hearted men vs women's match (with the men required to bat and field left-handed). These games were played in 1891, with the latter a novel-enough occurrence to make the front page of the city's dailies.[52]

Not until the final years of the century did Philadelphia women become involved with cricket on an organized, competitive basis when the women's team organized at Chestnut Hill took on its counterparts at the Germantown club in 1898, the latter also playing the women's team organized at the Philadelphia club the following year.[53]

These contests, hailed as "a red letter day in the history of Philadelphia feminine athletics," would, however, be the full extent of organized women's cricket among the Halifax Cup clubs, whose female members showed an overwhelming preference for the emerging sports of tennis and golf, though Bryn Mawr, Haverford College's all-female sister college, was still offering cricket as part of its physical education program in 1907.[54]

Like overseers of other institutions alarmed by the evident decline of its social world, Philadelphia cricket authorities turned to youth to revitalize their game. The most significant effort toward this end began in 1897, when a "colts" (U-23) match was included in the slate of games with Warner's visiting English team. Long advocated by Daniel and Bob Newhall, these matches, contested up to the Australian visit of 1912, did passably well in their intended objective of introducing the city's most promising young cricket players to high-level cricket.[55]

And it certainly wasn't that Philadelphia couldn't turn out good cricket players at this stage in its history. Germantown's young player Bobby Anderson, "fascinating, daring, and brilliant," was not only recognized locally as the "most talented fielder in the city" but also proclaimed by Australian manager R.B. Benjamin to be the "finest slip fielder [player positioned behind the batter to make cat-quick catches of balls deflected "back to the screen"] I have seen since [English player Len] Braund." Fellow Australian Warren Bardsley felt Merion fast bowler Henry Pearce had the makings of a "match winning bowler" while the *American Cricketer*

Twelve. Decline, Denial, and Dreams

The William Penn Charter school cricket team, Interacademic League cricket champions in 1909. The fourteen games played by the school that year would be the most by a Philadelphia school. Holding the ball is Bobby Anderson, who within a few years would be internationally acclaimed as one of the game's finest fielders (*Penn Charter Class Record*).

believed the young Philadelphia bowler Herbert Goodall "might emulate the prowess of a King or Clark."[56]

Anderson, along with a cadre of young, talented players who were on the Germantown team that toured England in 1911, so impressed A.G. Groom that the Englishman confided to the *American Cricketer* he'd "dearly wish that five of the Germantown young 'uns were qualified to play for my old county Gloucestershire."[57]

These players, however, would represent the last standouts in Philadelphia's final generation of cricketers. Local cricket clubs were now finding it increasingly harder to recruit, retain, and motivate young players, the *American Cricketer* noticing, on the eve of the First World War, a marked "listlessness in the junior cricketers of today," players who "somehow do not show the promising qualities that made cricket giants one, two, or three decades ago."[58]

But then, the Philadelphia cricket community should have known that it could no longer attract aspiring young athletes to a sport that could only offer to its participants the shrinking competitive horizons of a single city while the emerging sports of football, basketball, tennis and golf could hold out to its followers the expanding competitive horizons of an entire nation, even the world. To the very end, Philadelphia cricket's hopes for its survival would rest on an infusion of young blood, but in scanning the horizons for new talent in 1919, the *American Cricketer* was forced to conclude that "at this moment there is no material, and little in sight."[59]

The one bright spot during this period of decline was schools cricket. Six schools were still fielding cricket teams between 1915 and 1917, only one fewer than had been playing ten years earlier. Twenty-one school matches were played in 1916, seven by Frankford High School alone. With superior facilities, coaching and alumni support, the private schools continued to maintain their competitive superiority, but even lopsided wins like Penn Charter's 143–26 win over Northeast Manual in 1916 didn't seem to dampen interest among the public schools. At least there existed enough interest among students at Northeast Manual that four members of the school's cricket team won varsity letters that same year.[60]

All this seems to not only cast doubts on Lester's claim that "the first decline of interest in cricket among the young is noticeable in the schools" but also reveals what appears to have been a less than supportive stance for this area of Philadelphia cricket. Played by young men who demanded excitement over propriety with their sport, school cricket seems to have always shown a restlessness with the moral straitjacket of Philadelphia's adult ethos and for that reason never won the full approval of Lester, who found "the desire to win was so keen that the standards of sportsmanship suffered."[61]

This may account for the apparently benign neglect senior Philadelphia cricketers seemed to show towards school cricket. Only a handful off the private schools, such as Haverford Grammar and Penn Charter (whose team Lester himself briefly coached in 1905), had a regular coach while the city's top senior players never seemed to feel they were under any serious obligation to assist the game at this level.[62]

The *American Cricketer* had itself expressed concern about this neglect of school cricket in 1915 but not until the end of the First World War did the cricket community seem to awaken to its failings. George Newhall, at war's end, proclaimed a crusade ("let it take a century") to revive cricket at schools, which had contracted during U.S. involvement in the war (the Interscholastic League had suspended, or greatly reduced, its sports activity in 1918). To conscientious observers, however, declarations like this must have appeared hollow and ineffective given the previous decades of senior disinterest. Only one school, Penn Charter, revived its cricket after the war, in 1922, but finding no other schools to play, disbanded its team the following year, bringing the history of organized Philadelphia school cricket to an end.[63]

Twelve. Decline, Denial, and Dreams

The *Philadelphia Inquirer* may still have been optimistically declaring, in 1916, that "cricket is not dead even in these days" but all trends in the game were pointing to its termination. The city's presence in international cricket was now nothing more than pro forma. The Incogniti team that arrived in 1913 was the first English team to visit Philadelphia in six years and wouldn't be followed by another for seven more years. And the U.S.-Canada match of 1912 would be the last in the series' seventy-year history, as the Philadelphians were unwilling to meet the Canadians' demand to travel to Winnipeg for the 1913 match and Canada's entry into the First World War the following year made it all but impossible to continue the world's hereto oldest international sporting rivalry.[64]

The competitive standard of the city's cricket was also going into free fall. The Halifax Cup competition, supposedly comparable, in 1906, to Australia's "Pennant" league, had deteriorated, by 1913, to a level, it was claimed, of being no better than English club cricket. The New York club, which had been admitted to the Halifax Cup competition in 1915 to replace the disbanded Moorestown club, won the competition in 1917 and 1919 (the Halifax Cup was suspended in 1918), reclaiming for that city the competitive superiority that it had lost to Philadelphia half a century ago.[65]

Germantown dismantled its cricket grandstand in 1915 while the Merion cricket team was "going backwards," outright forfeiting some Halifax Cup matches that year. A representative Halifax Cup side lost two of three matches against the more vibrant and immigrant-dominated Interstate League that same year and all but conceded competitive superiority to that organization when the Halifax clubs allowed, also beginning that year, its members to play for Interstate clubs.[66]

King had effectively "retired" in 1913 but returned the following year to lead the Philadelphia club, which he and teammate Eddie Cregar had joined after their old Belmont club had disbanded, to that club's first Halifax Cup championship. After that final moment of accomplishment, however, Philadelphia's greatest cricketer retreated into the role of honored senior statesman, now just basking in such adulations as *Sporting Life's* glorifying 1916 article titled "American the Greatest Cricketer," or reminiscing about past glories with his old teammates, the *American Cricketer* proclaiming that "their very records blaze like the handwriting on the wall."[67]

At the very time Philadelphia's cricket world was fast fading, many of the original architects, actors and supporters of this sporting world were also passing on. William Rotch Wister, now the acknowledged "Father of Philadelphia cricket," who had been involved with the game from its beginnings in the 1840s, died in 1911, his brother Jones in 1917. William Morgan, one of the founders of the Merion club, died in 1921, while John P.

Green, one of the founders of the Belmont club, passed away in 1924. In the span of eleven years between 1910 and 1921, three of the celebrated Newhall brothers—Robert (1910), Dan (1913) and George (1921)—all passed away. Charles Venou died in 1919, and John B. Thayer had gone down with the *Titanic* in 1912. It must have been deeply and personally sad for these creators of Philadelphia cricket to see unfold before their eyes, in the span of barely fifty years, the birth, rise, and now extinction of their sporting world.[68]

And the sporting world that these first and second generations of Philadelphia cricketers had worked to construct was now disintegrating under the eyes of its third generation, and not without increasing personal anxiety and trepidation. Terrified by increasing rumors, as the United States drew closer to war, that their sport was in danger of being eliminated in even some of the Halifax Cup clubs themselves, cricket supporters countered with the only card left in their hand: a plea for the game's social values. "Take away the cricket life with all its traditions" from these clubs, the *American Cricketer* cried, and all that would be left would be "a graven image without a vestige of the warm heartedness and human kindness that helps so much." Without cricket, it was further warned, "these clubs would lose their very souls and exist merely as utilitarian enterprises for the promotion of health" and would outright "fall by the wayside."[69]

To all but the most hardened cricket supporters, these warnings must have appeared as much a sign of desperation as the wild claim, at war's end, that cricket was somehow "on the verge of an opportunity to burst back." The suggestion that Philadelphia undertake a national cricket tour as part of the country's 150th celebration in 1924 was at least not as forlorn as George Newhall's dream of hosting a grand, international tournament involving Philadelphia, Canada, England and Australia in 1918, though both schemes, given the reality of the times, were equally illusory.[70]

Contacts with England were reestablished at war's end and the motherland of cricket obligingly sent a team, the Incogniti, to Philadelphia in 1920. However, this team just further confirmed Philadelphia's status as no more than a shadow on the periphery of world cricket when it won every game it played in the city. The Philadelphians could at least lay claim, with this visit, of having crossed paths with future England captain Douglas Jardine who would gain infamy, a decade later, as the mastermind behind one of cricket's most notorious episodes: the "Bodyline Series" between England and Australia.[71]

On the invitation of the Incogniti, Philadelphia made a return visit to England the following year—its fourteenth visit, and what would be the final, overseas trip by a representative Philadelphia cricket team. This side, now playing under the diminished title of the Philadelphia Pilgrims, was a combination of aging veterans like C.C. Morris and John Mason and several now forgotten heroes of Germantown's 1913 Australian match, Bobby Anderson and William O'Neil, giving the English public a tantalizing final glimpse of Philadelphia cricket. With a slate of matches against mostly military and unchallenging country house sides, the tour was little more than a trip down memory lane, meeting old acquaintances like the seventy-year-old Lord Harris (who had played the Philadelphians as a member of the Band of Brothers), while "some charming ladies ... were giving us a house party." Returning home from such a socially delightful excursion that included a banquet at the House of Commons, these Philadelphians could perhaps not be faulted in clinging even tighter to their dreams that back in their homeland, cricket "will come into its own again in this country."[72]

Back home, the condition of the game, in reality, could present its supporters with little, and even scantier, evidence that cricket in Philadelphia "was not dead, only sleeping."[73]

Cricket at the University of Pennsylvania, after its wartime suspension in 1918, did make a modest revival, with twenty-five students turning

The Germantown side that defeated the all-conquering Australians in 1913, bringing to a close Philadelphia's long history in first-class cricket in a memorable fashion. Top row, left to right: R.L. Pearson, Tom Irving (umpire), J.H. Savage, A.G. Priestman, R.P. Anderson, F.H. Tripp, George Woolley (umpire), F.A. Greene; middle row: Percy H. Clark, W.P. O'Neill (captain), W.P. Newhall; bottom row: C.M. Graham, J.R. Stewart, H.S. Harned (*American Cricketer*).

out for the university team in 1920. Thanks to the university's admission, along with Haverford College, to the Philadelphia Cup competition, the school was able to put together a thirteen-match schedule in 1922. Its official status as a "minor sport" among the university's athletic offerings, however, always placed cricket in constant jeopardy of defunding or even worse. In evaluating this sport that was now being played by mostly foreign students and a few novices, and one that contributed little to the institution's athletic reputation, the university's athletic association, which for years had not been "offering any assistance, either moral or financial," to the university's cricket team, made the fateful but not unexpected decision in 1924 to drop cricket from its officially recognized sports. A last-ditch plea by the university's cricket-playing alumni to reconsider the decision was ignored, and the university's apostolic sport, whose long history had been "practically the history of cricket in Philadelphia," came to an end.[74]

At Haverford College, the forces of decline met more determined resistance in the post–First World War years. Fewer and fewer school and junior club cricketers meant fewer and fewer cricket-familiar students at the college (only two of the students on the 1926 team had previously played cricket), it becoming an accepted fact that the college cricket team, by now, "seldom draws any first class athletes."[75]

All this was evident enough during the college's final tour in England in 1925, the side returning home with only a single win, its batting so inept that the side could only put up three first innings runs against Repton and its bowling so feeble that it gave up a massive 414 runs against Haileybury.[76]

Around the college, cricket was disintegrating. There were no more representative sides to play for and the Halifax clubs offered the college fewer and fewer matches (none after 1930), necessitating the college team to seek non-traditional opponents like the exclusively foreign student teams at Ursinus College and the Princeton graduate school.[77]

Yet cricket's roots at the college ran deep and were sustained, even then, by the power of small-group loyalty. After students were asked, in an informal 1921 survey, which sport, baseball or cricket, should be dropped by the college, cricket supporters must have been pleased, and probably relieved, to find the final vote, 44–32, in favor of keeping cricket.[78]

And so Haverford College would continue to play cricket, in increasing isolation and declining proficiency, but still it played, the college able to claim it never had abandoned cricket so much as Philadelphia cricket had abandoned the college.

Now absent from schools and postsecondary institutions, and with a dwindling number of clubs and native players, Philadelphia cricket limped along over its final years on "the momentum of the past," kept alive by aging veterans (Percy Clark was still bowling for his Germantown club at age 54) who persevered in the fanciful dream "that they must keep the sport alive in hopes that someday it will come back." Philadelphia cricket's true believers would cling as tenaciously to the delusion of their game's future as they had clung to their demonstrative inability to sustain its presence.[79]

In the end, these hopeless expectations of imminent revival gave way to an even more lamentable delusion of a quasi-messianic return. "Sports and pastimes move in cycles," the *American Cricketer* would still prophesize in its penultimate year of publication. "Let us hope that the present period through which we are passing is only a temporary one." Yet the reality had been everywhere apparent, for years, that cricket in the city "has passed more or less into the discard." Philadelphia cricket was destined to "die in a dream."[80]

The last and longest surviving actors in this disappearing world themselves finally exited. The match between the Philadelphia and Frankford clubs in 1926 would be the 300th, and final, Halifax Cup match, bringing to an end the forty-five-year-old "World Series pennant" of cricket. Three years later, the *American Cricketer*, the very voice and image of Philadelphia cricket, ceased publication with its April 1929 issue. With its demise, Philadelphia's era of cricket had come to an end.[81]

Epilogue

In its October 26, 1839, issue the *Spirit of the Times*, one of America's earliest sporting journals, and one of the first to carry extensive cricket reports, queried, in one of its reports on the game, "What can be done to naturalize this beautiful game in America?"[1]

In this single, brief, and straightforward statement is summarized the challenge that cricket would face throughout its entire history in America. Here was a sport that had something Americans almost instinctively and immediately found appealing. There was certainly something here they found "beautiful," something engaging, in this sporting experience. But ... but there was also something in this game that Americans found inherently repellent, something that was just "out of sync" with their own preconditioned sporting tastes and expectations. And unless these dissonant features could somehow be distilled out—could be "naturalized" to conform to Americans' excitement expectations while staying true to the game's given format—cricket would have little hope of ever integrating itself into America's sporting culture no matter what other benefits the sport could assert (technical sophistication, internationalism, character building, etc.) on its behalf.

For more than half a century, Philadelphia would stand as the greatest cultural battleground in the struggle to resolve this cultural dissonance, to somehow achieve a workable balance between the culturally inherited English features in structure and tradition with the excitement expectations that Americans demanded from any form of bat-and-ball play. It was a heroic, even Herculean, undertaking but one that Philadelphia's cricket community ultimately failed to achieve. The city was never able to fully recognize, or bring about, in its cricket that elusive yet critical "potent agency" that the *Clipper* had pinpointed, as early as 1861, was so essential for the game's incorporation into America's sporting culture.[2]

Philadelphia was able to build an impressive and imposing sporting edifice with its cricket, but it could never carry it to a stage of full cultural integration nor beyond the point observed by a reporter in 1889: "For a half century or more our little congregation of cricket clubs here and there have gone through their somewhat conventional yearly series of friendly contests, developing a degree of skill of which we need not be ashamed, pleasing the circles of their immediate friends and admirers, receiving from the newspapers a generous measure of space and intelligent comment—yet still never arousing the public at large from its apathy towards cricket."[3]

With the passing of Philadelphia cricket, America's sporting culture that first began to emerge with baseball in the mid–19th century had only now reached is full, final, and settled state of cultural development. The history of Philadelphia cricket is more the story of a sporting ethos than the story of a single sport in a single city, an ethos of what sport *should be* in its content and end purpose rather than sport *as it is*, one whose content was solely contained in its emotional immediacy. The former was an ethos that attempted to subordinate the core excitement expectations contained in America's bat-and-ball sports to cricket's desirable extraneous and extra-cultural values and ends. This, however, was completely contrary to the cultural content of all popular American team sports which, beginning with the pathway laid out by baseball, would arise and develop solely from these core excitement expectations regardless of the potential social or personal consequences.

With the demise of Philadelphia cricket, the last island of "rational asceticism" in American team sports, a realm that had been receding since the appearance of organized baseball, had now been finally subsumed under the irrepressible sporting ethos of "impulsive enjoyment." Henceforth there would not and could not be ever again a sustainable alternative to this now dominant American sporting world.

Though the world of Philadelphia cricket has long vanished, its vestiges remain to this day. Of the "Big Five" Halifax Cup clubs three continue to live on—Germantown, Merion and Philadelphia—all now long since evolved into social clubs given over primarily to golf and tennis, the two sports their cricket founders had most feared now reigning supreme, though there remains "a certain charm in the anomaly" in these club's name retention of their founding sport.[4]

The game continues to be played at its age-old stronghold, Haverford College, although its scale is a shadow of its renowned past and it is played on a fully coed basis. The lower floor of the team's pavilion houses the C.C. Morris Cricket Library, established through an endowment of the longtime Philadelphia cricketer and maintained by a staff of dedicated volunteers. This one-of-a-kind library, with its extensive literary collection, manuscripts and memorabilia, stands as the "keeper of the flame" for the cricket legacy of Philadelphia as well as all America.[5]

Many figures from this legacy lived on long past its golden era:

Cope Field in the early 20th century, then as now the home ground of Haverford College cricket (author's collection).

"Around its throne they stand as executors of its actualization and as signs and ornaments of its grandeur." Henry Pleasants, former Haverford cricketer of the early 19th century, was still running into many old cricketers on his walks down Chestnut and Walnut streets in the late 1940s. One of these may have been George Wharton Pepper, who, at the age of eighty, claimed he still remembered the names of the Philadelphia team members who had faced the Australian side in 1878—he had attended the match as an eleven-year-old. Lester claims at least forty former members of the Gentlemen of Philadelphia teams were still alive at the time he authored his history in 1951, with eight of these past Philadelphia greats on hand to greet the MCC team that stopped in Philadelphia as part of the centennial commemoration of England's 1859 tour to North America.[6]

Two of these former players eventually made nostalgic and celebrated late-life returns to their now long vanished cricket past. When the English press learned that Henry Sayen had once played for the Gentlemen of England side during Philadelphia's 1908 England tour, the former Merion fast bowler became "the talk of London" during his visit to England in 1953, the whole experience eventually leading to the publication of his *A Yankee Looks at Cricket*.[7]

Charles Winter was also honored by the Kent County Cricket Club during his sentimental return to England in 1957, the former Gentlemen of Philadelphia wicket keeper astonished to meet, during his visit to the county grounds, Bill Fairservice, the club's scorekeeper who had been on the Kent side that had played against the Philadelphians almost half a century before.[8]

Longevity blessed many other former Philadelphia cricket standouts, some, like Winter, Lester, C.C. Morris, and Harold Furness, surviving into the Super Bowl era—a brief, forgotten yet symbolic moment when America's most ancient sporting tradition was in tangent with its most modern.

As for King, he married (no children) and, like the other towering figures of Philadelphia cricket, lived on as a forgotten figure in a vanished sporting world, one of the "great men for things that do not exist." Haverford cricketer Amar Singh would remember a lean, gaunt, aged gentleman—unidentified but matching King's description—haunting, alone and silent, the college cricket grounds in the 1950s.[9]

He would settle into the insurance business and pass the decades uneventfully in the country club life of golf and bridge up to his death, two days short of his ninety-second birthday, in 1965.[10]

To this day, "America's cricket masterpiece" is absent from Pennsylvania's Sports Hall of Fame and no marker, plaque, or monument publicly honors the memory of one of the greatest cricket players in America and the world.[11]

Appendix: Casual Olympian

This previously unpublished short work, here reproduced in its entirety, is held by the C.C. Morris Cricket Library, in typewritten manuscript, undated and unsigned. Internal evidence strongly points to Lester as its author, though stylistically, there's a strong resemblance to Lester's friend and fellow Haverford College graduate, Christopher Morley. Passing reference to "this book" suggests it may have been composed around the time of A Century of Philadelphia Cricket, *perhaps even intended to be included in that work. In any event, the piece stands as an entertaining yet insightful pen portrait of John B. King, America's greatest cricketer.*

* * *

Casual Olympian

I must get this down quick, before the long shadows creep over the pitch, and the fates in the dust coats snip off the bails and pocket them and trudge toward the great pavilion. For all the stories in this book that start memories in me are tributaries which run at last into the same river or drain—have it your own way—John Barton King. Besides, I have some old scores to settle with this lad. When we were playing he slogged me and bowled me for twenty years, and he has been scandalizing me ever since.

Bart spent all his real life either playing cricket or talking about it. By *it* is meant here what Bart had done, or what Bart was going to do. To every audience he spoke of his own deeds with a contagious enthusiasm and a matchless imagination. Bart on his feet and well set after the toasts to the President and the King at cricket dinner—what memories!

I am willing to believe that at some time, somewhere, he began a speech with the honest intention to be brief and modest. But I never heard it. Someone would whisper, particularly if King had failed to score runs, "Tell them you *can* bat; tell them about that 200 against Belfield."[1] Then we were in for it. Egged on by our hints and by his own invention, he ranged from fantasy to fantasy, the dominating genius of everything that happened—himself.

No one objected to this self-adulation. It went with the man, and was as little offensive as if he were talking about Zeus. He disarmed us by that portentous burst of praise for some fellow cricketer with which he began. Whenever Bart commended another, we sat back and waited for the sequel, and in spite of every interruption it came.

"You would never think it to watch him, but Johnny on his day is a really fine bat. On his day, Johnny is one of the finest batsmen we have in America." And then came that ominous pause, a slow smile and a chuckle, and the voice up two tones:

"There's only one trouble with Johnny; *his day never comes.*"

The voice dropped, and the face resumed the expression of one who is now going to devote himself sternly to facts—no more nonsense.

"But once Johnny played a really magnificent innings against us. You remember that, Johnny, at Merion, when you scored all those runs?"

Frank Green broke in: "In 1905, Bart? Wasn't that when Christie gave you that pasting?"

"You're right, Frank; that's exactly right; you remember the very year, 1905." Do you know why Frank always remembers 1905? That was the very year *he got his wicket.* It was a great year for Johnny, too; that was when he got his runs against us. The first ball I sent down was the best ball I ever bowled and Johnny played it magnificently. It came back almost half way down the pitch. I walked over the [sic] Woodie,[2] and I said "Woodie, You've got to take me off after this over; this is really Johnny's day. You remember that second ball, Johnny, the one you snicked over short slip for two runs? I didn't think I would ever get you out." Then came the pause, the slow smile, the chuckle and the up-pitched voice.

"The trouble with Johnny was, those two runs made him over confident, and the next ball took away his leg stump. *You remember that, Johnny?*"

You couldn't really tell where King's talk ended and his cricket began. He *talked* some of his opponents out of their wickets at luncheon. If a not-out had a favorite shot he would praise it; the more unorthodox the shot, the more fulsome the praise. He would explain a double curve he was working on and show how it had to start with the wrist bent at right angles. That was the trouble, he said; you had to telegraph it, and the batsman always seemed to know what was coming. We knew what would come at the end of the long run with twisted wrist held high in air—a very fast straight yorker.

Wherever he went in Great Britain he talked, preferably to policemen and reporters. There was the cricket writer who interviewed Bart before our match at Brighton. That memory is marked by the great roar of laughter coming from Frank Bohlen, as I entered the breakfast room next morning. Bohlen is remembered among lawyers for his book on torts; he is remembered by us for the matchless grace and brilliance of some of his innings, and for that remark that settled the matter for all time, like the brief and final decision of a judge. He was reading from the interviewer's story; "I listened to many wonderful narratives of cricket from Mr. King, a tall American athlete, with a calm, intelligent face." Bohlen shouted out the verdict—

"If that's a calm intellectual face, then my ar … is like Shakespeare."

Frank's basic facts were indisputable, but I always thought he was a shade rough on Bart. On these tours he stalked through England like a causal Olympian down for a frisk, willing for mortals to gaze for a spell on his unclouded face.

It had a certain majesty to those ignorant of the immense vacuum behind it. For King's intellectual ceiling was *Casey at the Bat*. Toward the tail of a long cricket dinner, he was easily induced to recite the classic, and when he came to "there's no joy in Mudville" the Olympian lips quivered and a tear would course down the calm intellectual face. How we reverenced the tear!

Of all the bowlers I ever played against, Bart was the one I faced with the most reluctance, bar one, Hughie Trumble.[3] Both came from right over the head, but Hughie had three inches on Bart, there was more spin and under the hat. You felt Bart was hammering, Trumble probing. That said, when King was going downhill with a half gale over his left shoulder, I would take my chances with Trumble. The only batsman who could break King were either of the Jessop type, with the feet of a cat and the wrists of a riveter, or with the tall, loose, rangy build of a George Gunn and F.J. Ford. On a hard, true, wicket, they were the lads who could make Bart come in for his gruel. Jessop would hit him high or low, anywhere so long as it was hard, willing to take his chance in the outfield. It was worth taking; there wasn't much there—only Frank Bohlen. The long-reach boys could get at King's pitch and brush him past mid-off or mid-on to the boundary, as if they were sweeping marbles off the back porch. Jessup would *jump* Bart; Ford would *push* him.

I remember those long outings more vividly than my own innings. There was that interminable day against Somerset in 1897. Palairet[4] had us collared. He treated Bart like a poodle he had of his own on a private leash, giving him an airing on the Taunton grounds. That's when the stuff of a bowler shows, and the best thing about John Barton was not his fast inswinger, but his courage, his eagerness to go to it again when we were licked, looking into the bowling barrel, and nothing there but the bottom. We developed a little ritual for occasions like this—and there were more than one of them—just between the two of us. I took the ball at the end of the over and walked to Bart at mid-off—

"Are you 'urt, John Barton?"
"No, Johnny, but I'm h'injured."
"All right then, 'ave another go."

And he would. Later, when we were dressing, he would hand me one of the customary cables (still among my treasures) to his brother in Philadelphia, "To Edwin King, Tioga: Home immediately, disgusted, Bart."

As a bowler, King could shift a sixpence when guaranteed it would be his if moved. The best evidence I recall of his accuracy is how he spotted the Major in 1908. Prince Ranjitsinhji, now the Jam of Nawanagar,[5] was back in England that summer, and he took a team to play a two-day match with the Yorkshire Gentlemen at Gilling in Yorkshire, to help his former Cambridge tutor, now rector, to restore the beautiful old parish church. We had just finished our match against Ireland in Dublin, and he wired for Bart and me to join him. What an eleven he had brought us! There was the Jam Sahib, C.B. Fry, Archie MacLaren, Quaife, Lilly, the best wicketkeeper in England, and others like them. The Yorkshiremen were a trifle ruffled at the strength of the opposition, particularly when they lost the toss and fielded out all through the first day. In the middle of our long innings some trifling difference arose, and the Yorkshire skipper, a gallant but peppery soldier, led his team from the field, and Ranji had to exercise all that charming tact of his to get the game going again.

Midmorning of the second day, with the Yorkshiremen scrambling for runs, there came the Major down the club house steps to stop the rot, and Ranji said to Bart,

"Here comes the blighter that made all the trouble. Do you think you could *spot him one*, Bart?"

King said nothing. He went to the pitch at the lower end. There was a worn spot on the leg wicket, a trifle short of a good length for a fast bowler; a heelmark, rolled in, but, as King saw it, quite usable. Ranji was at point, smiling to the Major as he walked in to get his guard. Bart passed him and held up three fingers, and then went to finish his over from the upper end—there were four more balls to go. The first three of them rose sharply and, one by one decorated the Major's left leg just above the pad, in a very pretty pattern.[6] It was a good leg, fleshy and hairy as I remember it under the showers, where the Major displayed it that evening with some pride. "All in front," he said. It showed three prize carnations applique, pink, but fading to a greenish yellow at the rims, one above the other, spaced neatly one inch apart. After each ball the Jam Sahib insisted on the Major lying flat on his back, while he rubbed, and Bart driveled condolences. After the fourth ball, a fast yorker, had spread eagled the wickets and the Major had limped in, and we were treading down the heelmark, Ranji said to Bart,

"But I told you to spot him *one*." And Bart replied, "I did it, Skipper. One for you. You forgot Johnny and me. You weren't the only one the Major h'injured."

That's how Bart spotted the Major. The Jam Sahib thought it was hardly cricket, but Bart told him anyone that took his team off the field deserved a marking, and went on about how he had spotted Tom Collins, the "Duke of York" at Toronto, and....

It was accuracy too that got King his runs—an exact, keen and accurate eye. He watched the bowler's hand; you couldn't fool him about which way the ball was going to turn. He was a clubbing batsman, at his best against fast bowling on a hard wicket; fast-footed, with reach, a left shoulder into the pitch, and great power in low drives to the off. His runs were made in front of the wicket; I cannot remember ever seeing King cut behind point. He would get his left foot over to a short one, and slap it hard to the left of cover. The best batting ever done by an American in England was his 98 and 113 not out at the Oval in 1903, against Richardson, Hayes, Dowson and Lees, and his best bowling that marvelous feat in the second innings against Lancashire at Old Trafford in the same year, when he got nine wickets, clean bowling eight men.

When King was at the top of his game, I suppose he was better known at sight to Englishmen than any other American. He was, indeed, a roving ambassador in cricket flannels, mowing down wickets and sowing good will. Cricket does that as nothing else can. For fifty years English teams visited America and American teams visited England, creating not "incidents," but friendships as lasting as these memories. I think the memories last because we were doing something more than knocking and chasing a red ball. There was something at the heart of it that holds on through life.

And beyond it, old chap! There's where I'm really going to get even with you. A little this side of felicity, W.G. is waiting by a bright cricket field, the stripes of the old I Zingari cap shining red and yellow. The left hand will still be under the right elbow, the right hand cupping the beard over his mouth—*you remember that, Bart?* There will be faint shouts coming from inside, and now and then that sharp crack of wood on leather. W. G.'s eyes will sparkle a little, but he will only growl, "I thought you'd be coming."

That's where I'll 'ave another go at you, Bart!

Chapter Notes

Prologue

1. Melvin Adelman, *A Sporting Time: New York City and the Rise of Modern Athletics, 1820-1870* (Urbana: University of Illinois Press, 1986) p. 119.
2. George Kirsch, *Baseball and Cricket: The Creation of American Team Sports, 1838-1872* (Urbana: University of Illinois Press, 1989) pp. 21-56; Adelman, *A Sporting Time*, pp. 97-121; J. Thomas Jable, "Social Class and the Sport of Cricket in Philadelphia, 1850-1880," *Journal of Sport History*, vol. 18, no. 2 (Summer 1991), pp. 205-223; Timothy Lockley, "'The Manly Game': Cricket and Masculinity in Savannah, Georgia, in 1859," *International Journal of the History of Sport*, vol. 20, no. 3 (Sept. 2003), pp. 77-98.
3. Adelman, *A Sporting Time*, p. 109. For early 19th-century English cricket, see Rowland Bowen, *Cricket: A History of Its Growth and Development Throughout the World* (London: Spottiswoode, 1970) pp. 68-87.
4. For changing social attitudes towards sports, see Adelman, *A Sporting Time*, pp. 99-100; Kirsch, *Baseball and Cricket*, pp. 12-13.
5. For cricket's development in England see Bowen, *Cricket: A History*, pp. 115-116, Derek Birley, *A Social History of English Cricket* (London: Aurum, 1999) pp. 67-68; John Ford, *Cricket: A Social History, 1700-1935* (Newton Abbot: David & Charles, 1972) pp. 74-79; 106-107.
6. For early baseball see Adelman, *A Sporting Time*, pp. 166-168; Kirsch, *Baseball and Cricket*, pp. 247-253; Tom Melville, *Early Baseball and the Rise of the National League* (Jefferson, NC: McFarland, 2001) pp. 13-14.

7. In Lester's eyes, the high standard of play Philadelphia achieved with its cricket was the sole "justification for telling the story [of Philadelphia cricket] at all," a preoccupation that restricts his otherwise excellent treatment of the subject. John Lester, *A Century of Philadelphia Cricket* (Philadelphia: University of Pennsylvania Press, 1951) p. 3.

Chapter One

1. For pre-modern ball playing, see Kirsch, *Baseball and Cricket*, pp. 1-4; David Block, *Baseball Before We Knew It* (Lincoln: University of Nebraska Press 2005) pp. 152-162; Tom Melville, "Pre-1840 Cricket and the Formation of a National Sporting Culture," *Sporting Traditions*, vol. 27, no. 1 (May 2010), pp. 49-65.
2. "Philosophy of the National Sport," *Nation*, Aug. 26, 1869, p. 168.
3. "Rules for the 1795 Richmond Cricket Club" held by the Virginia State Library; Helmut von Erffa, *The Paintings of Benjamin West* (New Haven: Yale University Press, 1986) p. 24; Melville, "Pre-1840 Cricket," pp. 56-59.
4. *Spirit of the Times*, Oct. 24, 1840, p. 397. William Rotch Wister, *Some Reminiscences of Cricket in Philadelphia Before 1861* (Philadelphia: Allen, Scott, 1904) p. 140.
5. *Spirit of the Times*, Sept. 12, 1840, p. 330; John Marder, *The International Series: The Story of the United States vs Canada at Cricket* (London: Kaye & Ward, 1968) pp. 16-25.
6. Very few inter-city sporting contests are known before the 1840s. The Norfolk, Virginia, cricket club challenged the

Petersburg, Virginia, cricket club in 1811 and 1817, though it's unknown if the challenges were accepted. *Star* [Raleigh, NC], Oct. 18, 1811, p. 167; *American Beacon & Commercial Diary* [Norfolk, VA], Jan. 11, 1817, p. 3. The town of Hamden, New York, challenged residents of Delaware County, New York, to a baseball game in 1825; Dean Sullivan, *Early Innings: A Documentary History of Baseball, 1825–1908* (Lincoln: University of Nebraska Press, 1995) p. 2; Wister, *Some Reminiscences*, p. 141.

7. *New York Morning News*, Aug. 29, 1845, p. 2; *New York Herald*, Aug. 27, 1845, p. 2. William Brown, *America: A Four Years' Residence in the United States and Canada* (Leeds: Kemploy, 1849) p. 87.

8. *Anglo-American*, July 27, 1844, p. 334; *Spirit of the Times*, Sept. 22, 1849, p. 6; May 27, 1848, p. 163; April 20, 1844, p. 90; July 16, 1844, p. 222; Sept. 13, 1845, p. 339; *Sun* [Baltimore], May 24, 1849, p. 4; *Chicago American*, Sept. 4, 1840, p. 3.

9. *New York Herald*, Sept. 6, 1845, p. 2.

10. Adelman, *A Sporting Time*, pp. 121–123; Kirsch, *Baseball and Cricket*, pp. 56–57. The fact that organized cricket and baseball both appeared in New York City at almost the same time, in the early 1840s, and lapsed into temporary decline at almost the same time, the late 1840s, raises some significant questions regarding possible causal relations between the two sports, a subject largely unaddressed by baseball historians in their preoccupation with the when and where of the "first" baseball game/club rather than the why. Scholars have long been aware of the contacts between New York cricket and baseball in the 1840s (Melvin Adelman, "The First Baseball Game, the First Newspaper References to Baseball and the New York Club: A Note on the Early History of Baseball," *Journal of Sport History*, vol. 7, no. 3 [Winter 1980], pp. 132–135) and the testimony of contemporaries. In his account of early New York baseball, published in the *San Francisco Examiner* (Nov. 27, 1887, p. 14) decades after the fact, William Wheaton claimed he and his acquaintances took to baseball because they found cricket "too slow and lazy." Another early baseballer, William Ladd, a member of the Knickerbocker club during this period, told John M. Ward, also decades later, that he and his friends took to baseball rather than cricket because they didn't want to play a game of "foreign invention" (Dean Sullivan, *Early Innings: A Documentary History of Baseball, 1825–1908*, Lincoln: University of Nebraska Press, 1995, p. 292). These and other testimonies raise important questions: (1) was cricket's organized presence in New York in the early 1840s a direct, possibly essential, catalyst, for either physical or ideological reasons, for the appearance of organized baseball in New York City and (2) why did this early baseball not exert enough staying power among its early followers for them to continue with the game? Wheaton himself, after the demise of his baseball club, actually returned to cricket, a game at which he was proficient enough to score sixty runs in one match (*Spirit of the Times*, Oct. 21, 1848, p. 414). As a preliminary explanation, this may seem to indicate cricket's social stature, at least in the 1840s, still considerably outbalanced, in the eyes of Americans, any emotional appeal of their homegrown game. In any event, the question continues to loom over this entire subject: What would have been the history, the path of development, of not only baseball but of all American team sports if cricket *had not* appeared in New York at the time and in the form that it did in the 1840s?

11. Sam Bass Warner, *The Private City: Philadelphia in Three Periods of Its Growth* (Philadelphia: University of Pennsylvania Press, 1968) pp. 69, 71; Tanja Bueltmann and Donald MacRaild, *The English Diaspora in North America: Migration, Ethnicity and Association, 1730s—1950s* (Manchester: Manchester University Press, 2017) p. 31.

12. *Philadelphia Inquirer*, Dec. 4, 1833, p. 2; *Saturday Morning Transcript* [Philadelphia], Nov. 16, 1833, p. 43; *Pennsylvania Inquirer and Daily Courier* [Philadelphia], Oct. 3, 1839.

13. *Public Ledger*, Dec. 10, 1841, p. 2; Dec. 15, 1841, p. 2.

14. Along with the extensive reminiscences of William Rotch Wister, other reports of early Philadelphia cricket can be found in Jones Wister's *Reminiscences* (Philadelphia, 1920), Richard Ashurst's account in the *American Cricketer* (March 1, 1899, p. 11), Robert Waller's in that same

publication (May 3, 1893, p. 28), and Barnet Phillips' "Cricket in the Forties," *Harper's Weekly*, Sept. 22, 1894, pp. 908–909.

15. Wister mistakenly has Harry Wright as the manager of Philadelphia's professional baseball club in the 1850s, thirty years too early (Wister, *Some Reminiscences*, p. 51) while Jones Wister has Englishman Lord Hawke as captain of the Australian national cricket team (Jones Wister, *Reminiscences*, p. 121).

16. Wister, *Some Reminiscences*, p. 9; *North American* [Philadelphia], Oct. 11, 1843, p. 2; *Spirit of the Times*, Sept. 14, 1844, p. 340.

17. Wister, *Some Reminiscences*, p. 8; *Spirit of the Times*, Oct. 24, 1840, p. 397. Waller continued to live in New York until his death in 1909 and was very active in that city's St. George Society, *History of the St. George Society of New York from 1770 to 1913* (New York, 1913) p. 97.

18. Wister, *Some Reminiscences*, p. 142. It was claimed that Waller was a person who liked to "settle things in his own fashion" (*Clipper*, Feb. 20, 1858, p. 348). He seems to have been a competent, if indifferent, player who would smoke while fielding (*New York Tribune*, July 20, 1855, p. 5).

19. *Spirit of the Times*, June 3, 1843, p. 162.

20. *Spirit of the Times*, Aug. 9, 1845, p. 279.

21. Marder, *The International Series*, p. 14; *True Sun* [New York], July 30, 1844, p. 2.

22. *North American*, Aug. 13, 1846, p. 2; Aug. 14, 1846, p. 2.

23. *Anglo-American*, Oct. 14, 1843, p. 598; Wister, *Some Reminiscences*, p. 12.

24. Anna Burr, *Weir Mitchell: His Life and Letters* (New York: Duffield, 1929) p. 40; Edward Bushnell, ed., *A History of Athletics at the University of Pennsylvania, 1873–1908* (Athletic Association, 1909) vol. II, p. 123; Wister, *Some Reminiscences*, p. 12; *North American*, Oct. 28, 1845, p. 2; *Spirit of the Times*, Sept. 18, 1847, p. 347; *New York Herald*, Oct. 29, 1845, p. 3.

25. *Litchfield Monitor*, April 11, 1798, p. 3; Ralph Hill, ed., *College On the Hill* (Hanover: Dartmouth University Press, 1964) pp. 265–266; Robert Gannon, *Up to the Present: The Story of Fordham* (New York: Doubleday, 1967) inside front cover illustration; Henry Hubbart, *Ohio Wesleyan's First Hundred Years* (Delaware, OH, 1943) p. 24, 280; Thomas Wentworth Higginson, *Cheerful Yesterdays* (New York: Arno, 1968) p. 27, 60.

26. *Public Ledger*, Aug. 13, 1922, p. 8; E. Digby Baltzell, *Philadelphia Gentlemen: The Making of a National Upper Class* (Glencoe: Free Press, 1958) p. 75.

27. J. Thomas Jable, "Philadelphia Cricket Comes of Age," in *Philly Sports: Teams, Games and Athletes from Rocky's Town* (Fayetteville: University of Arkansas Press, 2016) p. 41.

28. *Public Ledger*, Sept. 30, 1845, p. 2; *Spirit of the Times*, Oct. 4, 1845, p. 380; Wister, *Some Reminiscences*, pp. 13, 15; Anna Burr, *Weir Mitchell*, p. 41.

29. *North American*, Sept. 1, 1846, p. 2; *Anglo-American*, Sept. 19, 1846, p. 526; Marder, *The International Series*, p. 22.

30. *Anglo-American*, Sept. 19, 1846, p. 526; *Spirit of the Times*, July 17, 1847, p. 239. Dominic Malcolm interprets the Helliwell incident as representing "the non-standardized character of cricket laws at that time and the variety of playing customs and traditions of the game which co-existed both in England and thus in America at this time." Dominic Malcolm, "The Diffusion of Cricket to American: A Figurational Sociological Examination," *Journal of Historical Sociology*, vol. 19, no. 2 (June 2006), p. 161. Even if correct, the fact that the incident led to an outbreak of violence reveals the far more significance deep class divisions within North American cricket at that time.

31. *Spirit of the Times*, Sept. 18, 1847, p. 347; July 8, 1848, p. 234; Sept. 7, 1850, p. 343.

32. *Brooklyn Evening Star*, Sept. 1, 1846, p. 2.

33. *New York Herald*, Sept. 6, 1846, p. 2.

34. John Thorn, *Baseball in the Garden of Eden* (New York: Simon & Schuster, 2011), p. 3. Unless the new Brooklyn baseball club announced in the *Brooklyn Daily Eagle* on July 6, 1846, p. 2, was a reference to one known at that time, there could have been a sixth New York baseball club during this period.

35. Sullivan, *Early Innings*, p. 15.

36. For sectional animosities in early English sports see Robert Malcolmson, *Popular Recreations in English Society*,

1700-1850 (Cambridge: Cambridge University Press, 1973) p. 83. North/South animosity had led to the breakup of the early All-England cricket teams. Christopher Brooks, *English Cricket* (London: Weidenfield, 1978) pp. 114–116.

37. Intra-club dissention was not limited to Philadelphia cricket clubs; *New York Herald*, Nov. 19, 1845, p. 2.

38. Wister, *Some Reminiscences*, pp. 11, 141.

39. *Ibid.*, p. 15.

40. *American Cricketer*, May 3, 1893, p. 28; Wister, *Some Reminiscences*, p. 15. Dudson would reappear on other Philadelphia cricket teams in the 1850s; *Clipper*, Nov. 29, 1856, p. 254; Nov. 21, 1857, p. 244.

41. *Spirit of the Times*, Sept. 18, 1847, p. 347.

42. Wister, *Some Reminiscences*, p. 18.

43. Jones Wister, *Reminiscences*, p. 113.

44. For hostile reports of "ball playing," see *Boston Traveler*, Dec. 26, 1828, p. 2 ("obscene language"); *Boston Recorder*, Jan. 8, 1829, p. 7 ("idle and dissolute young men"); and *Baltimore Sun*, April 12, 1838, p. 2 ("a fine state of affairs in a land of steady habits").

45. Wister, *Some Reminiscences*, p. 15. George Newhall would recall that "the beer and betting" of the English residents was highly objectionable to his circle of proper Philadelphians; George Newhall, "The Cricket Grounds of Philadelphia and a Plea for the Game," *Site and Relic Society of Germantown*, March 11, 1910, p. 182.

46. Sam Bass Warner, *The Private City*, p. 142.

Chapter Two

1. *Spirit of the Times*, Sept. 3, 1853, p. 343; Marder, *The International Series*, pp. 36–40; *New York Herald*, Aug. 25, 1853, p. 4.

2. *Spirit of the Times*, Nov. 19, 1853, p. 476; Oct. 29, 1853, p. 432; Sept. 24, 1853, p. 384; July 16, 1853, p. 264; *Clipper*, Oct. 1, 1853, p. 2.

3. *Clipper*, Sept. 20, 1856, p. 174.

4. *New York Times*, April 21, 1855, p. 4; *Spirit of the Times*, Oct. 27, 1855, p. 438.

5. *Spirit of the Times*, Oct. 15, 1853, p. 409; *New York Times*, July 9, 1860, p. 1.

6. Jones Wister, *"A Bawl" for American Cricket* (Philadelphia, 1893), p. 7.

7. *New York Tribune*, Sept. 21, 1854, p. 6; Sept. 5, 1855, p. 5; Wister, *Some Reminiscences*, pp. 20, 26.

8. *Spirit of the Times*, May 31, 1851, p. 177; Dec. 7, 1850, p. 500. *Philadelphia Inquirer*, April 23, 1898, p. 9. Jarvis, who lived in Philadelphia for the rest of his life, and was honored with free admission to the Germantown club ground at any time, was tragically hit and killed by a trolley car in 1898; *Philadelphia Inquirer*, Aug. 29, 1897, p. 32; April 23, 1898, p. 12.

9. *Spirit of the Times*, May 13, 1854 p. 150; *Saturday Evening Gazette* [Boston], Sept. 4, 1858, p. 3; *Chicago Daily Tribune*, May 26, 1857, p. 1; *Sun* [Baltimore], Dec. 2, 1859, p. 2.

10. Wister, *Some Reminiscences*, p. 19.

11. *Ibid.*, p. 22; *American Cricketer*, July 1927, p. 152.

12. *Clipper*, Nov. 12, 1853, p. 4; Sally (Butler) Wister, *Walter S. Newhall: A Memoir* (Philadelphia: Sanitary Commission, 1864) p. 14.

13. Wister, *Some Reminiscences*, p. 22; H.M. Lippincott, *History of the Philadelphia Cricket Club* (1954), p. 10; *American Cricketer*, March 1, 1899, p. 11; *Public Ledger*, Aug. 31, 1854, p. 2.

14. *Clipper*, Dec. 12, 1868, p. 284; Adelman, *A Sporting Time*, p. 103; Kirsch, *Baseball and Cricket*, pp. 21–22.

15. Wister, *Some Reminiscences*, p. 24.

16. *Ibid.*, p. 24; *American Cricketer*, July 27, 1927, p. 152.

17. Wister, *Some Reminiscences*, p. 24.

18. J. Thomas Jable, "Social Class and the Sport of Cricket in Philadelphia, 1850–1880," p. 215; Wister, *Some Reminiscences*, p. 25.

19. Wister, *Some Reminiscences*, p. 20.

20. *Ibid.*, pp. 36, 88; *New York Herald*, Oct. 3, 1853; *American Cricketer* July 1927, p. 155.

21. Wister, *Some Reminiscences*, p. 29. Other sources state the Germantown club was established on June 14, 1855, though this may have been the date of its formal organization; *Germantown Cricket: Charter and By-Laws* (Philadelphia, 1880) p. 5; *Philadelphia Inquirer*, June 26, 1855, p. 1; *Philadelphia Times*, May 30, 1886, p. 7.

22. Wister, *Some Reminiscences*, p. 30.

23. *Clipper*, Nov. 1, 1856, p. 220; Wister, *Some Reminiscences*, p. 44; *North American*, June 14, 1859, p. 1.

24. *Clipper,* June 11, 1859, p. 100; Wister, *Some Reminiscences,* p. 88; *Clipper,* Nov. 7, 1857, p. 231.
25. Wister, *Some Reminiscences,* pp. 46–47, 79.
26. *Ibid.,* p. 31; *Constitution and By-Laws of the Young American Club of Germantown* (Philadelphia: Dando, 1876) [p.1]; Sally (Butler) Wister, *Walter S. Newhall,* p. 14; *Brentano's Aquatic Monthly* (April 1880), p. 452.
27. *Clipper,* June 26, 1858, p. 75; "Cricket in America," *Lippincott's Magazine,* May 1873, p. 594; Wister, *Some Reminiscences,* p. 49.
28. *Clipper,* Nov. 15, 1856, p. 236; *Pennsylvanian,* May 22, 1858, p. 2; *Philadelphia Inquirer,* Sept. 10, 1858, p. 1; Wister, *Some Reminiscences,* pp. 83, 100.
29. *Clipper,* Nov. 12, 1859, p. 236.
30. Lester devotes virtually no attention to the non-Halifax Cup clubs while Wister (*Some Reminiscences,* p. 71) dismissively declares "many clubs were formed at this time, too many for the good of the game."
31. *New York Herald,* Nov. 6, 1853, p. 4; Sally (Butler) Wister, *Walter S. Newhall,* p. 14. For a list of known American cricket clubs in the 19th century, see Tom Melville, *The Tented Field: A History of Cricket in America* (Popular Press, 1998) pp. 211–267. Since that publication the author has located more than two hundred additional 19th-century American cricket clubs; Tom Melville, *Directory of American Cricket Clubs, 1837–1914: Supplement* [unpublished manuscript], pp. 1–19.
32. *Public Ledger,* Nov. 16, 1858, p. 1; *Clipper,* March 10, 1860, p. 372; *American Cricketer,* July 1927, p. 154; Wister, *Some Reminiscences,* p. 41; *Clipper,* June 6, 1857, p. 53.
33. Charles Peverelly, *Book of American Pastimes* (New York, 1866) p. 545; *Clipper,* Sept. 17, 1859, p. 172; *Public Ledger,* June 21, 1861, p. 8; Anthony Lampe, "The Background of Professional Baseball in St. Louis," *Bulletin* (Missouri Historical Society), vol. 7 (Oct. 1950), p. 31.
34. *Gazette* [Montreal], Aug. 24, 1857, p.2; *Clipper,* May 16, 1857, p. 27; June 5, 1858, p. 52; July 16, 1859, p. 99; April 20, 1861, p. 2.
35. *Clipper,* Oct. 24, 1857, p. 213. Kephardt served in the Civil War along with his four brothers, three of whom died in the conflict; Eugene Stackhouse, *Germantown in the Civil War* (Charleston: History Press, 2010) p. 118; Wister, *Some Reminiscences,* p. 81; *Clipper,* Oct. 11, 1856, p. 197; Oct. 24, 1857, p. 213; April 17, 1858, p. 411.
36. *Philadelphia Press,* May 19, 1859, p. 3; *Clipper,* June 27, 1857, p. 75; Nov. 26, 1859, p. 236; *Philadelphia Inquirer,* Sept. 7, 1897, p. 11; *Sunday Mercury* [New York], Sept. 16, 1860, p. 5.
37. *Clipper,* April 11, 1857, p. 403; Dec. 17, 1856, p. 283; *North American,* June 1, 1857, p. 1.
38. *Clipper,* July 27, 1878, p. 143; "Cricket," *Ichnolite* [Amherst College], May 1860, p. 337; Kristen Peterson, *Waltham Rediscovered* (Randall, 1988) p. 75.
39. *Daily Evening Bulletin* [Philadelphia], June 2, 1857, p. 2; *Turf, Field, and Farm,* Oct. 16, 1868, p. 680; *Boston Daily Advertiser,* Sept. 14, 1865, p. 1. The *Clipper* (March 10, 1860, p. 372) claimed ten cricket matches were being played weekly on Philadelphia's Powelton Fairgrounds in 1860, engaging as many as three hundred young men.
40. *Porter's Spirit of the Times,* Sept. 20, 1856, p. 42; *Philadelphia Press,* Nov. 17, 1859, p. 2; Jones Wister, *Reminiscences,* p. 115; *Clipper,* Oct. 22, 1859, p. 212; Jason Kaufman and Orlando Patterson, "Cross-National Cultural Diffusion: The Global Spread of Cricket," *American Sociological Review,* vol. 70 (Feb. 2005), p. 98.
41. *Clipper,* April 25, 1857, p. 3; *North American,* Oct. 12, 1859, p. 1.
42. Wister, *Some Reminiscences,* pp. 64, 89, 126, 130.
43. *New York Tribune,* July 6, 1859, p. 5; *Clipper,* June 18, 1859, p. 69; Wister, *Some Reminiscences,* p. 111; Lester, *A Century,* p. 26; *Philadelphia Press,* Oct. 13, 1859, p. 2.
44. *New York Evening Express,* June 2, 1856, p. 4; *New York Herald,* Aug. 4, 1855, p. 1; *Clipper,* Sept. 6, 1856, p. 159; *Porter's Spirit of the Times,* Oct. 15, 1859, p. 100; *Utica Daily Gazette,* Aug. 28, 1848, p. 2.
45. Wister, *Some Reminiscences,* pp. 61, 68.
46. *Ibid.,* pp. 77, 81; *Clipper,* July 3, 1858, p. 84; Nov. 27, 1858, p. 253; Sept. 22, 1860, p. 179; Wister, *Some Reminiscences,* p. 132.
47. *Clipper,* Aug. 12, 1854, p. 2; Wister, *Some Reminiscences,* p. 35.

48. *Clipper,* Oct. 18, 1856, p. 204.
49. *Spirit of the Times,* July 7, 1858, p. 271.
50. *Philadelphia Inquirer,* July 6, 1860, p. 4.
51. *Ibid.;* Wister, *Some Reminiscences,* p. 73.
52. *Clipper,* Oct. 27, 1860, p. 218; March 10, 1860, p. 372.
53. The growing respect American cricketers were gaining in Philadelphia was indicated by the challenge from a resident English team to the Americans who had been on the Philadelphia side in the match against the visiting All-England cricket team in 1859; *Philadelphia Press,* Oct. 20, 1859, p. 3; Fred Lillywhite, *The English Cricketers' Trip to Canada and the United States in 1859* (World's Work, 1980) pp. 38-42; Lester, *A Century,* p. 19.
54. Adelman, *A Sporting Time,* p. 111.
55. *Clipper,* July 4, 1857, p. 83. Wister credits Waller as being "an earnest advocate of all measures that tended to bring forward American players" (*Some Reminiscences,* p. 143), though only, evidence seems to indicate, if they were under English direction and control, at least in New York cricket.
56. *Clipper,* May 21, 1859, p. 35; March 10, 1860, p. 372; June 30, 1860, p. 85; *Wilkes' Spirit of the Times,* June 16, 1860, p. 229.
57. *Daily Age* [Philadelphia], June 3, 1865, p. 3; *Clipper,* Sept. 3, 1859, p. 154.
58. *Clipper,* Sept. 3, 1859, p. 154; Wister, *Some Reminiscences,* p. 111.
59. *Clipper,* Aug. 21, 1858, p. 141; Aug. 11, 1860, p. 130; Adelman, *A Sporting Time,* pp. 111-112; Kirsch, *Baseball and Cricket,* pp. 31-32.
60. *Clipper,* Sept. 7, 1861, p. 164; Aug. 11, 1860, p. 130; Oct. 7, 1868, p. 220; *World* [New York], Sept. 17, 1868, p. 10; *Clipper,* Dec. 12, 1868, p. 284.
61. *New York Herald,* Nov. 6, 1853, p. 4; May 7, 1855, p. 1; *Ninth Annual Report of the Board of Commissioners for the Central Park, 1865* (New York: Bryant, 1866), p. 46; *New York Leader,* July 10, 1858, p. 5; *Porter's Spirit of the Times,* April 2, 1859, p. 68.
62. *Wilkes' Spirit of the Times,* Aug. 16, 1862, p. 37; *New York Evening Express,* Oct. 24, 1856, p. 2.
63. Marder, *The International Series,* p. 36.
64. *North American,* Aug. 7, 1860, p. 2; Wister, *Some Reminiscences,* pp. 130-131.
65. *Clipper,* Aug. 11, 1860, p. 130.
66. *Ibid.*
67. *Porter's Spirit of the Times,* May 9, 1857, p. 156; *Clipper,* May 21, 1859, p. 37; May 19, 1860, p. 37.
68. *Clipper,* May 18, 1861, p. 36.
69. *Ibid.,* May 3, 1862, p. 18.
70. *Ibid.,* May 24, 1862, p. 43.

Chapter Three

1. *New York Morning Express,* Oct. 6, 1859, p. 4; *Clipper,* July 16, 1859, p. 98; April 10, 1858, p. 402; *North American,* Oct. 2, 1859, p. 1.
2. *Clipper,* Sept. 20, 1856, p. 174.
3. For an overview of early American ball playing, see Adelman, *A Sporting Time,* p. 31; Kirsch, *Baseball and Cricket,* pp. 3-4, David Block, *Baseball Before We Knew It* (Lincoln: University of Nebraska Press, 2005) pp. 152-162; Albert Spalding, *America's National Game* (Lincoln: University of Nebraska Press, 1992) pp. 29-47; Benjamin Rader, *Baseball: A History of America's Game* (Urbana: University of Illinois Press, 1997) p. 2.
4. *New York Herald,* Nov. 3, 1854, p .2.
5. Adelman, *A Sporting Time,* p. 127; Spalding, *America's National Game,* p. 69. It was about this time that Daniel "Doc" Adams of the Knickerbocker Baseball Club claimed to, or is credited with, "inventing" the shortstop position in baseball, though a fielding position by that name appears on the diagram of an American cricket field as early as 1838; "Gymnastics," *Parley's Magazine,* Jan. 1, 1838 [p. 247]; Sullivan, *Early Innings,* p. 15; Robert W. Henderson, "Adams of the Knickerbockers" [typewritten manuscript], p. 4.
6. *North American,* Nov. 24, 1859, p. 1; *Philadelphia Press,* Nov. 23, 1859, p. 2; Wister, *Some Reminiscences,* p. 7.
7. John Shiffert, *Baseball in Philadelphia: A History of the Early Game, 1831-1900* (Jefferson, NC: McFarland, 2005), p. 43; *Clipper,* Nov. 17, 1860, p. 242; Henry Chadwick, *American Cricket Manual* (Dewitt, 1873), p. 99.
8. Peverelly, *Book of American Pastimes,* p. 545; *Philadelphia Press,* Sept. 12, 1865, p. 4; *Public Ledger,* Jan. 19, 1863, p.

1; Kirsch, *Baseball and Cricket*, p. 54; *Clipper*, May 10, 1862, p. 27.

9. *Philadelphia Age*, Nov. 26, 1862, p. 27; *Press* [Philadelphia], June 1, 1865, p. 4; *Philadelphia Inquirer*, Aug. 8, 1863, p. 8; *Press* [Philadelphia], Sept. 7, 1865, p. 4; *North American*, Nov. 26, 1863, p. 1; *Clipper*, July 7, 1866, p. 99.

10. *Public Ledger*, July 7, 1860, p. 1; July 16, 1860, p. 1; *Clipper*, Dec. 15, 1860, p. 276; June 27, 1857, p. 75; Sept. 12, 1860, p. 180.

11. *Brooklyn Eagle*, June 24, 1864, p. 2; *Clipper*, July 20, 1861, p. 106; Sept. 16, 1862, p. 18. McBride, with his unorthodox underarm bowling, would victimize English cricket batters as a member of the Athletics/Boston Red Stockings baseball team during their baseball/cricket tour to England in 1874 (K. Martin Tebay, *Harry's Mission: An Account of the American Baseball Players Tour of the British Isles, 1874* [Red Rose, 2019] pp. 14, 17). Shiffert gives only passing mention to the careers of McBride and Pratt as "cricketeers" (a clothing line; a cricket player is no more a "cricketeer" than a baseball player is a "baseballeer"); Shiffert, *Baseball in Philadelphia*, p. 32.

12. *Philadelphia Inquirer*, Oct. 17, 1865, p. 4; *Press* [Philadelphia], Aug. 30, 1865, p. 4; *Philadelphia Inquirer*, May 22, 1863, p. 8; Nov. 5, 1861, p. 8.

13. *Clipper*, May 3, 1862, p. 19; *Public Ledger*, Oct. 26, 1860, p. 1.

14. *Sunday Mercury* [Philadelphia], May 6, 1866, p. 4; July 8, 1866, p. 4.

15. *Philadelphia Inquirer*, Aug. 31, 1865, p. 2; *Turf, Field, and Farm*, Sept. 15, 1868, p. 616; *Clipper*, Aug. 12, 1865, p. 140; *North American*, Sept. 1, 1865, p. 1. One of the two most persistent urban legends purporting to explain cricket's disappearance in America (the other will be addressed in Chapter Eleven, note 20) claims that the Civil War effectively "killed" the game, an explanation held predominantly by laymen (*Germantown Cricket Club: Charter and By Laws*, p. 6; Marder, *The International Series*, p. 15) but by some academic scholars as well (Adelman, *A Sporting Time*, p. 109; Sandiford, *Cricket and the Victorians*, p. 148; Dean Allen, "'The Game of the English': Cricket and the Spread of English Culture, 1830-1900" in *English Ethnicity & Culture in North America*, ed. David Gleeson [Columbia: University of South Carolina Press, 107], p. 184). The Civil War certainly disrupted cricket activity around the country, but it equally disrupted baseball activity while cricket, during the conflict, still maintained a not inconsiderable presence among Civil War soldiers (Melville, *The Tented Field*, pp. 54-55). The Civil War may serve as a convenient demarcation point for cricket's decline vis-à-vis baseball but there's no compelling evidence it was the direct cause of this trend. The Civil War, in short, just "accelerated a shift in [America's] sporting culture that would have taken place anyway"; Scott Reeves, *The Champion Band: The First English Cricket Tour* (Sheffield: Chequered Flag, 2014) p. 241.

16. *Clipper*, Sept. 2, 1865, p. 163; *Daily Evening Bulletin* [Philadelphia], June 24, 1864, p. 5; *Philadelphia Inquirer*, Aug. 25, 1870, p. 2; *North American*, Aug. 7, 1865, p. 1; J. Thomas Jable, "Latter Day Cricket Imperialism: The British Influence on the Establishment of Cricket in Philadelphia, 1842-1872" in J.A. Mangan, ed., *Pleasure, Profit, and Proselytism* (London: Cass, 1988) p. 180.

17. On the rise of "modern" American sports see Adelman, *A Sporting Time*, pp. 5-11; Kirsch, *Baseball and Cricket*, pp. 5-14.

18. For an "elitist" interpretation see Jason Kaufman and Orlando Patterson, "Cross National Cultural Diffusion," pp. 82-110, and Carl Stempel, "Towards a Historical Sociology of Sport in the United States, 1825-1875" (PhD thesis, University of Oregon, 1992) p. 278. For an interpretation based on playing facilities, see Kirsch, *Baseball and Cricket*, p. 107; for the argument that "certain groups legitimized" sports, see S.W. Pope, *Patriotic Games* (Oxford University Press, 1997) p. 79; for the nationalist argument, see Boria Majumdar and Sean Brown, "Why Baseball, Why Cricket: Differing Nationalisms, Differing Challenges," *International Journal of the History of Sport*, vol. 24, no. 2 (Feb. 2007) pp. 139-156; Dominic Malcolm, "The Diffusion of Cricket to America" pp. 151-173; Steve Ickringil, "American Sporting Isolationism: Cricket, Baseball and the Wright Brothers," in K. Versluys, ed., *The Insular Dream* (Amsterdam: V.U. University Press, 1995) pp. 141-155; Allen Guttmann, "The Diffusion of

Sports and the Problem of Cultural Imperialism," in E. Dunning, ed., *The Sports Process* (Champaign: Human Kinetics, 1993) pp. 125–137.

19. The "elitist" interpretation will be discussed in Chapter Nine. The "lack of facilities" interpretation contends that cricket's requirement of a specially prepared playing area, since the bowler usually throws the ball to the batter on the bounce, put the game at a marked disadvantage to baseball, which requires no specially prepared ground, since the baseball pitcher throws the ball to the batter on the fly. As anyone who's ever played cricket knows, however, batting is inconvenienced very little, even on a rough playing area, if the bowling is underarm, which was the predominant form of bowling in the 1840s and 1850s. In time, Philadelphia's larger, more affluent, cricket clubs would erect facilities with grounds as fine as anywhere in the world, yet the availability of such facilities couldn't save their game. The assertion that baseball "out-promoted" cricket rests largely on the perceived influence of such prominent early baseball organizers as Albert Spalding to "legitimize" the game with the American public. Spalding and other early baseball promoters, however, didn't impact the game until the 1870s by which time Americans had already passed cultural judgement in favor of baseball over cricket. Individuals like Spalding expanded, even exploited, baseball's popularity but they themselves didn't create its appeal and certainly not to cricket's direct detraction. If, indeed, "it is superficial thinking which clings to abstractions" (Hegel), then the difficulty with the "want of a national pastime" abstraction can be elucidated with a simple thought experiment. Let us assume one of the rapid -transition, circular scoring, "safe haven" British ball games identified by David Block in his *Pastime Lost* (Lincoln: University of Nebraska Press, 2019) pp. 181–195, had, early on, developed as England's "national game," and that this baseball-structured game, and not cricket, had been introduced, in a modern, advanced, form, to the United States in the 1840s by English immigrants. Then, according to proponents of this explanation, who claim Americans would never accept any team sport of foreign origin as their "national pastime," we would have to expect, of necessity, the bizarre, unimaginable, historical scenario of Americans explicitly rejecting a baseball-type game as "foreign"!

20. Andei Markovits and Steven Hellerman, *Offside: Soccer and American Exceptionalism* (Princeton: Princeton University Press, 2001) p. 10.

21. Thomas W. Higginson, "Gymnastics," *Atlantic Monthly* (March 1861), p. 287.

22. *World* [New York], Sept. 19, 1872, p. 4; "Philosophy of the National Game," *Nation*, Aug. 26, 1869, pp. 167–168.

23. *Patriot* [Harrisburg], Sept. 20, 1871, p. 1; *Sunday Mercury* [New York], Oct. 23, 1859, p. 5; *Wilkes' Spirit of the Times*, May 4, 1872, p. 185; *World* [New York], Sept. 13, 1874, p. 2.

24. *History of Haverford College for the First Sixty Years* (Philadelphia: Porter, 1892) p. 339.

25. *Washington Reporter* [Washington, PA], Nov. 16, 1859, p. 1. For a rebuff to the Doesticks lampoon see *Knickerbocker Magazine*, vol. 50 [Sept. 1857], p. 311.

26. *Chicago Times*, April 17, 1889, p. 3 (the author has found considerable amusement, over the years, challenging members of the baseball community to identify the Baseball Hall of Fame member who preferred cricket to baseball as a participant activity). Wright's description anticipates, by over seventy years, C.L.R. James' claim for cricket of "infinite variety" in its batting, whose players "can shape to hit practically round the points of the compass"; C.L.R. James, *Beyond A Boundary* (Durham: Duke University Press, 2013) pp. 207, 206.

27. A.S. Draper, ed., *Sports, Pastimes, and Physical Culture* (St. Louis: Self Culture, 1907) p. 94.

28. Sullivan, *Early Innings*, p. 27.

29. Block, *Baseball Before We Knew It*, p. 82. The "21 run rule" seems to have been more of a general guideline that an inflexible rule, some early Knickerbocker games concluding with scores as high as 71. It seems the early Knickerbockers simply concluded a game when they grew tired of playing; Harold Peterson, *The Man Who Invented Baseball* (New York: Scribner, 1973), p. 75; *Porter's Spirit of the Times*, Sept. 22, 1855, p. 373; *Brooklyn*

Daily Eagle, Oct. 15, 1855, p. 2; Peverelly, *Book of American Pastimes*, pp. 348–349.
30. *Porter's Spirit of the Times*, March 7, 1847, p. 5; March 10, 1858, p .37.
31. *World* [New York], Sept. 19, 1872, p. 4.
32. *Lancaster Gazette* [England], Aug. 29, 1874, p. 2; R.A. Fitzgerald, *Wickets in the West* (London: Tinsley, 1873) p. 292.
33. James D'Wolf Lovett, *Old Boston Boys and the Games They Played* (Boston: privately printed, 1907), p. 78; *Clipper*, April 10, 1869, p. 3.
34. Malcolm MacLean, "Ambiguity Within the Boundary: Re-Reading C.L.R. James's Beyond A Boundary" *Journal of Sport History* (Spring 2010), p. 101.
35. George Wright, *Record of the Boston Base Ball Club* (Boston: Rockell & Churchill, 1874) p. 5; Jacob Burckhardt, *Reflections on History* (Indianapolis: Liberty, 1979) p. 93.
36. Barnet Phillips, "Cricket in the Forties," *Harper's Weekly*, Sept. 22, 1894, p. 909; Virginia Woolf, *Books and Portraits* (New York: Harcourt, 1981), p. 73.
37. Majumdar and Brown, "Why Baseball, Why Cricket," p. 143.
38. *New York Times*, Sept. 15, 1872, p. 5.
39. *Clipper*, Nov. 8, 1879, p. 258; Sept. 12, 1856, p. 165; *New York Times*, April 10, 1870, p. 4.
40. *Anglo-American*, Aug. 27, 1853, p. 416.
41. *Beadle's Dime Base-Ball Player*, (1872), p. 10.

Chapter Four

1. Stempel, "Towards A Historical Sociology of Sport," p. 260; Adelman, *A Sporting Time*, pp. 168–169; Kirsch, *Baseball and Cricket*, pp. 247–248; Spalding, *America's National Game*, pp. 65–67.
2. *Philadelphia Inquirer*, Nov. 16, 1860, p. 2.
3. Charles King Newcomb, *The Journals of Charles King Newcomb* (Providence: Brown University Press, 1946), pp. 280–281; *Philadelphia Inquirer*, Sept. 9, 1865, p. 4; *Clipper*, Sept. 8, 1860, p. 164; May 24, 1862, p. 43.
4. *Clipper*, Aug. 2, 1865, p. 138; Oct. 24, 1868, p. 226.
5. R. Terry Furst, *Early Professional Baseball and the Sporting Press* (Jefferson, NC: McFarland, 2014) pp. 110, 143.
6. *Boston Herald*, Aug. 19, 1868, p. 2; *Ball Players' Chronicle*, June 6, 1867, p. 5; Feb. 6, 1869, p. 18.
7. *Detroit Free Press*, July 3, 1870, p. 6.
8. *New York Times*, March 8, 1872, p. 4; *Evening Telegraph* [Philadelphia], Oct. 2, 1866, p. 4.
9. Rev. J.T. Crane, *Popular Amusements* (Cincinnati: Hitchcock & Walden, 1870) p. 81; *Wilkes' Spirit of the Times*, Jan. 23, 1869, p. 359.
10. Spalding, *The National Game*, p. 7.
11. *New York Times*, Aug. 30, 1881, p. 4. A decade earlier, the *New York Times* (March 6, 1871, p. 6) had claimed that the best classes had been driven away from baseball.
12. This class orientation has given rise to the stereotype with Americans, which persists to this day, that cricket is an "aristocratic" game while the more popular baseball is a "democratic" game, a categorization favored by Albert Spalding: "Cricket is essentially a game for the aristocracy while base-ball ... is a game for the people" (Albert Spalding, "Base-Ball," *Cosmopolitan*, vol. 7 [1889], p. 609). Demographically this claim is unsupportable, cricket being a popular sport at that time and to this day with all social classes in all cricket-playing countries. Structurally, in only one sense can this claim possibly be made. Whereas each player on a cricket team bats only once (or twice in a two innings game) in an entire game, each player in baseball will get at least three or four times at bat. Under these restrictions cricket might be said to be "aristocratic" insofar as it incorporates more *intolerance* to failure than "democratic" baseball which incorporates "second and third" chances. Just the opposite, however, is the case with pitching/bowling. Whereas the baseball pitcher may fail after only a handful of pitches right from the start and be pulled from the game, the cricket bowler, who's participating in a much higher scoring game, can be "successful" even if many runs are given up.
13. John Ford, *Cricket, A Social History, 1700–1835* (Newton Abbot: David & Charles, 1972) pp. 96–108; Malcolmson, *Popular Recreations in English Society*, p. 41.

14. "Cricket in 1907," *Fortnightly Review*, Sept. 1907, p. 506; *American Cricketer*, April 15, 1904; Andrew Hignell, *History of the Glamorgan County Cricket Club* (London: Helm, 1983), p. 11; Peter Davies and Robert Light, *Cricket and Community in England* (Manchester: Manchester University Press, 2012) pp. 41, 51.

15. Bowen, *Cricket: A History*, pp. 89–90; Keith Sandiford, "Amateurs and Professionals in Victorian County Cricket," *Albion*, vol. 15, 1983, pp. 32–51; W.F. Mandle, "The Professional Cricketer in England in the Nineteenth Century," *Labour History*, vol. 23 (1972), pp. 1–16; Erik Nielsen, *Sport and the British World, 1900-1930* (Basingstoke: Palgrave, 2014) pp. 66–67.

16. Pope, *Patriot Games*, pp. 27–28.

17. H.J. Whigham, "American Sport From an English Point of View," *The Outlook*, vol. XCIII (Sept.–Dec. 1909), pp. 738–744.

18. Ibid., pp. 739, 740, 741, 742.

19. George Newhall, "The Cricket Grounds of Germantown," p. 175.

20. *Rochester Union and Advertiser*, Oct. 23, 1858, p. 3; *Philadelphia Times*, May 23, 1880, p. 3.

21. *Wilkes' Spirit of the Times*, July 24, 1869, p. 360; Newcomb, *Journals*, p. 80; George Newhall, "Cricket in America" *Outing*, Oct. 1884, p. 48; *Philadelphia Times*, Sept. 27, 1879, p. 2; July 5, 1879, p. 2.

22. Baltzell, *Philadelphia Gentlemen*, p. 268. Biographical information was gathered from individual obituaries and Wikipedia entries.

23. Baltzell, *Philadelphia Gentleman*, p. 41; *New York Herald*, May 3, 1886, p. 3; *Clipper*, March 26, 1887, p. 27; *Philadelphia Inquirer*, Jan. 20, 1916, p. 6.

24. Howard McNutt, "Philadelphia Cricket, Past and Future," *Outing*, Aug. 1888, p. 458.

25. *American Cricketer*, July 1927, p. 160; *Clipper*, May 11, 1867, p. 35; *Philadelphia Inquirer*, March 26, 1883, p. 2.

26. Lester, *A Century*, p. 45; *Halifax Cricket Tournament: Visit of the American Twelve of Philadelphia, August, 1874* (Philadelphia: J.B. Lippincott, 1874), p. 4.

27. *Daily Evening Bulletin* [Philadelphia], Oct. 6, 1868, p. 5. Wilshire had predicted the Philadelphians wouldn't make forty runs in their second innings and, in fact, they made only thirty-five. *New York Herald*, May 7, 1879, p. 6; *Forest & Stream*, Jan. 8, 1880, p. 977; *Philadelphia Times*, Oct. 12, 1879, p. 1.

28. *Clipper*, Oct. 11, 1879, p. 242.

29. Richard Daft, *Kings of Cricket* (Bristol: Arrowsmith, 1893), p. 250; *Clipper*, May 15, 1880, p. 58; *Philadelphia Inquirer*, April 30, 1881, p. 3; *Philadelphia Times*, April 16, 1887, p. 2; *American Cricketer*, Sept. 1924, p. 210; *Lillywhite's Cricketers' Annual, 1880*, p. 6.

30. *Clipper*, Oct. 15, 1881, p. 481; *Philadelphia Inquirer*, Oct. 10, 1881, p. 2; *Philadelphia Times*, Oct. 14, 1882, p. 2.

31. *Clipper*, Oct. 9, 1869, p. 211; May 28, 1870, p. 59; *American Cricketer*, July 1927, p. 160; *Philadelphia Inquirer*, June 5, 1882, p. 2; *Daily Evening Bulletin* [Philadelphia], May 10, 1869, p. 6; *Philadelphia Inquirer*, May 16, 1870, p. 2; Sept. 29, 1879, p. 2.

32. *New York Herald*, Oct. 29, 1883, p. 5; *Philadelphia Times*, Oct. 14, 1882, p. 4. More specifically, it was the policy of the Halifax club's International Committee, which, during these years, always included at least one Newhall; *Philadelphia Inquirer*, Oct. 20, 1888, p. 3; George Patterson, "Cricket in the United States," *Lippincott's Magazine*, vol. 50 (1892), p. 660.

33. *Philadelphia Inquirer*, Aug. 23, 1896, p. 6. George Patterson emphatically insisted this would be the only title under which Philadelphia's representative teams would play; *Philadelphia Inquirer*, Jan. 23, 1899, p. 4.

34. *Philadelphia Inquirer*, April 4, 1885, p. 2; April 23, 1885, p. 2.

35. *Philadelphia Times*, Aug. 27, 1882, p. 2; May 16, 1886, p. 11.

36. *Philadelphia Inquirer*, April 30, 1890, p. 6.

37. Ibid., March 15, 1888, p. 2; Aug. 31, 1885, p. 3; *Philadelphia Times*, May 24, 1884, p. 2.

38. *Philadelphia Times*, July 23, 1882, p. 2; *Clipper*, July 15, 1882, p. 271; Oct. 24, 1885, p. 506; *Philadelphia Inquirer*, Oct. 20, 1888, p. 3; *Philadelphia Times*, July 29, 1888, p. 2; *Philadelphia Inquirer*, July 8, 1889, p. 6.

39. *American Cricketer*, April 1903, p. 58; Lester, *A Century*, p. 79.

40. *Haverfordian*, May 1889, p. 17; *Cricket: A Weekly Record of the Game* (hereafter referred to as *Cricket*), May 19, 1910, p. 127.

41. Melville, *The Tented Field*, pp. 80–81; *Clipper*, Sept. 17, 1870, p. 186.
42. *Wilkes' Spirit of the Times*, Jan. 19, 1867, p. 324.
43. *Philadelphia Inquirer*, Sept. 25, 1872, p. 2; W.G. Grace, "W.G": *Cricket Reminiscences* (London: Bowden, 1899) p. 59; Fitzgerald, *Wickets in the West*, p. 244; *Wisden's Cricketers' Almanack, 1873*, p. 100; *Clipper*, June 21, 1856, p. 71; *Ball Players' Chronicle*, June 6, 1867, p. 5.
44. *Boston Globe*, June 29, 1875, p. 5; Sept. 3, 1875, p. 5; *Sunday Mercury* [Philadelphia], Dec. 10, 1876, p. 4; *Philadelphia Times*, July 13, 1875, p. 4; Oct. 15, 1875, p. 4; *Chicago Tribune*, Nov. 26, 1876, p. 7; Spalding, *America's National Game*, pp. 161, 222.
45. *Philadelphia Times*, Sept. 20, 1885, p. 4.

Chapter Five

1. *North American*, Sept. 1, 1865, p. 1; *Philadelphia Age*, June 9, 1865, p. 2; *Public Ledger*, Nov. 1, 1865, p. 1.
2. *Clipper*, May 21, 1864, p. 43; *American Cricketer*, July 1927, p. 160; *Philadelphia Inquirer*, Oct. 19, 1866, p. 2; *Clipper*, Oct. 27, 1866, p. 227.
3. *Clipper*, May 13, 1865, p. 34; *North American*, July 7, 1865, p. 1; *Daily Age* [Philadelphia], Sept. 12, 1865, p. 4; *Clipper*, Aug. 12, 1865, p. 140.
4. *The Merion Cricket Club, 1865–1965* (privately printed, 1965), [p. 1]; *Philadelphia Inquirer*, April 23, 1916, p. 61; *Philadelphia Times*, May 18, 1892, p. 8; Aug. 17, 1884, p. 2; Peverelly, *Book of American Pastimes*, p. 548.
5. *Belmont Cricket Club of Philadelphia* (Philadelphia, 1884), p. 62; *American Cricketer*, Aug. 1924, p. 171; *Philadelphia Inquirer*, June 11, 1885, p. 3; Feb. 25, 1912, p. 9; J. Thomas Jable, "Philadelphia Cricket Comes of Age," in Ryan Swanson and David Wiggins, ed., *Philly Sports* (Fayetteville: University of Arkansas Press, 2016), p. 42.
6. *Evening Telegraph* [Philadelphia], June 8, 1870, p. 8; Jable, "Philadelphia Cricket Comes of Age," pp. 42–43.
7. *Daily Age* [Philadelphia], June 22, 1865, p. 2; Oct. 8, 1868, p. 1; Tanja Bueltmann and Donald MacRaild, *The English Diaspora*, p. 49; Edwin Brown, "English Tour to America, 1879," *The Cricket Statistician*, vol. 39 (Oct. 1982), p. 32.
8. *Philadelphia Inquirer*, April 20, 1890, p. 7; *Clipper*, July 24, 1869, p. 123; June 7, 1873, p. 74; *Philadelphia Inquirer* June 17, 1872, p. 2; June 21, 1875, p. 2. The Linden cricket club was made up almost entirely of immigrant mill workers (*Philadelphia Times*, Oct. 2, 1895, p. 2); while the players on the Girard cricket club seem to have been mostly immigrants from Nottinghamshire and Yorkshire (*New York Herald*, April 14, 1882, p. 14).
9. *Clipper*, Dec. 7, 1881, p. 634; *North American*, Sept. 23, 1872, p. 1; *Clipper*, June 30, 1877, p. 106; Nov. 11, 1865, p. 242; *Public Ledger*, June 2, 1873, p. 1; *Philadelphia Inquirer*, June 27, 1874, p. 2; May 8, 1876, p. 3. A William Hargreaves reportedly assumed leadership of the Star cricket club from its founder William Jarvis in 1853 (Norman Keyer, *History of Old Germantown* [Philadelphia: McCann, 1902], p. 189). John Hargreaves prematurely died at the age of 29 (*Clipper*, Jan. 3, 1880, p. 322).
10. *Philadelphia Times*, Sept. 14, 1880, p. 4; Lester, *A Century of Philadelphia Cricket*, p. 31; *Philadelphia Times*, June 25, 1877, p. 4; *Philadelphia Inquirer*, Sept. 15, 1877, p. 2.
11. *Brentano's*, April 1879, p. 452; *Clipper*, July 16, 1870, p. 117.
12. *Clipper*, Oct. 16, 1866, p. 203; *New York Times*, July 28, 1860, p. 5.
13. *Daily Evening Bulletin* [Philadelphia], June 16, 1864, p. 8; *Clipper*, June 26, 1873, p. 115; *Sportsman's Oracle and Country Gentlemen's Newspaper*, July 1866, p. 133. Though the Young America/St. George rivalry was intense, it always seemed to be cordial, the St. George players "enthusiastic" over the abilities of their American opponents (letter in Philadelphia Cricket Club records, 1858–1883, Pennsylvania Historical Society).
14. *Press* [Philadelphia], Nov. 21, 1864, p. 4; *World* [New York], Sept. 22, 1865, p. 5; *Daily Evening Bulletin* [Philadelphia], Sept. 23, 1865 p. 1; *Philadelphia Inquirer*, Sept. 23, 1867, p. 4; July 10, 1868, p. 2; *Clipper*, June 23, 1877, p. 103.
15. *Daily Evening Bulletin* [Philadelphia], Sept. 23, 1869, p. 6; *Clipper*, June 26, 1875, p. 99; Oct. 2, 1869, p. 205; *Philadelphia*

Inquirer, June 25, 1870, p. 8; *Clipper*, Sept. 20, 1873, p. 194.

16. Lester, *A Century of Philadelphia Cricket*, p. 23; Baltzell, *The Philadelphia Gentlemen*, p. 378.

17. *Spirit of the Times*, July 17, 1858, p. 27; *Philadelphia Inquirer*, Sept. 14, 1891, p. 5; *Philadelphia Times*, Oct. 4, 1878, p. 1; *New York Herald*, Oct. 8, 1888, p. 8.

18. *Philadelphia Inquirer*, Sept. 29, 1881, p. 2; W.G. Grace, *"W.G": Cricket Reminiscences*, p. 59; *New York Times*, Sept. 22, 1872, p. 1; Lester, *A Century of Philadelphia Cricket*, pp. 27–28.

19. *Philadelphia Inquirer*, Sept. 14, 1891, p. 5; Lester, *A Century of Philadelphia Cricket*, p. 29; *New York Herald*, Oct. 2, 1881, p, 8.

20. *New York Herald*, Sept. 18, 1885; *Patriot* [Harrisburg, PA], Oct. 12, 1883, p. 1; *Philadelphia Times*, Oct. 5, 1879, p. 3; *The Irish in the United States 1879* (Dublin: Lawrence, 1880) p. 65.

21. *New York Herald*, Aug. 29, 1881, p. 5; *American Cricketer*, Sept. 1913, p. 223; *Clipper*, Oct. 8, 1864, p. 204; *Boston Globe*, May 20, 1888, p. 2; *American Cricketer*, Aug. 1913, p. 190.

22. *Outing*, March 1886, p. 686; *International Cricket Fete: Official Handbook* (Philadelphia: J.B. Lippincott, 1872) pp. 9–11.

23. *Clipper*, June 8, 1867, p. 228; *National Chronicle*, May 7, 1870, p, 142.

24. *Philadelphia Inquirer*, July 6, 1885, p. 3; *Daily Age* [Philadelphia], Sept. 19, 1865, p. 2; *Forest & Stream*, Sept. 11, 1879, p. 635; *Philadelphia Inquirer*, July 7, 1883, p. 2.

25. *New York Herald*, April 13, 1881, p. 11.

26. Wister, *Some Reminiscences*, p. 40; Jones Wister, *A "Bawl" for American Cricket*, p. 7.

27. Lester, *A Century of Philadelphia Cricket*, p. 34; Fitzgerald, *Wickets in the West*, p. 244.

28. *Halifax Cricket Tournament: Visit of the American Twelve of Philadelphia, August, 1874* (Philadelphia: J.B. Lippincott, 1874) p. 4. The policy didn't seem to be absolute at this time, with two Hargreaves men on the Philadelphia team against the Canadian side during its return visit to Philadelphia the following year (*Philadelphia Times*, Sept. 14, 1875, p. 1).

29. *Clipper*, June 26, 1880, p. 107; *New York Herald*, June 19, 1880, p. 8; *Philadelphia Times*, Feb. 23, 1890, p. 9. Newhalls did not appear on the U.S. team that played the visiting "Garrison Knickerbockers" team from Canada in 1868, nor on the U.S. team that played Canada in 1865 (though they were invited to play), nor on the U.S. team that faced an English team in 1872 (though Hargreaves men were on the U.S. side)—possibly because they protested the inclusion of immigrant English players on the "American" sides (*Clipper*, July 25, 1868, p. 125; *Philadelphia Inquirer*, Sept. 4, 1865, p. 1; Sept. 30, 1872, p. 1).

30. Five members of the Hargreaves family were on the Melrose cricket club in 1891, and men of the family were still playing on English-identified Philadelphia cricket clubs as late as 1918 and 1921 (*Philadelphia Inquirer*, Sept. 14, 1891, p. 3; Aug. 25, 1918, p. 14; July 27, 1921, p. 14).

31. *Daily Evening Bulletin* [Philadelphia], Sept. 23, 1869, p. 6; *New York Herald*, Oct. 8, 1882, p. 16; *American Cricketer*, July 7, 1887, p. 162; *Philadelphia Times*, Aug. 26, 1883, p. 2; *Philadelphia Inquirer*, Aug. 21, 1880, p. 21; Mark Leopard, *Philadelphia and North American Cricketers 1878 to 1972* (Association of Cricket Statisticians and Historians, 2004), p. 12.

32. Newhall, *The Cricket Grounds of Germantown*, p. 185; *New York Herald*, June 27, 1880, p. 10; *Philadelphia Inquirer*, July 3, 1882, p. 3.

33. *Philadelphia Inquirer*, Aug. 3, 1878, p. 2; *Clipper*, July 3, 1880, p. 115; *Detroit Free Press*, June 22, 1880, p. 1; *New York Herald*, Sept. 11, 1882, p. 8; Aug. 24, 1882, p. 8; Oct. 7, 1883, p. 17; Patrick Adams, *A History of Canadian Cricket: An Immigrant's Game?* (Lulu, 2010), pp. 61–63.

34. *American Cricketer*, April 31, 1900, p. 71.

35. Lester, *A Century of Philadelphia Cricket*, pp. 77–83.

36. George Newhall, "Cricket in America," *Outing*, pp. 48, 49.

37. *Philadelphia Inquirer*, Sept. 18, 1885, p. 4; *New York Herald*, Sept. 20, 1885, p. 14; *Philadelphia Inquirer*, Aug. 17, 1885, p. 3.

38. Guy Wyatt, *Tour of the West Indian Cricketers, August & September, 1886* (Demerara, 1887), p. 85; *Philadelphia*

Inquirer, Sept. 23, 1888, p. 13; Lester, *A Century of Philadelphia Cricket*, pp. 98–110. Charles Newhall's presence on the International Selection Committee during these years certainly must have ensured an All-American selection policy (*American Cricketer*, Sept. 20, 1886).
 39. *Philadelphia Inquirer*, April 20, 1890, p. 7; April 23, 1885, p. 2; *Sporting Life*, May 6, 1885, p. 9. At least five smaller English-dominated cricket clubs were playing in the Germantown area alone (*Philadelphia Inquirer*, April 23, 1887, p. 2).
 40. Patterson, "Cricket in the United States," p. 656; *Philadelphia Times*, Aug. 31, 1891, p. 3; June 10, 1895, p. 8.
 41. *American Cricketer*, Oct. 28, 1891, p. 202; *Philadelphia Times*, Sept. 14, 1892, p. 6.
 42. *Philadelphia Times*, Jan. 11, 1891, p. 3; Ric Sissons, *The Players: A Social History of the Professional Player* (Sydney, 1988), p. 85; Marder, *The International Series*, p. 160. Philadelphia had considered adopting the English two-year residency requirement for its cricket (*Philadelphia Inquirer*, Oct. 5, 1890, p. 9); July 2, 1892, p. 3.
 43. *Philadelphia Inquirer*, Aug. 2, 1896, p. 10; Sept. 1, 1896, p. 5.
 44. Thomas Wharton, "Inter-city and International Cricket in America," *Outing*, June 1892, p. 180.
 45. *Philadelphia Inquirer*, Aug. 12, 1890, p. 5; Sept. 21, 1890, p. 5; Dec. 21, 1890, p. 7.
 46. *Ibid.*, Oct. 9, 1890, p. 5; Sept. 21, 1890, p. 5; April 6, 1890, p. 6; Oct. 24, 1890, p. 3.
 47. *American Cricketer*, Aug. 7, 1879, p. 22; *Philadelphia Inquirer*, Nov. 23, 1890, p. 12.
 48. *Philadelphia Inquirer*, Dec. 14, 1890, p. 3; *American Cricketer*, Aug. 30, 1893, p. 164; *Philadelphia Inquirer*, Sept. 26, 1890, p. 7.
 49. *Philadelphia Inquirer*, July 20, 1890, p. 9; *Sporting Life*, Jan. 3, 1891, p. 10.
 50. *Philadelphia Inquirer*, Oct. 9, 1890, p. 5; *American Cricketer*, Aug. 14, 1890, p. 74; *Philadelphia Times*, March 26, 1891, p. 4.
 51. *Philadelphia Inquirer*, May 30, 1887, p. 3; *Philadelphia Times*, Dec. 12, 1890, p. 6; *American Cricketer*, April 22, 1891, p. 2.
 52. *Philadelphia Times*, July 26, 1891, p. 4; Aug. 4, 1891, p. 1; *Philadelphia Inquirer*, Aug. 6, 1891, p. 8; *Philadelphia Times*, April 12, 1891, p. 4.
 53. Wharton, "*Inter-City and International Cricket in America*," p. 178; *Philadelphia Inquirer*, Sept. 12, 1891, p. 5; Sept. 14, 1891, p. 3. *American Cricketer*, May 17, 1894, p. 33.
 54. "Cricket in the United States," *Lippincott's*, p. 649; *Outing*, June 1905, p. 321; *American Cricketer*, July 14, 1881, p. 171; Feb. 1893, p. 5; *Philadelphia Times*, July 2, 1885, p. 4.
 55. *American Cricketer*, Feb. 1926, p. 219; *Philadelphia Times*, May 9, 1892, p. 6; *Philadelphia Inquirer*, Sept. 11, 1883, p. 3; *Philadelphia Times*, June 20, 1886, p. 10; *Philadelphia Inquirer*, June 28, 1889, p. 6; *American Cricketer*, June 27, 1889, p. 45.

Chapter Six

 1. Robeson Perot, *A History of Athletics of the Germantown Academy* (Philadelphia: Jenkins, 1910), p. 72.
 2. *Cricket*, Nov. 26, 1906, p. 449; Keith Sandiford, *Cricket and the Victorians* (Routledge, 1994) p. 145; James Bradley, "The MCC, Society and Empire: A Portrait of Cricket's Ruling Body, 1860–1914," *International Journal of the History of Sport*, vol. 7, no. 1 (1990), p. 11.
 3. *Wilkes' Spirit of the Times*, Oct. 26, 1867, p. 190; Douglas Wallop, *Baseball: An Informal History* (New York: Norton, 1969), p. 121.
 4. Spalding, *America's National Game*, pp. 175–188; 251–268; A.G. Spalding, "Base-Ball," *Cosmopolitan*, vol. 7 (1889), p 612.
 5. Harry Palmer, *Sights Around the World with the Base Ball Boys* (New York: Edgewood, 1892), p. 279. In light of the recent and projected Major League baseball games played in England, this unfulfilled obsession still seems to lurk deep in the heart of American baseball.
 6. *Brentano's Aquatic Monthly*, April 1879, p. 68.
 7. *American Cricketer*, March 1920, p. 739; Newhall, "The Cricket Grounds of Germantown and a Plea for the Game," 172. The Australian *Leader* (Oct. 7, 1893, p. 18) consoled its readers on their national cricket team's bad loss to the Philadelphians that year by pointing out that the

Australians had at least lost to a team of "British stock."

8. *Lillywhite's Cricketers' Annual 1885*, p. 49.

9. *Pall Mall Gazette*, June 8, 1897, p. 5.

10. Marder, *The International Series*, pp. 72–76.

11. *The Cricketers Association of the United States: Proceedings of Convention Held in Philadelphia, April 17, 1878* (Philadelphia, 1878); Marder, *The International Series*, p. 75.

12. *American Cricketer*, March 29, 1883, p. 15. The 1886 match was held at the Seabright Lawn Tennis and Cricket Club in Rumson, New Jersey; *Philadelphia Inquirer*, Aug. 9, 1886, p. 3; Marder, *The International Series*, p. 128.

13. *The International Cricket Match Played October, 1859 in the Elysian Fields at Hoboken on the Grounds of the St. George's Cricket Club* (New York: Vinten, 1859) pp. vii–viii; Fitzgerald, *Wickets in the West*, p. 244; *Lillywhite's Cricketers' Annual 1880*, p. 5.

14. Fred Lillywhite, *The English Cricketers Trip to Canada and the United States in 1859* (World's Work, 1980), p. 40; Fitzgerald, *Wickets in the West*, p. 244; *Lillywhite's Cricketers' Annual 1880*, p. 5; David Beaumont, *From Third Man to Third Base: Richard Daft's Tour to Canada and the USA in 1879* (privately printed, 2015), p. 121.

15. *Official Report of the International Cricket Fete at Philadelphia*, p. 3; *Cricket in Ireland* (1955), p. 64.

16. *Clipper*, Oct. 17, 1868, p. 22; *Philadelphia Inquirer*, Sept. 25, 1872, p. 2.

17. *Philadelphia Inquirer*, Sept. 23, 1872, p 4.

18. *Ibid.*, Sept. 27, 1886, p. 4; Oct. 2, 1886, p. 3; *Official Handbook of the Program of Arrangements During the Visit of the English Gentlemen* (Philadelphia, 1872), p. 11.

19. *Philadelphia Inquirer*, Jan. 31, 1876, p. 3.

20. *Clipper*, Oct. 12, 1878, p. 226; *New York Herald*, Oct. 6, 1878, p. 7; *Philadelphia Inquirer*, Oct. 7, 1878, p. 1; Lester, *A Century of Philadelphia Cricket*, pp. 63–64.

21. Chris Harte, *A History of Australian Cricket* (London: Deutsch, 1993), pp. 101, 108; John Lazenby, *The Strangers Who Came Home: The First Australian Cricket Tour to England* (London: Bloomsbury, 2015) p. 123; *Owens and Murray Advertiser* [Australia], Dec. 7, 1878, p. 3; *New York Times*, Jan. 29, 1879, p. 8. Conway was also suspected of trying to shortchange the Philadelphia hotel where he was staying (*Philadelphia Inquirer*, Oct. 19, 1878, p. 3).

22. *Owens and Murray Advertiser* [Australia], Dec. 7, 1878, p. 9. Other sources state the Australians voted 8–3 to resume the match (*Philadelphia Inquirer*, Oct. 7, 1878, p. 1). Dan Newhall, *How to Play Cricket: A Manual for Americans* (Philadelphia: Dando, 1881), p. 35.

23. *Sporting Life*, July 2, 1884, p. 7; *Chicago Tribune*, June 29, 1884, p. 10; *Forest and Stream*, May 1, 1879, p. 256; *Philadelphia Inquirer*, Aug. 31, 1885, p. 5.

24. *Philadelphia Times*, Oct. 6, 1882, p. 3; *World* [New York], Oct. 2, 1878, p. 4; H.S. Altham, *A History of Cricket*, vol. I (London: Allen & Unwin, 1962), p. 153; [John P. Green], *The Tour of the "Gentlemen of Philadelphia" in Great Britain in 1884* (Red Rose, 2002), pp. 27–28.

25. *The Tour of the Australian Eleven Through England, America and Colonies with Conway's Australian Cricketers Annual* (Melbourne: Bailliere, 1879), p. 283; *Clipper*, Oct. 21 1882, p. 501.

26. Altham, *A History of Cricket*, p. 152; *Philadelphia Times* Oct. 14, 1882, p. 2. Attempts to bring the Australians to Philadelphia in 1886 and 1888 were unsuccessful; *Clipper*, July 17, 1886, p. 274; *Philadelphia Times*, April 1, 1888, p. 2.

27. *World* [New York], Oct. 6, 1878, p. 1.

28. *Philadelphia Times*, July 27, 1879, p. 3.

29. *New York Herald*, May 6, 1879, p. 7; *New York Tribune*, May 9, 1879, p. 5.

30. *New York Herald*, Oct. 3, 1879, p. 8; *North American*, Oct. 18, 1879, p. 2; Oct. 24, 1879, p. 1; *Philadelphia Times*, Oct 24, 1879, p. 3. Three of the Hargreaves men played along with the English cricketers (something that most likely didn't endear them to Philadelphia's pro-American contingent) as did George and Harry Wright, the latter probably playing in his last international cricket match (Beaumont, *From Third Man to Third Base*, p. 257).

31. *North American*, Oct. 4, 1879, p. 4.

32. *New York Herald*, Nov. 12, 1881, p. 5; Oct. 2, 1881, p. 8.

33. *Clipper*, Oct. 11, 1879, p. 227; *Philadelphia Inquirer*, Oct. 5, 1881, p. 3.

34. *Clipper,* Sept. 20, 1879, p. 203; *The Irish Cricketers in the United States* (Dublin, 1880), p. 7; *Philadelphia Inquirer,* Sept. 26, 1879, p. 2.

35. There had been discussions of sending an American cricket team to England as early as 1869 (*Wilkes' Spirit of the Times,* March 20, 1869, p. 71) and a Philadelphia team as early as 1879 (*Clipper,* Dec. 20, 1879, p. 309); *Philadelphia Inquirer* May 19, 1884, p. 4.

36. *Cricket,* July 11, 1889, p. 245.

37. *Boston Herald,* Oct. 7, 1884, p. 8; *Lillywhite's Cricketers' Annual 1885,* p. 46; *Clipper,* June 21, 1884, p. 215; *Nottinghamshire Guardian,* June 20, 1884, p. 12.

38. *Tour of the Gentlemen of Philadelphia in Great Britain,* pp. 13–16; *Outing,* July 2, 1884, p. 7; July 9, 1884, p. 10.

39. *Birmingham Daily Post,* July 19, 1884, p. 6; *Tour of the Gentlemen of Philadelphia in Great Britain,* pp. 23–25, 30–31.

40. Lester, *A Century of Philadelphia Cricket,* p. 84.

41. *Lillywhite's Cricketers' Annual 1885,* p. 48; *Philadelphia Times,* April 12, 1885, p. 2.

42. *New York Herald,* Sept. 19, 1885, p. 6; *Philadelphia Inquirer,* Sept. 19, 1888, p. 8; *Cricket,* Oct. 29, 1885, p. 439.

43. *Philadelphia Inquirer,* Sept. 27, 1886, p, 4; Sept. 16, 1886, p. 3.

44. *Plain Dealer* [Cleveland], Dec. 22, 1887, p. 6; *Philadelphia Inquirer,* Feb. 18, 1888, p. 3; *American Cricketer,* April 26, 1888, p. 1; *Cricket,* April 19, 1888, p. 78.

45. *Philadelphia Inquirer,* Sept. 23, 1888, p. 13.

46. *Morning Post* [London], July 22, 1889, p. 2; July 23, 1889, p. 3; *Philadelphia Inquirer,* Aug. 8, 1889, p. 4.

47. *Sporting Life,* Aug. 28, 1889, p. 8; *New York Times,* Sept. 5, 1889, p. 8; Jable, "Philadelphia Cricket Comes of Age," p. 42; *Philadelphia Times,* May 9, 1886, p. 12.

48. *Cricket,* Oct. 23, 1883, p. 423; Rowland Bowen, *Cricket: A History of Its Growth and Development Throughout the World* (London: Spottiswoode, 1970), pp. 125, 134; Marder, *The International Series,* p. 9.

Chapter Seven

1. Bowen, *Cricket: A History,* p. 139.
2. *Boston Herald,* Jan. 6, 1888, p. 3.

3. *American Cricketer,* April 27, 1892, p. 26; April 27, 1898, p. 2; *Public Ledger,* April 14, 1892, p. 8; April 9, 1895, p. 15; April 22, 1897, p. 17; April 13, 1898, p. 19; March 29, 1899, p. 17; *Philadelphia Inquirer,* April 13, 1898, p. 4. Since these were only the formally scheduled matches among the established clubs in the spring, they would not include what must have been many informal matches and those arranged later in the season.

4. *Clipper,* Dec. 21, 1895, p. 608; *Philadelphia Inquirer,* Nov. 21, 1897, p. 20; May 7, 1899, p. 13.

5. *Sporting Life,* March 24, 1894, p. 8; *The Merion Cricket Club* [p. 21]; *The City of Philadelphia as it Appears in the Year 1893* (Philadelphia: Harris, 1894), pp. 126–127.

6. *Philadelphia Inquirer,* Oct. 23, 1891, p. 3; July 13, 1903, p. 10; Aug. 5, 1907, p. 6.

7. *American Cricketer,* April 1894, p. 17. On the testimony of Cornelius Weygandt, below this stratum of organized cricket was a vast array of unorganized, ad hoc cricket. In addition to the young men with whom Weygandt played as a youth in the 1870s and 1880s "a hundred other such groups were cricketing in this informal fashion in a hundred other yards or playgrounds" (Cornelius Weygandt, *Philadelphia Folks* [New York: Appleton-Century, 1938, p. 42]).

8. *Sporting Life,* Nov. 6, 1888, p. 6; *New York Herald,* Nov. 28, 1887, p. 9; *Clipper,* Nov. 26, 1887, p. 596; *American Cricketer,* Thanksgiving Day, 1887, p. 170.

9. *Philadelphia Times,* July 8, 1888, p. 2; *Philadelphia Inquirer,* June 12, 1888, p. 3; *New York Herald,* May 22, 1888, p. 8; *Sporting Life,* Sept. 28, 1887, p. 8; *Philadelphia Inquirer,* June 28, 1887, p. 3.

10. *Philadelphia Inquirer,* April 12, 1889, p. 6; *American Cricket Annual for 1891,* p. 14; Lester, *A Century of Philadelphia Cricket,* p. 312.

11. *Cricket,* Nov. 26, 1891, p. 477; *Philadelphia Inquirer,* June 22, 1890, p. 7; June 29, 1890, p. 5.

12. *Daily Age,* May 22, 1866, p. 2; May 29, 1866, p. 2; *Clipper,* Oct. 5, 1872, p. 210; *American Cricketer,* June 28, 1877, p. 3; *Philadelphia Inquirer,* Sept. 17, 1880, p. 3.

13. *Philadelphia Inquirer,* Dec. 3, 1881, p. 3; *The Merion Cricket Club* [p. 19]; *Philadelphia Times,* Nov. 22, 1892, p. 3.

14. *Clipper,* Jan. 11, 1896, p. 716; Oct.

3, 1896, p. 494; *Philadelphia Times*, Sept. 25, 1896, p. 3; *International Studio*, April 1908, p. 80.

15. Jable, "Social Class and the Sport of Cricket," p. 220; *Philadelphia Inquirer*, Sept. 26, 1897, p. 9.

16. *North American*, Aug. 20, 1877, p. 4; *Philadelphia Record*, June 12, 1885, p. 3; *American Cricket Annual for 1891*, p. 15.

17. *Philadelphia Inquirer*, May 16, 1885, p. 2; Sept. 16, 1885, p. 3; April 24, 1886, p. 2; May 24, 1886, p. 2.

18. *Ibid.*, May 4, 1888, p. 2; *Philadelphia Times*, Aug. 14, 1893, p. 10.

19. *Spalding's Official Cricket Annual, 1910* (New York: American Sports Publishers) p. 25; *Philadelphia Times*, June 22, 1879, p. 3.

20. *New York Herald*, April 30, 1882, p. 16; *Philadelphia Inquirer*, June 20, 1888, p. 3; David Contosta, *A Philadelphia Family* (Philadelphia: University of Pennsylvania Press, 1988) p. 28; David Contosta, *Suburb in the City* (Columbus: Ohio State University Press, 1992) pp. 87–88; Baltzell, *Philadelphia Gentlemen*, p. 206.

21. *Philadelphia Inquirer*, April 24, 1885, p. 8; July 6, 1885, p. 3.

22. *Philadelphia Times*, April 12, 1885, p. 2; *Philadelphia Inquirer*, May 21, 1888, p. 3; *Philadelphia Times*, July 15, 1888, p. 2; *Philadelphia Inquirer*, July 24, 1889, p. 5; *Haverfordian*, July 1890, p. 55; *Philadelphia Inquirer*, Sept. 14, 1890, p. 5; May 11, 1890, p. 3.

23. *Philadelphia Times*, July 14, 1894, p. 9; Dec. 15, 1895, p. 16; *Philadelphia Inquirer*, Feb. 8, 1897, p. 12. The Philadelphia clubhouse was also destroyed by fire in 1908, the only cricket club fire to claim a fatality *(American Cricketer*, Oct. 1908, p. 219); *Philadelphia Inquirer*, Sept. 11, 1908, p. 6.

24. *Philadelphia Inquirer*, Sept. 1, 1890, p. 3.

25. *Clipper*, June 4, 1881, p. 171; *Philadelphia Inquirer*, June 7, 1884, p. 2; *Clipper*, July 20, 1882, p. 303; *Forest and Stream*, March 25, 1880, p. 149; *Philadelphia Inquirer*, July 29, 1880, p. 3; July 2, 1880, p. 8.

26. *Philadelphia Inquirer*, Sept. 11, 1876, p. 3; *Clipper*, July 8, 1893, p. 289; *Philadelphia Inquirer*, July 4, 1893, p. 2; July 27, 1890, p. 12.

27. *Philadelphia Inquirer*, Aug. 23, 1901, p. 6.

28. *Philadelphia Inquirer*, June 23, 1895, p. 9; *Clipper*, July 21, 1900, p. 459; *Philadelphia Inquirer*, July 30, 1894, p. 4.

29. Lester, *A Century of Philadelphia Cricket*, p. 111.

30. *Outing*, June 1905, p. 321; *Cricket*, April 12, 1888, p. 49.

31. *Philadelphia Inquirer*, Sept. 18, 1886, p. 2; Lester, *A Century of Philadelphia Cricket*, pp. 109, 128; *Philadelphia Inquirer*, Sept. 21, 1895, p. 6.

32. *Outing*, June 1905, pp. 321–322; *Sun* [New York], Oct. 3, 1895, p. 5; Lester, *A Century of Philadelphia Cricket*, p. 85.

33. *Philadelphia Inquirer*, June 30, 1885, p. 2; *Philadelphia Times*, July 5, 1889, p. 3; Lester, *A Century of Philadelphia Cricket*, p. 108.

34. *Evening Express* [Cardiff], June 27, 1903, p. 4; *Cricket*, Dec. 28, 1893, p. 475; Lester, *A Century of Philadelphia Cricket*, p. 130.

35. Lord Hawke, *Recollections and Reminiscences* (London: Williams & Norgate, 1924), p. 278; *Clipper*, June 16, 1894, p. 238; *Cricket*, June 27, 1894, p. 179. Bohlen was reportedly sponsored in his MCC membership by Somerset cricketer H.T. Hewitt (*Philadelphia Times*, May 2, 1894, p. 8). At least one other international Philadelphia cricketer, Walter Hinchman, was also a playing member of the MCC; Walter Hinchman, *The Only Paradise* (Wakefield: Murray, 1952) p. 61.

36. Lester, *A Century of Philadelphia Cricket*, p. 120; *American Cricketer*, Nov. 1910, p. 248; *Spalding's Official Cricket Guide, 1909*, p. 9.

37. Lester, *A Century of Philadelphia Cricket*, pp. 96, 123; *Philadelphia Inquirer*, March 9, 1896, p. 5.

38. *Philadelphia Times*, Sept. 9, 1895, p. 8; *Philadelphia Inquirer*, Aug. 2, 1896, p. 10.

39. Lester, *A Century of Philadelphia Cricket*, pp. 124; 204; *Manchester Guardian*, July 20, 1903, p. 4.

40. *Clipper*, Aug. 21, 1858, p. 138; *Porter's Spirit of the Times*, Oct. 15, 1859, p. 100.

41. *Clipper*, Oct. 2, 1860, p. 213; *Wilkes' Spirit of the Times*, Oct. 18, 1862, p. 116.

42. Alfred Spink, *The National Game* (St. Louis, 1910) p. 4; *New England Base Ballist*, Sept. 3, 1868, p. 18; *Clipper*, Oct. 13, 1878, p. 226; *American Cricketer*, July

24, 1879, p. 16; *Paterson Daily Press*, Oct. 2, 1878, p. 3.

43. *World* [New York], Sept. 13, 1879, p. 2; *New York Herald*, Oct. 4, 1879 p. 8; Richard Daft, *Kings of Cricket* (Bristol: Arrowsmith, 1893) p. 169; *Lillywhite's Cricketers' Annual*, 1880, p. 9.

44. *New York Herald*, Sept. 2, 1885, p. 8; *New York Tribune*, Sept. 15, 1886, p. 2. Poole also excelled against the England-bound Canadian team that played at Seabright in 1887, returning figures of 6-40; *Cricket Across the Sea, or the Wanderings of the Gentlemen of Canada* (Toronto, 1887) p. 29.

45. G.L. Jessop, *A Cricketer's Log* (London: Hodder & Stoughton, 1926) p. 134; Marder, *the International Series*, p. 221.

46. *Canadian Cricket Guide* (Ottawa, 1876) p. 119.

47. *Saturday Review* (Aug. 9, 1884), p. 171.

48. *Philadelphia Inquirer*, Sept. 7, 1897, p. 11; Fitzgerald, *Wickets in the West*, p. 263; Lester, *A Century of Philadelphia Cricket*, pp. 29-30.

49. *Philadelphia Times*, June 7, 1896, p. 11; *Lillywhite's Cricketers' Annual*, 1898, p. 31. During Philadelphia's 1897 England tour Bates was 1-12 against Oxford Past and Present, King 1-30. Against Gloucestershire he was 2-17, King 2-100, against the MCC he was 1-41, King 1-67 (*Lillywhite's Cricketers' Annual*, 1898, p. 33); *American Cricketer*, Sept. 1897, p. 131; *Wisden's Cricketers' Almanack*, 1898, p. 318.

50. *Philadelphia Times*, Aug. 1, 1892, p. 6; *Outing*, July 1890, p. 84; *Philadelphia Inquirer*, Sept. 27, 1899, p. 5; P.F. Warner, *Cricket in Many Climes* (London: Heinemann, 1900), p. 96.

51. *Philadelphia Inquirer*, Sept. 1, 1907, p. 14; Henry Sayen, *A Yankee Looks at Cricket* (London: Putnam, 1956) p. 32.

52. *Philadelphia Inquirer*, June 28, 1913, p. 12.

53. *American Cricketer*, Dec. 1913, p. 316.

54. *Philadelphia Inquirer*, Sept. 24, 1889, p. 6; *Philadelphia Times*, June 6, 1889, p. 3.

55. *Philadelphia Inquirer*, Sept. 18, 1891, p. 3; *Cricket Club Life*, July 7, 1898, p. 3; *Philadelphia Inquirer*, Sept. 15, 1890, p. 3; Aug. 17, 1890, p. 5; *Philadelphia Times*, Sept. 6, 1891, p. 14; Sept. 21, 1891, p. 3. Leopard erroneously has King attending Frankford High School (Mark Leopard, *Philadelphia and North American Cricketers, 1878 to 1972* [Association of Cricket Statisticians and Historians, 2004] p. 7). For King's early life see Stephen Musk and Roger Mann, *Bart King of Philadelphia* (Leicestershire: Matador, 2022) pp. 26-27.

56. *Philadelphia Times*, June 19, 1892, p. 15; July 10, 1892, p. 14; July 17, 1892, p. 14. In his encounters with King up to 1895 Patterson was averaging barely five runs per at bat (*Philadelphia Inquirer*, June 16, 1895, p. 9).

57. *American Cricketer*, Dec. 1925, p. 171; *Philadelphia Inquirer*, Aug. 21, 1892, p. 14; Marder, *The International Series*, pp. 161-162.

58. *Philadelphia Times*, June 4, 1893, p. 9; Lester, *A Century of Philadelphia Cricket*, p. 161. King himself claimed he strengthened his fingers through a regimen of lifting weights with each individual finger; Stephen Musk and Roger Mann, *Bart King*, p. 286.

59. *Cricket*, July 29, 1897, p. 310; Lester, *A Century of Philadelphia Cricket*, p. 165; *Philadelphia Times*, Sept. 19, 1885, p. 2; July 11, 1892, p. 6; July 18, 1892, p. 3; *Ottawa Journal* [Canada], July 7, 1888, p. 5.

60. David Allen, *Cricket's Silver Lining* (London: Willow, 1987) p. 210; *Harper's Weekly*, Oct. 21, 1899, p. 1074; Horace Hutchinson, *Cricket* (London: Newnes, 1903) p. 392.

61. Lester, *A Century of Philadelphia Cricket*, pp. 166-167; F.M. Gilbert, "What Makes a Cricket Ball Curl in the Air?" *Strand Magazine*, vol. 15 (1906), pp. 730-731; Herbert Hordern, *Googlies* (Sydney: Angus & Robertson, 1932) p. 55; *Cricket*, July 29, 1897, p. 309.

62. *American Cricketer*, April 1913, p. 77; *Manchester Guardian*, July 27, 1903, p. 5; *American Cricketer*, July 10, 1903, p. 123; *Manchester Guardian*, July 7, 1903, p. 5. A cartoon depicting King's run up shows him taking a long, meandering path (*Philadelphia Inquirer*, Sept. 20, 1901, p. 16).

63. Lester, *A Century of Philadelphia Cricket*, p. 166; *Public Ledger*, Sept. 21, 1896, p. 16; *Philadelphia Inquirer*, Sept. 6, 1896, p. 9; *Pall Mall Gazette*, June 8, 1897, p. 5; *American Cricketer*, Oct. 12, 1912, p. 248.

64. P.F. Warner, *British Sportsmen* (1903 Scrapbook in C.C. Morris Cricket Library); *Public Ledger*, Sept. 28, 1901, p. 20; *Philadelphia Inquirer*, Oct. 3, 1903, p. 2; "The Cricket Season of 1908," *Fortnightly Review* (Sept. 1908), p. 486.

65. *Sydney Morning Herald*, Oct. 9, 1912, p. 5; *American Cricketer*, July 29, 1897, p. 309; *Philadelphia Inquirer*, July 11, 1897, p. 20; Allen, *Cricket's Silver Lining*, p. 209; "The Cricket Season of 1908" *Fortnightly Review*, p. 486; *Nottingham Evening Post*, June 19, 1903.

66. *Cricket*, July 23, 1908, p. 299; Allen, *Cricket's Silver Lining*, p. 209. An examination of the 1908 tour statistics shows Hordern taking only twelve catches off King.

67. Altham, *A History of Cricket*, vol. I, p. 163; *Public Ledger*, Sept. 26, 1893, p. 10.

68. *Clipper*, Sept. 2, 1899, *Cricket*, July 9, 1903, p. 260; *New York Tribune*, Aug. 12, 1903, p. 7; Hordern, *Googlies*, p. 147; *American Cricketer*, Sept. 1912, p. 212.

69. *American Cricketer*, April 1910, p. 81. This was only the total number of hat tricks King had taken up to 1910.

70. Lester, *A Century of Philadelphia Cricket*, p. 188.

71. *American Cricketer*, Aug. 15, 1903, p. 129; Allen *Cricket's Silver Lining*, p. 321.

72. Allen, *Cricket's Silver Lining*, p. 209; *American Cricketer*, April 1913, p. 77; Oct. 1912, p. 247. Warner finished with a lower batting average in his two American visits than in any of his other overseas tours, Gerald Howat, *Plum Warner* (London: Allen & Unwin, 1987), [p. 226].

73. *Cricket*, May 2, 1914, p. 98.

74. *Philadelphia Inquirer*, July 18, 1896, p. 5; *Clipper*, May 18, 1895, p. 174; *Philadelphia Times*, Aug. 8, 1899, p. 10.

75. *Philadelphia Inquirer*, Sept. 7, 1900, p. 10; *Philadelphia Inquirer*, June 23, 1905, p. 10; *Cricket*, Aug. 30, 1906, p. 370.

76. *American Cricketer*, Oct. 5, 1892, p. 173.

77. *Ibid.*, Oct. Aug. 1903, p. 159; Lester, *A Century of Philadelphia Cricket*, p. 213; *Philadelphia Inquirer*, July 5, 1905, p. 13.

78. *Clipper*, Jan. 22, 1898, p. 780.

79. *Philadelphia Inquirer*, Sept. 28, 1912, p. 46; Aug. 3, 1902, p. 12; Sept. 27, 1903, p. 14; Adams, *A History of Canadian Cricket*, p. 117.

80. *Cricket Quarterly*, vol. IV (1966), p. 61; Lester, *A Century of Philadelphia Cricket*, p. 367; *Philadelphia Inquirer*, Dec. 3, 1911, p. 12.

81. *Clipper*, May 12, 1860, p. 31; *Sporting Life*, March 13, 1903, p. 7; *American Cricketer*, Dec. 1920, p. 992; *New York Times*, Aug. 12, 1903, p. 6; Ralph Baker, *The Great Bowlers* (London: Chatto, 1967), p. 129; *American Cricketer*, April 1913, p. 78. Like other sports heroes, King has had legends assigned to him, the most famous being the game in which he supposedly called off his entire team and then bowled the last batter to an empty field. The veracity of the incident, however, hasn't been definitively confirmed, primarily because its exact place and date has never been firmly established. The earliest mention of the feat appears in Arthur Wood's account in *Cricket* (Nov. 26, 1903, p. 450), which can be taken as a *terminus ante quem* for the incident. Lester personally queried King about the feat, which the Belmont bowler confirmed, but even then, no place nor date is given (Lester, *A Century of Philadelphia Cricket*, pp. 162–163). Most accounts state it occurred in a match between Belmont, King's club, and the Trenton cricket club, though no known match report between these two clubs specifically mentions the incident. The *American Cricketer* (Oct. 1919, p. 607) claims the feat actually occurred in a match against a New York club while P.F. Warner claims King bowled not one, but three, batters to an empty field (P.F. Warner, *My Cricketing Life* [London: Hodder & Stoughton, 1921] p. 84).

82. Lester, *A Century of Philadelphia Cricket*, pp. 77, 119.

83. *South Australian Register*, Nov. 26, 1896, p. 7; Lester, *A Century of Philadelphia Cricket*, pp. 168, 361–363.

84. "Lord Hawke's Cricketers in America," *The Illustrated American*, Oct. 17, 1891, p. 391.

85. Derek Birley, *A Social History of English Cricket* (London: Aurum, 1999) p. 135; Bradley, "The MCC, Society and Empire," p. 12; Altham, *A History of Cricket*, vol. I, p. 295. Hawke seems to have decided on his American trip only after a planned tour to India that year fell through (*Cricket*, Aug. 6, 1891, p. 323).

86. *American Cricketer*, Sept. 23, 1891, p. 178; *Public Ledger*, Sept. 26, 1891, p. 3; *American Cricketer*, Sept. 30, 1891, p. 187;

Philadelphia Inquirer, Oct. 5, 1891, p. 3; *Outing*, June 1892, p. 179; *Philadelphia Inquirer*, Sept. 27, 1891, p. 1.
  87. *American Cricketer*, Sept. 30, 1891, p. 185; *Philadelphia Inquirer*, Sept. 29, 1891, p. 2.
  88. *Philadelphia Inquirer*, Oct. 11, 1891, p. 12; Oct. 18, 1891, p. 12; Oct. 9, 1891, p. 8; Oct. 6, 1891, p. 5. The author's efforts to locate the transcript of this burlesque, if one still exists, have, to date, been unsuccessful.

Chapter Eight

  1. *American Cricketer*, Sept. 30, 1891, p. 187; *Outing*, June 18912, p. 179.
  2. *Philadelphia Inquirer*, Sept. 12, 1891, p. 3; Oct. 8, 1891, p. 3. Harry Wright and his pro baseballers would occasionally attend Philadelphia cricket matches, but in most instances, they went away unimpressed with the game (*New York Herald*, Oct. 3, 1886, p. 14; *Philadelphia Inquirer*, Sept. 21, 1895, p. 5).
  3. *American Cricketer*, Oct. 5, 1892, p. 170; Lester, *A Century of Philadelphia Cricket*, p. 129; *American Cricketer*, Oct. 5, 1892, pp. 171, 173.
  4. *American Cricketer*, Oct. 5, 1892, pp. 170, 178.
  5. *American Cricket Annual, 1894*, p. 17; *Philadelphia Inquirer*, Aug. 20, 1893, p. 2; *Philadelphia Times*, Sept. 29, 1893, p. 2.
  6. *Sun* [New York], Sept. 1893, p. 3; *Philadelphia Inquirer*, Oct. 1, 1893, p. 3; *Australasian*, Nov. 18, 1893, p. 902.
  7. *Public Ledger*, Sept. 30, 1893, p. 6; *Cricket*, Oct. 26, 1893, p. 444.
  8. *Philadelphia Inquirer*, Sept. 30, 1893, p. 3; Oct. 1, 1893, p. 3.
  9. *Public Ledger*, Oct. 2, 1893, p. 3; *Sporting Life*, Oct. 7, 1893, p. 11; Peter Sheppard, *The Prince and the Doctor* (Four O'Clock Press, 2007), p. 203. The Australians played their New York match at Staten Island, not, as Sheppard states, in Central Park (*ibid.*, p. 207).
  10. *Australasian*, Oct. 7, 1893, p. 633.
  11. *Philadelphia Times*, Sept. 22, 1894, p. 1.
  12. *Public Ledger*, Sept. 15, 1894, p. 11; Sept. 25, 1894, p. 1; *Philadelphia Inquirer*, Sept. 30, 1894, p. 2; Beaumont, *From Third Man to Third Base*, p. 163.
  13. *Philadelphia Inquirer*, Oct. 5, 1891, p. 3; Sept. 24, 1894, p. 4.
  14. Lester, *A Century of Philadelphia Cricket*, p. 126; *Philadelphia Times*, Oct. 1, 1895, p. 9; George Orton, ed., *A History of Athletics at Pennsylvania, 1873–1896* (Athletic Association), p. 170.
  15. *Public Ledger*, Sept. 28, 1895, p. 1; *Cricket*, Oct. 31, 1895, p. 439; *Philadelphia Inquirer*, Feb. 22, 1896, p. 5.
  16. Harte, *A History of Cricket in Australia*, p. 189; Lester, *A Century of Philadelphia Cricket*, p. 126; *Philadelphia Times*, Sept. 13, 1896, p. 19.
  17. *American Cricket Annual, 1897*, p. 8; *Australasian*, Nov. 7, 1896, p. 902; *Philadelphia Inquirer*, Sept. 22, 1896, p. 4. The author's personal visit to the Germantown grounds confirmed that the markings are long gone.
  18. *Cricket*, Oct. 29, 1896, p. 440.
  19. *Philadelphia Inquirer*, Sept. 29, 1896, p. 5; *Sun* [New York], Sept. 28, 1896, p. 8.
  20. *Australasian*, Dec. 26, 1896, p. 18.
  21. George Giffen, *With Bat & Ball* (London: Ward, Lock, 1897), p. 97; *Philadelphia Inquirer*, Oct. 11, 1896, p. 22.
  22. *Cricket*, June 10, 1897, p. 193; *Public Ledger*, Aug. 21, 1896, p. 5. Mitchell reportedly helped arrange the Philadelphia schedule in England (*Public Ledger*, Aug. 29, 1897, p. 4); *Cricket*, June 10, 1897, p. 193.
  23. *Public Ledger*, Oct. 2, 1893, p. 13; *Philadelphia Inquirer*, Feb. 28, 1894, p. 1. Also disappointed was the South African cricket team that toured England in 1894, which had to cancel what would have been an historic encounter with Philadelphia scheduled to be played at the Oval (*Cricket*, April 26, 1894, p. 440).
  24. Patterson, "Cricket in the United States," p. 651.
  25. *Haverford News*, Oct. 1901, p. 82.
  26. *Sheffield Telegraph*, June 28, 1897, p. 11; Lester, *A Century of Philadelphia Cricket*, p. 188.
  27. *Public Ledger*, Aug. 5, 1897, p. 3; Derek Birley, *A Social History of English Cricket*, p. 168; Altham, *A History of Cricket, vol. I*, p. 226.
  28. *Philadelphia Times*, June 18, 1897, p. 9; *American Cricketer, Midsummer, 1897*, p. 115; *Wisden's Cricketers' Almanack, 1898*, p. 309.

29. *Wisden's Cricketers' Almanack, 1898*, p. 314.
30. *American Cricketer*, Sept. 1897, p. 146.
31. David Firth, *The Golden Age of Cricket, 1890-1914* (Hertfordshire: Omega Books, 1983), p. 20; *Public Ledger*, July 12, 1897, p. 16; *Philadelphia Inquirer*, July 11, 1897, p. 20.
32. *Public Ledger*, July 12, 1897, p. 16; *Sheffield & Rotherham Independent*, June 29, 1897, p. 8; *Cricket*, Sept. 6, 1900, p. 385.
33. *American Cricketer*, Midsummer, 1897, p. 119.
34. *Ibid.*, Sept. 1897, p. 131; *Wisden's Cricketers' Almanack, 1898*, p. 317; S.M.J. Woods, *My Reminiscences* (London: Chapman, 1925), p. 92.
35. *American Cricketer*, Sept. 1897, p. 146; "Cricket Old and New," *Fortnightly Review*, vol. 68 (Sept. 1897), p. 401.
36. *Wisden's Cricketers' Almanack 1898*, p. 308; *Cambridge Review*, June 17, 1897.
37. *American Cricketer*, Sept. 1897, pp. 131, 134.
38. *Wisden's Cricketers' Almanack, 1898*, p. 131; *Times* [London], July 24, 1897, p. 14.
39. *Wisden's Cricketers' Almanack, 1898*, pp. 309, 316; *American Cricketer*, Midsummer, 1897, p. 119.
40. *Wisden's Cricketer's Almanack, 1898*, p. 302.
41. *Cricket*, Aug. 1897, p. 334; *Philadelphia Inquirer*, June 13, 1897, p. 22.
42. *Pall Mall Gazette*, June 11, 1897, p. 10; *Sheffield & Rotherham Independent*, June 28, 1897, p. 8; *Wisden's Cricketers' Almanack, 1898*, p. 310.
43. *Philadelphia Inquirer*, May 30, 1897, p. 23; *Wisden's Cricketers' Almanack, 1898*, p. 303.
44. *New York Tribune*, June 10, 1897, p. 3; *Philadelphia Times*, Oct. 14, 1896, p. 8; *Public Ledger*, Aug. 5, 1897, p. 3.
45. *Public Ledger*, June 3, 1897, p. 17; *Harper's Weekly*, Aug. 14, 1897, p. 816. Even the *Philadelphia Inquirer* (Feb. 14, 1897, p. 9) came up short in its prediction that the Philadelphians would win at least 25 percent of their matches.
46. *Cricket*, Aug. 5, 1897, p. 334; *Cricket Club Life*, Sept. 1, 1897, p. 5; *American Cricketer*, Sept. 1897, p. 146.
47. *Wisden's Cricketers' Almanack, 1898*, p. 304; *Lillywhite's Cricketers' Annual, 1898*, p. 26; *Philadelphia Inquirer*, Feb. 13, 1898, p. 11; *American Cricketer*, Sept. 1897, p. 134.
48. *Lillywhite's Cricketers' Annual, 1898*, p. 26; *Morning Post* [London], June 28, 1897, p. 2; *Cricket*, Aug. 5, 1897, p. 325.
49. *Cricket*, July 22, 1897, p. 297; Aug. 5, 1897, p. 325.
50. *Wisden's Cricketers' Almanack, 1898*, p. 302; *Derby Mercury*, June 30, 1897, p. 4; *Public Ledger*, June 18, 1897, p. 6.
51. *Philadelphia Inquirer*, Oct. 5, 1891, p. 3; *Cricket Club Life*, Sept. 1, 1897, p. 5.
52. *American Cricket Annual, 1898*, p. 15.
53. *Cricket*, Aug. 5, 1897, p. 324; *Lillywhite's Cricketers' Annual, 1898*, p. 27; *Cricket*, May 3, 1913, p. 147; Beaumont, *From Third Man to Third Base*, p. 162.
54. P.F. Warner, *Cricket in Many Climes* (London: Heinemann, 1900) p. 87.
55. Birley, *A Social History of Cricket*, p. 168; Bradley, "The MCC, Society, and Empire," p. 14.
56. Lester, *A Century of Philadelphia Cricket*, p. 171.
57. Warner, *Cricket in Many Climes*, p. 106; *Philadelphia Inquirer*, Sept. 25, 1897, p. 12
58. Warner, *Cricket in Many Climes*, p. 106.
59. *Ibid.*, pp. 162-163; *Philadelphia Times*, Oct. 2, 1898, p. 8; P.F. Warner, *My Cricketing Life* (London: Hodder and Stoughton, 1921) p. 99.
60. *Clipper*, Sept. 2, 1899, p. 542; Lester, *A Century of Philadelphia Cricket*, p. 173; Ross, *Ranji*, p. 113.
61. *New York Tribune*, Sept. 19, 1899, p. 4; *Philadelphia Inquirer*, Oct. 3, 1899, p. 4.
62. Percy Standing, *Cricket of Today*, vol. I (London: Caxton, 1900) p. 132; *Philadelphia Times*, Oct. 11, 1899, p. 11; *Cricket*, Oct. 26, 1899, p. 446.
63. *Cricket Club Life*, Oct. 1899, p. 6; *Cricket*, Oct. 26, 1899, p. 446.
64. Warner, *Cricket in Many Climes*, p. 82.

Chapter Nine

1. *Outing*, Oct. 1884, p. 52.
2. A.G. Bradley, *Other Days* (London: Constable, 1913) p. 416.
3. *Philadelphia Times*, June 13, 1879, p.

1; Sandiford, "Amateurs and Professionals in Victorian County Cricket," p. 34.

4. *American Cricketer,* Sept. 30, 1886, p. 132; June 28, 1877, p. 1.

5. For a directory of Philadelphia cricket clubs, see Lester, *A Century of Philadelphia Cricket,* pp. 371–375, and Melville, *The Tented Field,* pp. 255–258.

6. *Philadelphia Inquirer,* July 28, 1883, p. 3; *Clipper,* July 8, 1882, p. 251; *Philadelphia Inquirer,* May 24, 1905, p. 15; May 23, 1892, p. 3.

7. *Clipper,* May 12, 1860, p. 31. The Merion and Philadelphia cricket club veterans' teams played each other five times in 1891 (*Philadelphia Times,* Aug. 28, 1891, p. 3).

8. *Philadelphia Inquirer,* April 26, 1889, p. 6; *Philadelphia Inquirer,* March 13, 1898, p. 12.

9. *Philadelphia Inquirer,* Nov. 26, 1880, p. 3; *Public Ledger,* Dec. 9, 1880, p. 2; *New York Herald,* May 22, 1887, p. 14.

10. *American Cricketer,* April 26, 1888, p. 1; *Philadelphia Inquirer,* April 29, 1892, p. 3; *American Cricketer,* Feb. 17, 1900, p. 19; *Philadelphia Inquirer,* May 16, 1899, p. 4.

11. *Philadelphia Inquirer,* March 19, 1891, p. 5; Oct. 29, 1891, p. 3; June 24, 1900, p. 15; July 13, 1903, p. 10.

12. Kaufmann and Paterson, "Cross National Cultural Diffusions," p. 105.

13. *Philadelphia Inquirer,* Sept. 14, 1895, p. 7; *The City of Philadelphia as it Appears in the Year 1893,* p. 126.

14. Jable, "Social Class and the Sport of Cricket in Philadelphia," p. 210. Cricket matches between teams made up entirely of doctors and lawyers testify to the game's particular appeal to the city's professional classes (*Philadelphia Inquirer,* June 25, 1891, p. 2; July 11, 1883, p. 2).

15. Newhall, "The Cricket Grounds of Germantown," p. 189; *American Cricketer,* May 18, 1898, p. 13; April 30, 1900, p. 71; *Philadelphia Inquirer,* Aug. 5, 1891, p. 3; David Contosta, *A Philadelphia Family,* p. 28; Baltzell, *Philadelphia Gentlemen,* p. 206.

16. *Philadelphia Inquirer,* June 16, 1888, p. 2; Baltzell, *Philadelphia Gentlemen,* p. 97.

17. [John P. Green], *The Tour of the "Gentlemen of Philadelphia" in Great Britain in 1884* (Red Rose, 2002) p. 89.

18. Baltzell, *Philadelphia Gentlemen,*

pp. 115, 202. Biographical information was gleaned from individual entries in Wikipedia. This social composition was largely replicated with the subscribers to the guarantee fund for the Gentlemen of Philadelphia's England tour of 1903, with five of the non–cricket-playing subscribers to the 1884 fund still contributing in 1903: A.J. Cassatt, Allen Evans, Lincoln Godfrey, C.A. Griscom and H.H. Kingston (*Spalding's Official Cricket Guide, 1904,* pp 10–11).

19. *American Cricketer,* Aug. 1915, p. 183; *Philadelphia Inquirer,* Sept. 29, 1894, p. 4; Newhall, "The Cricket Grounds of Germantown," p. 174; *Philadelphia Times,* July 22, 1889, p. 2.

20. *Philadelphia Inquirer,* April 12, 1890, p. 2; *Clipper,* April 21, 1888, p. 94; Lester, *A Century of Philadelphia Cricket,* pp. 365–366.

21. *Philadelphia Inquirer,* Aug. 24, 1891, p. 3; May 18, 1891, p. 3; June 1, 1891, p. 2.

22. *American Cricketer,* Dec. 1895, p. 216; *Philadelphia Inquirer,* Aug. 15, 1895, p. 5; Jan. 6, 1891, p. 3; *Philadelphia Times,* July 23, 1893, p. 8; *Philadelphia Inquirer,* Aug. 5, 1894, p. 2.

23. *Philadelphia Inquirer,* Aug. 3, 1883, p. 2; Aug. 13, 1884, p. 2; July 16, 1884, p. 3; *Philadelphia Times,* July 23, 1893, p. 8; *Philadelphia Inquirer,* Aug. 5, 1894, p. 2.

24. *Philadelphia Times,* Aug. 4, 1890, p. 2; July 11, 1892, p. 6.

25. Players from non–Halifax Cup clubs were selected, however, for the city's representative "colts" (U-21) sides in their matches, beginning in 1897, against visiting foreign teams (*Philadelphia Times,* Aug. 17, 1898, p. 6).

26. *Philadelphia Inquirer,* Sept. 20, 1893, p. 3; *Philadelphia Times,* July 24, 1892, p. 14; Sept. 2, 1888, p. 2; *Philadelphia Inquirer,* June 18, 1899, p. 15; Oct. 14, 1891, p. 7.

27. *Clipper,* Oct. 22, 1859, p. 236. Central High School reportedly had eight class teams in 1860 (*Fitzgerald's City Item,* May 5, 1860, p. 2). *Wilkes' Spirit of the Times,* June 22, 1861, p. 245; *Clipper,* May 12, 1860, p. 5; *Sunday Mercury* [New York], April 22, 1860, p. 5.

28. Perot, *A History of Athletics of the Germantown Academy,* p. 79; *Sporting Life,* Oct. 13, 1886, p. 6.

29. Robert Pruter, *The Rise of American*

High School Sports and the Search for Control, 1880-1930 (Syracuse: Syracuse University Press, 2013), p. 37. Pruter makes no mention of cricket in Philadelphia schools. Charles Latham, *The Episcopal Academy, 1785-1984* (Devon, PA:Cooke, 1984) p. 96; The *Academy Scholium* [Episcopal Academy], Sept. 1889, p. 5; *Philadelphia Inquirer*, May 10, 1891, p. 8.

30. *The Index: Extra Number* (Haverford College Grammar School, Fall 1901), pp. 13, 31; Perot, *A History of Athletics of the Germantown Academy*, pp. 80, 82.

31. Baltzell, *Philadelphia Gentlemen*, p. 60; *Westonian* [Westtown School], vol. I, no. 8, p. 120.

32. Lester, *A Century of Philadelphia Cricket*, p. 90; *Philadelphia Inquirer*, March 14, 1909, p. 9; *William Penn Charter Record* (class of 1909-1910), p. 77; *American Cricketer*, March 1910, p. 51.

33. *Philadelphia Inquirer*, May 21, 1908, p. 10; *Westonian* [Westtown School], vol. 15, 1909, p. 174.

34. *Philadelphia Inquirer*, April 17, 1903, p. 10; *Index* (Haverford Grammar School, 1901), pp. 31, 32. Central High School also reportedly had indoor cricket facilities (*Philadelphia Inquirer*, April 1, 1905, p. 10).

35. *Philadelphia Inquirer*, June 29, 1908, p. 10; April 24, 1910, p. 30; May 21, 1913, p. 11; Perot, *A History of Athletics of Germantown Academy*, p. 92.

36. *Drexel Institute Bulletin* (Philadelphia, 1904), p. 10; *Philadelphia Inquirer*, June 6, 1914, p. 13; *Spalding's Official Cricket Guide, 1911*, p. 22; E. Digby Baltzell, *Puritan Boston and Quaker Philadelphia* (Boston: Beacon, 1979), p. 234.

37. *Philadelphia Inquirer*, May 5, 1912, p. 16; *College Weekly* [Haverford College], May 19, 1913, p. 2; *Philadelphia Inquirer*, June 2, 1907, p. 13; *College Weekly*, June 7, 1909, p. 3; *Philadelphia Inquirer*, May 16, 1912, p. 11; *Daily Pennsylvanian* [University of Pennsylvania], May 22, 1913, p. 3; *The Record of the Class of 1901* (Central High School, June 1900), p. 175.

38. *Clipper*, Oct. 3, 1857, p. 188.

39. *Philadelphia Inquirer*, May 19, 1862, p. 8; *Clipper*, May 14, 1859, p. 28; May 27, 1865, p. 50; *Daily Age* [Philadelphia], May 3, 1866, p. 4.

40. Archibald Graham, *Cricket at the University of Pennsylvania* (privately printed, 1930), p. 10; Orton, *A History of Athletics at Pennsylvania*, p. 176; *Daily Evening Bulletin*, Sept. 25, 1866, p. 8; *Daily Age* [Philadelphia], p. May 22, 1866, p. 2; Frank Presbrey, *Athletics at Princeton: A History* (Presbrey, 1901), p. 557.

41. Graham, *Cricket at the University of Pennsylvania*, pp. 10-11; *A History of Haverford College for the First Sixty Years* (Philadelphia: Porter, 1892), pp. 320-321; *Clipper*, Oct. 25, 1873, p. 234.

42. Edward Cheney, *History of the University of Pennsylvania, 1740-1940* (Philadelphia: University of Pennsylvania Press, 1940), pp. 257-258, 314, 315; *University Magazine* [University of Pennsylvania], May 1877, p. 104

43. *New York Herald*, Feb. 13, 1887, p. 7. It was long claimed that Philadelphia's cricket clubs always provided more assistance to the university's cricket than that institution's athletic association (*Philadelphia Times*, April 29, 1895, p. 8).

44. *New York Herald*, Aug. 13, 1883, p. 6; *Philadelphia Times*, May 7, 1880, p. 3; Graham, *Cricket at the University of Pennsylvania*, pp. 36, 75; *Philadelphia Inquirer*, July 11, 1885, p. 5; Orton, *A History of Athletics at Pennsylvania*, pp. 172-173.

45. *University Magazine*, Oct. 1878, pp. 15-16; Oct. 1880, pp. 24-25.

46. Graham, *Cricket at the University of Pennsylvania*, p. 26; Lester, *A Century of Philadelphia Cricket*, p. 380; Orton, *A History of Athletics at Pennsylvania*, p.164; *Trinity Tablet* [Trinity College], May 14, 1881, pp. 55-56; *Cornell Daily Sun*, Jan .5, 1904, p. 1.

47. Lester, *A Century of Philadelphia Cricket*, pp. 380-381; *University Magazine*, May 20, 1883, p. 223; Orton, *A History of Athletics at Pennsylvania*, p. 182.

48. *Daily Pennsylvanian*, Dec. 3, 1894, p. 1; *Philadelphia Inquirer*, March 22, 1899, p. 4. The university had a succession of part-time coaches up to at least 1920 (*Daily Pennsylvanian*, April 27, 1920, p. 4).

49. *Daily Pennsylvanian*, Oct. 15, 1897, p. 3; Graham, *Cricket at the University of Pennsylvania*, p. 75; *American Cricketer*, June 1, 1907, pp. 111-112.

50. Cheney, *History of the University of Pennsylvania*, p. 270; *Old Penn: A Weekly Magazine*, March 11, 1907, p. 1; Orton, *A History of Athletics at Pennsylvania*, p. 174; *New York Evening Journal*, April 8, 1898,

p. 9; Allen Thomas, "Haverford College Cricket," *Outing*, June 1896, p. 238; *Philadelphia Inquirer*, April 27, 1904, p. 11; May 5, 1904, p. 11.

51. Edward Bushnell, ed., *A History of Athletics at the University of Pennsylvania, 1873-1908*, vol. II (Athletic Association, 1909), p. 124; *Daily Pennsylvanian*, May 8, 1905, p. 2; May 11, 1905, p. 1.

52. *Philadelphia Inquirer*, June 19, 1901, p. 6; Bushnell, *A History of Athletics at the University of Pennsylvania*, vol. II, p. 125.

53. *Daily Pennsylvanian*, Nov. 6, 1907, p. 1. Bushnell states the university alumni, as well as the students themselves, had to assume some of the tour expenses (Bushnell, *A History of Athletics at the University of Pennsylvania*, vol. II, p. 127).

54. Lester, *A Century of Philadelphia Cricket*, p. 96; *Cricket*, Aug. 15, 1907, p. 345.

55. *Spalding's Official Cricket Guide*, 1908, p. 7; *American Cricketer*, Sept. 1907, p. 193.

56. Altham, *A History of Cricket*, p 283; *American Cricketer*, Sept. 1907, p. 194.

57. *Philadelphia Inquirer*, July 25, 1907, p. 9. *Spalding's Official Cricket Guide, 1908* (p. 25), lists Hordern's average at the end of the tour as 9.58; Lester (*A Century of Philadelphia Cricket*, p. 96) gives it as 9.45.

58. *Daily Pennsylvanian*, Oct. 2, 1907, p. 1; *Philadelphia Inquirer*, March 22, 1902, p. 3; *Spalding's Official Cricket Guide, 1908*, p. 11; *Daily Pennsylvanian*, March 27, 1909, p. 1.

59. Lester, *A Century of Philadelphia Cricket*, p. 11; *History of Haverford College for the First Sixty Years*, p. 536; "Cricket at Haverford," *Harper's Weekly*, Oct. 3, 1896, p. 989; *Haverfordian*, Feb. 1887, p. 80; Feb. 1890, pp. 137-141.

60. *History of Haverford College for the First Sixty Years*, p. 6; Allen Thomas, "Haverford College Cricket," p. 236.

61. Thomas, "Haverford College Cricket," p. 236; *History of Haverford College for the First Sixty Years*, p. 259; *Appleton's Cyclopedia of American Biography*, vol. IV (1888), p. 69; Rufus Jones, *Haverford College: A History and Interpretation* (New York: Macmillan, 1933), p. 32. An alumnus from that period states there was no cricket at the college in 1856 (*Haverford News*, Oct. 22, 1928, p. 4).

62. Jones, *Haverford College*, p. 121;

Philadelphia Inquirer, Oct. 17, 1897, p. 36; Melville, *The Tented Field*, pp. 37, 47.

63. *Haverford News*, April,1908, p. 28; *Haverfordian*, March 1890, p. 153.

64. Thomas, "Haverford College Cricket," p. 237; *History of Haverford College for the First Sixty Years*, pp. 320, 591; *The Merion Cricket Club* [p. 17].

65. *Haverfordian*, March 1894, p. 144; Oct. 1881, p. xi; June 1887, pp 31-32; June 1888, pp. 34-36.

66. *Ibid.*, April 1, 1888, p. 164; Oct. 1887, p. 58.

67. *Ibid.*, Nov. 1887, p. 86; Dec. 1887, p. 95.

68. *Ibid.*, April 1888, p. 164.

69. *Ibid.*, May 1890, p. 7; May 1889, p. 17.

70. *Ibid.*, May 1889, p. 17; March 1893, p. 151; Feb. 1892, p. 129; July 1893, p. 51.

71. Lester, *A Century of Philadelphia Cricket*, p. 381; *Haverfordian*, July 1890, p. 52.

72. *Haverfordian*, May 1887, p. 2.

73. Lester, *A Century of Philadelphia Cricket*, p. 123; Thomas, "Haverford College Cricket," p. 239.

74. *American Cricketer*, July 15, 1903, p. 106; "Cricket at Haverford College," *Harper's Weekly*, p. 989; *Haverfordian*, Oct. 1896, p. 6; *Cricket*, June 25, 1896, p. 242.

75. *Haverfordian*, July 25, 1896, p. 74; *Cricket*, May 12, 1904, p. 113; *Haverfordian*, Oct. 1896, p. 16; Lester, *A Century of Philadelphia Cricket*, p. 124; *Times* [London], July 10, 1896, p. 11.

76. *Haverfordian*, July 1884, p. iv; Lester, *A Century of Philadelphia Cricket*, p. 96.

77. *Haverfordian*, July 1898, p. 61; *Outing*, June 1896, p. 238; *Clipper*, March 2, 1901, p. 18; *Philadelphia Inquirer*, Feb. 13, 1901, p. 5; *American Cricketer*, April 1893, p. 17; *Haverfordian*, Oct. 1901, p. 98.

78. *Haverfordian*, May 1903, p. 55; June 1903, p. 82.

79. *Philadelphia Inquirer*, June 10, 1894, p. 10; *Haverfordian*, Nov. 1900, p. 89.

80. *Haverfordian*, June 1904, p. 61; Oct. 1904, pp. 96-97; *Philadelphia Inquirer*, July 8, 1904, p. 6.

81. *Cricket*, June 25, 1896, p. 242. Because of the college's extensive interaction with English cricket the claim was made that Haverford was the only American college "affiliated" with Oxford

University (*Philadelphia Inquirer*, Feb. 22, 1914, p. 10).
82. *American Cricketer*, April 30, 1900, p. 71.
83. Quoted in Michael McCarthy, "The Unprogressive City," *Pennsylvania History*, vol. 54, no. 4 (1987), p. 269; Sally (Butler) Wister, *Walter S. Newhall*, p. 14.
84. *Philadelphia Inquirer*, Sept. 28, 1891, p. 4; Edwin Bateman Morris, *Pen and Ink* (Philadelphia, 1962), p. 159; *New York Tribune*, Oct. 3, 1879, p. 4; *New York Herald*, Sept. 3, 1883, p. 9.
85. *Philadelphia Inquirer*, Sept. 27, 1891, p. 2; Sept. 30, 1895, p. 1; Sept. 29, 1894, p. 1; *Philadelphia Times*, Sept. 25, 1892, p. 9; *Philadelphia Inquirer*, Sept. 27, 1897, p. 4; Oct. 1, 1898, p. 7; *Philadelphia Press*, July 17, 1904, p. 4; *Public Ledger*, Sept. 23, 1907, p. 2.
86. Lord Hawke, *Recollections and Reminiscences*, p. 219.
87. *Australasian*, Oct. 7, 1893, p. 633; *American Cricketer*, Jan. 31, 1884, p. 2; *Clipper*, May 9, 1885, p. 115; *Cricket*, May 12, 1887, p. 124. This modest American cricket publication, however, supposedly inspired C.W. Alcock to start his publication, *Cricket*, in 1882 (*Dominion Illustrated Monthly* [Canada], Nov. 1892, p. 502).
88. *Philadelphia Times*, Dec. 9, 1890, p. 2; *American Cricketer*, Jan. 15, 1904.
89. *Utica Daily Observer*, Oct. 28, 1878, p. 3; *World* [New York], July 28, 1882, p. 8; *Amsterdam Evening Recorder*, July 17, 1906, p. 2.
90. *Haverfordian* vol. I, no. 2 (1879), p. ix.
91. *Daily Evening Bulletin* [Philadelphia], Jan. 1, 1902, p. 8; *Philadelphia Times*, Sept. 28, 1891, p. 1; Dec. 24, 1889, p. 1; *Philadelphia Inquirer*, Feb. 13, 1898, p. 11. Prominent Philadelphia lawyer and United States senator George Wharton Pepper played several sports during his student days at the University of Pennsylvania but always remembered cricket as "the most interesting" (*Public Ledger*, Oct. 19, 1922, p. 20). One dedicated member of the West Philadelphia cricket club even set up an improvised pitch in his basement to practice during the winter (*Philadelphia Inquirer*, Nov. 16, 1908, p. 11).
92. *Patriot* [Harrisburg], Sept. 8, 1883, p. 1; *Detroit Free Press*, July 6, 1894, p. 2; *Plain Dealer*, May 4, 1900, p. 6; *Spalding's Official Cricket Guide*, 1910, p. 93.

93. *Forest and Stream*, March 5, 1874, pp .60-63; *Canadian Cricket Guide* (Toronto, 1877), pp. 114-115; *American Cricketer*, July 22, 1886, p. 80.
94. *Kansas City Times*, Nov. 2, 1885, p. 2; Kristyn McIver, *Legacy of the Twenty-Six: A Celebration of the First Hundred Years of the Multnomah Athletic Club* (Portland, 1991), pp. 16-17; *Morning Oregonian*, Aug. 25, 1895, p. 10; Craig Own Jones, "The History of Cricket in Oregon, 1870s-1920s," *Oregon Historical Quarterly*, vol. 120, no. 3 (Fall 2019), p. 289. Jones gives little attention to cricket at the Multnomah club although it was the one cricket organization in the area that seemed to have significant American participation, a number of its cricket players coming from baseball (*Morning Oregonian*, Aug. 4, 1901, p. 16). Ex-Young America players also helped organize a match between sailors from the American warship on which they were serving and a British warship in Piraeus, Greece, in 1880 (*United States Army & Navy Journal*, March 13, 1880, p. 646).
95. *Pioneer Press* [Minneapolis], Sept. 6, 1903, p. 3; *American Cricketer*, Aug. 15, 1903, p. 142. News of Roosevelt's membership soon brought to his cricket club a flood of match invitations, among them Philadelphia's Frankford club (*Philadelphia Inquirer*, Aug. 15, 1903, p. 12).
96. *Haverfordian*, Oct. 1904, pp. 96-97; Graham, *Cricket at the University of Pennsylvania*, p. 122.
97. *American Cricketer*, April 1, 1880, p. 97; *San Antonio Express*, Feb. 18, 1889, p. 7; *Sporting Life*, April 6, 1887, p. 7; *Detroit Free Press*, Sept. 11, 1890, p. 8; *Philadelphia Inquirer*, Oct. 6, 1904, p. 10. According to Thomas Gilbert, Jackie Kennedy Onassis was descended from a branch of the Vernou family (Thomas Gilbert, *How Baseball Happened* [Boston: Godine, 2020], p. 239).
98. Edmund Blunden, *Cricket Country* (London: Collins, 1944), p. 30.

Chapter Ten

1. *Philadelphia Times*, May 15, 1900, p. 8; *Clipper*, Aug. 16, 1900, p. 553; *Boston Journal*, Aug. 20, 1902, p. 3.
2. *Philadelphia Inquirer*, July 23, 1899, p. 15; *Philadelphia Times*, July 16, 1902, p.

Notes—Chapter Ten

6; Jack Pollard, *The Turbulent Years of Australian Cricket, 1893-1917* (North Ryde, NSW: Angus, 1987), p. 136.

3. *Philadelphia Inquirer*, Sept. 23, 1901, p. 6; Oct. 8, 1901, p. 6.

4. Lester, *A Century of Philadelphia Cricket*, pp. 182-183.

5. Plumptre, *The Golden Age of Cricket*, p. 117.

6. *American Cricketer*, May 15, 1903, p. 76.

7. *Nottingham Evening Post*, June 18, 1903; *Manchester Guardian*, July 7, 1903, p. 5; *Manchester Evening News*, July 6, 1903. In his history of this cricket period Alan Ross completely ignores the Philadelphians, stating there was "no touring side" in England in 1903 (Alan Ross, *Ranji* [Pavilion Library, 1983], p. 129).

8. John Lester, "Another Cricket Invasion of England," *Outing*, Oct. 1902, pp. 121-122.

9. *American Cricketer*, May 15, 1903, pp. 74, 76.

10. *American Cricketer*, July 15, 1903, pp. 116, 122; *Cricket*, July 23, 1903, p. 290; *Manchester Guardian*, June 11, 1903, p. 5.

11. *American Cricketer*, July 15, 1903, p. 112.

12. *Public Ledger*, June 24, 1903, p. 10; *American Cricketer*, July 15, 1903, p. 116.

13. *American Cricketer*, Aug. 15, 1903, p. 161; *Manchester Guardian*, July 7, 1903, p. 5; *American Cricketer*, Aug. 15, 1903, p. 129.

14. *American Cricketer*, Aug. 15, 1903, p. 131.

15. *Ibid.*, Sept. 15, 1903, p. 161.

16. *Manchester Guardian*, July 9, 1903, p. 4.

17. *American Cricketer*, July 15, 1903, p. 109.

18. *Public Ledger*, June 24, 1903, p. 10; *American Cricketer*, Sept. 15, 1903, p. 162; Lester, *A Century of Philadelphia Cricket*, p. 197.

19. *Times* [London], Aug. 7, 1903, p. 10; *American Cricketer*, Sept. 15, 1903, pp. 158, 160.

20. *American Cricketer*, Oct. 15, 1903, p. 187; July 15, 1903, p. 110; Lester, *A Century of Philadelphia Cricket*, p. 184; *Philadelphia Inquirer*, July 19, 1903, p. 12.

21. *American Cricketer*, Aug. 15, 1903, p. 131.

22. *Ibid.*, Oct. 15, 1903, p. 187; July 15, 1903, p. 111; Aug. 15, 1903, p. 131. Equally impressive was the fact that of the combined 178 wickets King and Clark took that summer, nearly half (77) were clean bowled; *American Cricketer*, Sept. 15, 1903, p. 162.

23. *Philadelphia Inquirer*, June 13, 1903, p. 10.

24. *American Cricketer*, Oct. 15, 1903, p. 187; *Manchester Guardian*, July 7, 1903, p. 5; *American Cricketer*, Aug. 15, 1903, p. 130; *Manchester Guardian*, July 8, 1903, p. 3; June 27, 1903, p. 5.

25. *Patriot* [Harrisburg], July 9, 1903, p. 7; *Manchester Guardian*, July 7, 1903, p. 5.

26. *Philadelphia Inquirer*, Aug. 2, 1903, p. 11.

27. *American Cricket Annual, 1904*, p. 13; *American Cricketer*, Aug. 15, 1903, pp. 116, 129.

28. *Cricket*, Aug. 22, 1903, p. 360.

29. *American Cricketer*, Sept. 15, 1903, pp. 156, 157.

30. Lester, *A Century of Philadelphia Cricket*, p. 191; *Nottingham Evening Post*, June 20, 1903.

31. *American Cricketer*, Sept. 15, 1903, p. 159.

32. *Ibid.*, Sept. 15, 1903, p. 157; *Philadelphia Inquirer*, Aug. 9, 1903, p. 11; *Times* [London], Aug. 10, 1903, p. 10.

33. The captain of the Derbyshire County side, in Philadelphia just before the tour, had predicted the Philadelphians would win at least six matches (*Philadelphia Inquirer*, May 24, 1903, p. 34).

34. The West Indian team that toured England in 1900 could only show a 5-8-1 record; the 1901 South African team a 13-9-3 record, though, overall, it played weaker sides than the 1903 Philadelphians; *Manchester Guardian*, June 27, 1903, p. 4; *American Cricketer*, July 15, 1903, p. 123. Philadelphia's moderate success on this tour in particular undermines John Nauright's assertion that a major reason for cricket's failure as an American sport was due to the fact that "Technical superiority was never achieved" by American cricketers. (John Nauright, "Cricket, Rugby, and Soccer in the United States," www.academia.edu/3987691/Cricket_Soccer_and_Rugby-in-the-USA).

35. *American Cricketer*, Aug. 15, 1903, p. 140; *New York Times*, Aug. 16, 1903.

36. *Pall Mall Gazette*, Aug. 6, 1897, p. 4.

Chapter Eleven

1. *American Cricketer,* Sept. 15, 1903, p. 166; *Illustrated Sporting News,* April 17, 1906, pp. 8-9.
2. *American Cricketer,* Oct. 15, 1903, p. 189. Lancashire had contemplated a visit to Philadelphia in 1885 and Nottinghamshire had considered a visit in 1896 (*Clipper,* Oct. 31, 1885, p. 526; *Philadelphia Inquirer,* Feb. 12, 1896, p. 5).
3. *American Cricketer,* July 15, 1903, p. 112; *Times* [London], Aug. 12, 1903, p. 9; *American Cricketer* Sept. 15, 1903, p. 160.
4. *Public Ledger,* July 26, 1905, p. 6. The Philadelphians were shocked at the extravagant expenses accrued by Ranji's team during its 1899 visit (*American Cricketer,* Nov. 3, 1899, p. 234); *Philadelphia Inquirer,* July 30, 1905, p. 12. From the start, it was clear this English cricket custom was "not going to take with the crowd" (*Philadelphia Inquirer,* July 26, 1905, p. 13).
5. Lester, *A Century of Philadelphia Cricket,* p. 217.
6. The Philadelphians seemed to have been persuaded to undertake the tour on the invitation of the visiting MCC team in 1907 (*Philadelphia Inquirer,* Oct. 3, 1907, p. 10).
7. Lester, *A Century of Philadelphia Cricket,* p. 221.
8. *Times* [London], June 20, 1908, p. 8.
9. *Manchester Guardian,* July 31, 1908, p. 9; *Daily News* [London], Aug. 21, 1908, p. 2.
10. *Spalding's Official Cricket Guide 1909,* p. 9; "The Cricket Season of 1908," *Fortnightly Review,* Sept. 1908, p. 486; *Spalding's Official Cricket Guide, 1909,* p. 7.
11. *Cricket,* April 22, 1897, p. 84; *Philadelphia Inquirer,* June 29, 1903, p. 10; *American Cricketer,* Oct. 1908, p. 222.
12. "Cricket Season of 1908," p. 486; *American Cricketer,* Oct. 1908, p. 222; *Wisden's Cricketers' Almanack, 1909,* p. 351.
13. *Spalding's Official Cricket Guide, 1909,* p. 7; *Wisden's Cricketers' Almanack 1909,* p. 363; *Philadelphia Inquirer,* July 12, 1908, p, 11.
14. *Public Ledger,* Aug. 21, 1908, p. 12; *Philadelphia Inquirer,* Aug. 23, 1908, p. 11.
15. *Spalding's Official Cricket Guide,* 1909, p. 9; Bowen, *Cricket: A History,* p. 362.
16. *American Cricketer,* Oct. 1908, p. 222; Eric Midwinter, *W.G. Grace, His Life and Times* (London: Allen & Unwin, 1981), pp. 23, 37, 68; *Cricket,* Oct. 29, 1908, p. 437.
17. *Cricket,* Aug. 20, 1908, p. 361; *Philadelphia Inquirer,* Aug. 26, 1908, p. 11.
18. *American Cricketer,* Sept. 1, 1908, p. 195. The 1908 Philadelphians would, nonetheless, find greater success in this, their final first-class England tour, than another emerging cricket nation, India, would in its first tour two years later; Prashant Kidambi, *Cricket Country: A Indian Odyssey in the Age of Empire* (Oxford: Oxford University Press, 2019), pp. 267–288.
19. *Cricket,* July 23, 1908, p. 297.
20. *Wisden's Cricketers' Almanack, 1909,* p. 350; *Fortnightly Review,* Sept. 1908, p. 486; *Boston Herald,* Nov. 25, 1883, p. 3. The second urban legend explaining cricket's disappearance in America lays the blame on the Imperial Cricket Conference for failing to extend Philadelphia an invitation to join that organization on its establishment in 1909. Aside from the fact that there is little evidence that organization, at its inception, seriously considered this idea (*Cricket,* June 17, 1909, p. 194; Aug. 9, 1909, p. 313), and no evidence Philadelphia even desired admission (the *American Cricketer,* the year before, had specifically stated it wouldn't be interested in joining England, Australia, and South Africa for any multi-team event since "cricket in Philadelphia is played because the men taking part in it love it for itself and not because the public demands it" [quoted in *Cricket,* Aug. 6, 1908, p. 330]), it must have, by that time, been apparent to English, Australian and South African cricket authorities that Philadelphia cricket was in decline and any prospect of that city reaching a competitive standard at all comparable to these charter members of the conference was effectively dead (*American Cricketer,* Sept. 1909, p. 203; *Philadelphia Inquirer,* Sept. 18, 1909, p. 11).
21. *American Cricketer,* Sept. 1909, p. 203, *Philadelphia Inquirer,* Sept. 18, 1909, p. 11.
22. *Clipper,* July 5, 1879, p. 114. Philadelphia's monopoly of the annual U.S.-Canada match was more than once the subject of criticism from other major American cricket clubs (*Philadelphia Times,* July 24, 1891, p. 2; *Philadelphia Inquirer,* Aug. 26, 1905, p. 13).
23. Even with no admission charge, the 1900 Canada match played in Philadelphia

was poorly attended (*Philadelphia Inquirer*, Sept. 21, 1900, p. 15).
24. *Philadelphia Times*, Jan. 22, 1891, p. 5; *Philadelphia Inquirer*, June 23, 1905, p. 10; *Cricket*, Aug. 16, 1913, p. 507; Lester, *A Century of Philadelphia Cricket*, p. 253.
25. *American Cricketer*, Jan. 25, 1899, p. 7; March 1925, p. 56; *Philadelphia Inquirer*, March 21, 1909, p. 7.
26. *Philadelphia Inquirer*, Dec. 10, 1910, p. 10.
27. *American Cricketer*, July 1911, p. 148; *Cricket*, Aug. 8, 1914, p. 488.
28. *Cricket*, Aug. 31, 1912, p. 472; Aug. 19, 1911, p. 438; Lester, *A Century of Philadelphia Cricket*, p. 330.
29. *Philadelphia Inquirer*, Sept. 28, 1901, p. 16; Fitzgerald, *Wickets in the West*, p. 244; *Philadelphia Inquirer*, Sept. 21, 1885, p. 3; *Philadelphia Times*, Sept. 22, 1888, p. 4.
30. *Philadelphia Inquirer*, Sept. 22, 1907, p. 13b; *Cricket*, Aug. 26, 1911, p. 464.
31. "Test Match Cricket of 1912," *Blackwood's Magazine*, Dec. 1912, p. 848; Pollard, *The Turbulent Years of Australian Cricket*, p. 251; Harte, *A History of Australian Cricket*, p. 255. There were, however, no reports of misconduct during the Australians' stay in America (*American Cricketer*, Jan. 1913, p. 4).
32. *American Cricketer*, Oct. 1912, p. 246.
33. Ibid., Oct. 1912, p. 247; *Philadelphia Inquirer*, Oct. 5, 1912, p. 2; *American Cricketer*, Oct. 1912, p. 247; *Sun* [Sydney], Sept. 30, 1912, p. 8.
34. Pollard, *The Turbulent Years of Australian Cricket*, p. 264; C.G. McCartney, *My Cricketing Days* (London: Heinemann, 1936) p. 83.
35. *Cricket*, Oct. 18, 1913, p. 673.
36. *Wilkes Barre Times*, Oct. 24, 1918, p. 13; *Schenectady Gazette*, June 24, 1913.
37. *Victorian Daily Times* [Canada], April 8, 1913, p. 8; *Cricket*, May 24, 1913, p. 236; *Calgary Herald*, May 1, 1913, p. 9.
38. *Cricket*, April 19, 1913, p 105. The Australian players, whose North American trip wasn't sanctioned by the Australian Cricket Board, had to sign agreements that their match results during the tour wouldn't be considered officially recognized (Pollard, *The Turbulent Years of Australian Cricket*, p. 266; *American Cricketer*, Feb. 1913, p. 28).

39. *Sydney Morning Herald*, Aug. 20, 1913, p. 5; *Cricket* July 19, 1913, p. 415; Aug. 30, 1913, p. 569.
40. *Cricket*, April 19, 1913, p. 105; *American Cricketer*, July 1913, p. 155; *Philadelphia Inquirer*, July 8, 1913, p. 11.
41. *American Cricketer*, Aug. 1913, p. 194.
42. Lester, *A Century of Philadelphia Cricket*, p. 246.
43. *American Cricketer*, Sept. 1913, p. 195.
44. Lester, *A Century of Philadelphia Cricket*, p. 245.
45. *American Cricketer*, Sept. 1913, p. 195; Lester, *A Century of Philadelphia Cricket*, p. 245; *Cricket*, Aug. 30, 1913, p. 570.
46. *Philadelphia Times*, Dec. 24, 1899, p. 4; *Philadelphia Inquirer*, Aug. 11, 1902, p. 10; *American Cricketer*, Aug. 1, 1908, pp. 171–172.
47. *Philadelphia Inquirer*, June 5, 1889, p. 6; *Philadelphia Times*, March 1, 1894, p. 6; *Philadelphia Inquirer*, Oct. 1, 1897, p. 4.
48. *Philadelphia Times*, April 29, 1888, p. 2; *Philadelphia Inquirer*, May 4, 1890, p. 7.
49. *Philadelphia Times*, Oct. 1, 1895, p. 9; *Philadelphia Inquirer*, July 29, 1903, p. 4; *Times* [London], Aug. 28, 1908, p. 7; *Clipper*, Oct. 1, 1882, p. 501; *Philadelphia Times*, Oct. 2, 1897, p. 8; *Philadelphia Inquirer*, Oct. 10, 1899, p. 5. This problem also plagued Halifax Cup matches, an important game between arch-rivals Germantown and Belmont finishing prematurely when the last batter had to leave before the match could be completed (*Philadelphia Times*, Sept. 1, 1890, p. 2).
50. *New York Tribune*, Sept. 5, 1885, p. 4.
51. *Philadelphia Inquirer*, Aug. 23, 1896, p. 6.
52. *Spalding's Official Cricket Guide*, 1904, p. 49; *Philadelphia Inquirer*, June 9, 1906, p. 11; April 27, 1908, p. 10.
53. *Philadelphia Inquirer*, March 28, 1909, p. 7.
54. Ibid., Sept. 12, 1909, p. 22; *American Cricketer*, Sept. 1915, p. 209.
55. *Clipper*, July 21, 1900, p. 459. Of the fifty matches Germantown scheduled in 1912, none were against Interstate or St. George league clubs (*Philadelphia Inquirer*, May 7, 1912, p. 12).

56. Leopard, *Philadelphia and North American Cricket*, p. 7; Marder, *The International Series*, pp. 232, 264.
57. *Philadelphia Inquirer*, June 27, 1905, p. 10; Aug. 22, 1911, p. 10; Lester, *A Century of Philadelphia Cricket*, p. 211.
58. *Cricket*, April 21, 1910, p. 78; Lester, *A Century of Philadelphia Cricket*, p. 211; *Philadelphia Inquirer*, Sept. 3, 1908, p. 6; Marder, *The International Series*, p. 253; *Spalding's Official Cricket Guide, 1910*, p. 27.
59. *Philadelphia Inquirer*, Sept. 17, 1903, p. 10; June 7, 1903, p. 11; *World* [New York], Sept. 24, 1903, p. 7; *Illustrated Sporting News*, Oct. 17, 1903, p. 14.
60. Lester, *A Century of Philadelphia Cricket*, p. 221.
61. *Philadelphia Inquirer*, March 7, 1909, p. 27; Aug. 24, 1909, p. 6; Marder, *The International Series*, pp. 258, 261; *Cricket*, Aug. 24, 1912, p. 456.
62. *American Cricketer*, Oct. 1909, p. 232.
63. *Philadelphia Inquirer*, Sept. 12, 1890, p. 3; *Philadelphia Times*, Sept. 27, 1891, p. 4.
64. *Ball Players' Chronicle*, June 30, 1867, p. 5; *The Cricketers Association of the United States. Proceedings of Convention Held in Philadelphia, April 17, 1878 and Constitution and Rules* (Philadelphia, 1878), p. 5.
65. *Clipper*, Dec. 12, 1885, p. 619; *Philadelphia Inquirer*, April 12, 1889, p. 6; April 12, 1890, p. 2.
66. *Philadelphia Inquirer*, March 10, 1891, p. 3; *American Cricketer*, Feb. 16, 1903, p. 24.
67. The suggestion, made in 1890, that the Gentlemen of Philadelphia should embark on a national tour to popularize the game "with the general public" was never acted upon (*Philadelphia Inquirer*, March 6, 1890, p. 6).
68. *New York Herald*, March 23, 1885, p. 3; *Philadelphia Inquirer*, June 20, 1887; *Cricket*, Aug. 5, 1911, p. 404. The local Philadelphia press itself urged city cricket authorities to send city teams to play clubs in other areas of the country (*Philadelphia Inquirer*, Oct. 19, 1890, p. 2).
69. *Clipper*, May 9, 1885, p. 115; *Daily Evening Bulletin* [Philadelphia], April 1, 1870, p. 3; *Philadelphia Times*, April 13, 1884, p. 2; *Philadelphia Inquirer*, July 20, 1885, p. 3; *Chicago Tribune*, July 19, 1885, p. 10.
70. *Philadelphia Inquirer*, Aug. 1, 1887, p. 3; *Detroit Free Press*, July 14, 1887, p. 8; *Philadelphia Inquirer*, Aug. 6, 1891, p. 8; July 13, 1890, p. 5; Aug. 8, 1899, p. 4; *American Cricketer*, July 10, 1910, p. 147; *Philadelphia Inquirer*, June 15, 1909, p. 6.
71. *Philadelphia Inquirer*, Sept. 10, 1911, p. 8; *Oregon Daily Journal*, Sept. 9, 1911, p. 9; Jones, "The History of Cricket in Oregon, 1870s-1920," p. 287; Lester, *A Century of Philadelphia Cricket*, p. 238; *Spalding's Official Cricket Guide, 1912*, p. 65.
72. *American Cricketer*, Aug. 15, 1904, p. 56; *Cricket*, July 1, 1911, p. 278; *Philadelphia Inquirer*, July 6, 1910, p. 11; *American Cricketer*, Aug. 1910, p. 171. With cricket having made a cameo appearance at the 1900 Paris Olympics, and the 1908 games to be held in cricket-playing Britain, a successful exhibition at the 1904 St. Louis Olympics could possibly have launched the game onto a path of extended, perhaps even permanent, presence in the Olympic Games.
73. *Philadelphia Inquirer*, Aug. 8, 1899, p. 4
74. *Philadelphia Times*, Aug. 3, 1884, p. 4.

Chapter Twelve

1. Quoted in *Cricket*, May 25, 1905, p. 154; Lester, *A Century of Philadelphia Cricket*, p. 207.
2. *Cricket*, Aug. 31, 1905, pp. 369–370.
3. *Daily Pennsylvanian*, May 22, 1906, p. 1; *Haverford News*, June 2, 1914, p. 3.
4. *College Weekly* [Haverford College], May 27, 1911, p. 4; *Cornell Daily Sun*, Jan. 5, 1904, p. 1; Feb. 26, 1913, p. 1.
5. *American Cricketer*, July 1913, p. 166; *College Weekly* [Haverford College], June 13, 1913, p.4.
6. *Daily Pennsylvanian*, Feb. 24, 1904, p. 1.
7. *Daily Pennsylvanian*, March 23, 1911, p. 1; April 2, 1912, p. 3; May 6, 1922, p. 1; *Public Ledger*, June 18, 1920, p. 16. The University Athletic Association reduced its funding for the cricket team from $813 in 1913 to a mere $50 the following year

(*Daily Pennsylvanian*, Dec. 10, 1913, p. 1; Dec. 17, 1914, p. 1).

8. *College Weekly* [Haverford College], Feb. 22, 1909, p. 1; April 4, 1910, p. 2; *American Cricketer*, June 1915, p. 125.

9. *College Weekly* [Haverford College], July 11, 1910, p. 1; *American Cricketer*, Sept. 1910, p. 198; *Spalding's Official Cricket Guide, 1911*, p. 11; *Haverford News*, Oct. 6, 1914, p. 4.

10. *Philadelphia Times*, Feb. 13, 1901, p. 9.

11. *American Cricketer*, Jan. 15, 1902, p. 8; *Cricket*, April 12, 1900, p. 61; Lester, *A Century of Philadelphia Cricket*, p. 177.

12. *American Cricketer*, Jan. 15, 1902, p. 3; Lester, *A Century of Philadelphia Cricket*, pp. 365–366.

13. *Philadelphia Times*, Dec. 13, 1896, p. 22.

14. *New York Tribune*, Dec. 23, 1898, p. 4; *Clipper*, Nov. 26, 1898, p. 664; *Philadelphia Inquirer*, Feb. 21, 1911, p. 2; April 16, 1911, p. 19; Feb. 16, 1913, p. 11; *Public Ledger*, Dec. 17, 1915, p. 15.

15. *Philadelphia Inquirer*, May 21, 1913, p. 2; *Philadelphia Board of Recreation Annual Report, 1913*, p. 6; *American Cricketer*, March 1913, p. 53; *Philadelphia Inquirer*, Jan. 26, 1914, p. 12.

16. *American Cricketer*, Jan. 1912, p. 4.

17. *Philadelphia Inquirer*, June 23, 1910, p. 8.

18. Lester, *A Century of Philadelphia Cricket*, p. 207.

19. *American Cricketer*, Dec. 1910, p. 267; *Public Ledger*, Dec. 6, 1917, p. 10; *Philadelphia Inquirer*, Nov. 1, 1888, p. 2; *Cricket Club Life*, Feb. 1900, p. 8; *Philadelphia Inquirer*, Sept. 7, 1913, p. 1; Lester, *A Century of Philadelphia Cricket*, p. 275.

20. *Philadelphia Inquirer*, Oct. 9, 1901, p. 8.

21. *Haverfordian*, Jan. 1898, p. 99; *Outing*, Oct. 1884, p. 48; Newhall, "The Cricket Grounds of Germantown and a Plea for the Game," p. 190.

22. *New York Times*, Aug. 21, 1903, p. 8.

23. *Outing*, Oct. 1884, p. 48; *Philadelphia Times*, Sept. 13, 1885, p. 7; *American Cricketer*, June 1, 1881, p. 161.

24. [Green], *The Tour of the "Gentlemen of Philadelphia,"* pp. 17–18; *Illustrated Sporting News*, Oct. 17, 1903, p. 18; *Philadelphia Times*, Oct. 5, 1879, p. 3; *Cricket*, Oct. 26, 1897, p. 445.

25. *Wilkes' Spirit of the Times*, June 6, 1874, p. 414; *Omaha World Herald*, Sept. 26, 1897, p. 20.

26. *American Cricketer*, Nov. 24, 1884, p. 221; April 13, 1913, p. 78; Dec. 15, 1902, p. 257.

27. *New York Times*, Sept. 20, 1885, p. 8.

28. *Detroit Free Press*, July 20, 1882, p. 1; *American Cricketer*, Oct. 5, 1882, pp. 176, 181; *Clipper*, June 8, 1872, p. 75; *International Cricket Fete, 1872, Official Hand Book* (Philadelphia: J.B. Lippincott, 1872) p. 47.

29. *Philadelphia Inquirer*, May 4, 1885, p. 3; May 7, 1890, p. 6; April 29, 1892, p. 3; *American Cricketer*, May 18, 1895, p. 34; *Spalding's Official Cricket Guide, 1912*, p. 43; *Cricket*, Aug. 31, 1912, p. 472; *American Cricketer*, April 1922, p. 60; June 15, 1915, p. 125.

30. *Outing*, June 3, 1888, p. 262; *Philadelphia Inquirer*, April 14, 1888, p. 2; *Public Ledger*, April 6, 1896, p. 21.

31. *Philadelphia Inquirer*, April 12, 1889, p. 6; Aug. 9, 1884, p. 2; *Clipper*, July 25, 1868, p. 125; *American Cricketer*, July 1915, p. 151; *Philadelphia Inquirer*, May 4, 1885, p. 3; *New York Times*, July 10, 1893, p. 2.

32. *Sporting Life*, May 6, 1885, p. 9; *American Cricketer*, May 21, 1885, p. 19; *Clipper*, May 30, 1874, p. 67; Dec. 20, 1879, p. 309.

33. *Clipper*, July 23, 1870, p. 125; *Philadelphia Inquirer*, July 26, 1905, p. 13.

34. *American Cricketer*, July 1911, p. 151.

35. Dan Newhall, *How to Play Cricket: A Manual for American Cricketers* (Dando, 1881), pp. 31–38.

36. *Philadelphia Inquirer*, July 27, 1875, p. 2; *Cricketers Association of the United States*, pp. 11–13; *Philadelphia Inquirer*, April 14, 1886, p. 2; May 6, 1900, p. 14.

37. *Philadelphia Record*, Aug. 9, 1885, p. 7; *Outing*, June 1890, p. 228; *Philadelphia Inquirer*, April 2, 1890, p. 6; Patterson, "Cricket in the United States," p. 658; *Philadelphia Inquirer*, April 7, 1890, p. 7; *Cricket*, April 14, 1890, p. 75.

38. *Haverfordian*, April 1890, p. 174; "Cricket at Harvard," *Outing*, Aug. 1890, p. 416. The author has also used a modified version of the "American Plan" with some success when working with Americans at cricket.

39. *Public Ledger,* March 28, 1911, p. 6; *Cricket,* Aug. 18, 1910, p. 343.

40. Newhall, *How to Play Cricket,* p. 38. It may not be entirely farfetched to see in the "Average System" a crude forerunner of the Duckworth-Lewis formula used to determine rain-delayed matches in contemporary cricket.

41. *Philadelphia Times,* March 9, 1890, p. 4; *Cricket,* Nov. 26, 1903, p. 450; *Philadelphia Times,* March 16, 1890, p. 3.

42. *American Cricketer,* July 1911, p. 147.

43. Newhall, *How to Play Cricket,* p. 31.

44. *Clipper,* May 22, 1858, p. 36; *Turf, Field & Farm,* Oct. 16, 1868, p. 680; *Philadelphia Inquirer,* Oct. 6, 1904, p. 10. For the practice games in 1860 of the American Cricket Club, a New York team composed mostly of baseball players, and for the Haverford alumni game in 1901, the players' time at bat was limited to fifteen total runs (*New York Leader,* Sept. 22, 1860, p. 8; *Haverfordian,* Oct. 1901, p. 95.

45. *American Cricketer,* March 24, 1881, p, 96; May 15, 1915, p. 99; *Haverfordian,* June 1886, p. 166; Patterson, "Cricket in the United States," p. 658.

46. *Cricket,* Aug. 21, 1902, p. 363; *Philadelphia Times,* Sept. 28, 1897, p. 6; *American Cricketer,* July 1915, p. 151; Nov. 1920, p. 963.

47. *Philadelphia Times,* Aug. 11, 1895, p. 6; Aug. 24, 1893, p. 6; *Philadelphia Inquirer,* Feb. 10, 1902, p. 10. Kirsch has shown, with his statistical analysis, that during the Civil War era many Philadelphia cricketers also resided in the city's 7th and 8th wards (Kirsch, *Baseball and Cricket,* pp. 128, 153).

48. *Philadelphia Times,* Jan. 30, 1887, p. 12; *Philadelphia Tribune,* May 3, 1913, p. 7; *Philadelphia Inquirer,* June 27, 1897, p. 23.

49. Newhall, "The Cricket Grounds of Germantown and a Pleas for the Game," p. 183; *Cricket,* Oct. 29, 1885, p. 439; *Philadelphia Times,* Sept. 23, 1891, p. 8.

50. *Philadelphia Times,* Aug. 7, 1887, p. 13; John S. White, "The New Athletics," *Proceedings of the American Association for the Advancement of Physical Education,* no. 3 (1889), p. 52.

51. *Sun* [New York], Sept. 2, 1888, p. 7; Aug. 23, 1895, p. 4; "The Outdoor Woman," *Harper's Bazar,* Nov. 23, 1896, p. 947; *Philadelphia Inquirer,* Aug. 19, 1895, p. 5. Lester makes no mention of women's cricket.

52. *American Cricketer,* Aug. 12, 1891, p. 134; *Philadelphia Inquirer,* July 18, 1891, p. 1.

53. *Philadelphia Times,* Oct. 9, 1898, p. 9; *Philadelphia Inquirer,* June 13, 1899, p. 4.

54. *Philadelphia Inquirer,* Oct. 9, 1898, p. 9; *History of Physical Education in Colleges for Women* (New York: Barnes, 1930), p, 29. Bryn Mawr reportedly had a women's cricket team as early as 1892 (*Philadelphia Inquirer,* June 12, 1892, p. 13).

55. *Philadelphia Inquirer,* June 12, 1897, p. 13; Lester, *A Century of Philadelphia Cricket,* p. 169.

56. *American Cricketer,* July 1921, p. 144; Aug. 1913, p. 188; *Sydney Morning Herald,* Aug. 22, 1913, p. 3; *Cricket,* Aug. 16, 1913, p. 507; *American Cricketer,* Jan. 1914, p. 5.

57. *American Cricketer,* Sept. 11, 1911, p. 195.

58. *Spalding's Official Cricket Guide,* 1911, p. 11; *American Cricketer,* Aug. 1913, pp. 188, 194.

59. *American Cricketer,* Dec. 1919, p. 656.

60. *Philadelphia Inquirer,* March 16, 1915, p. 10; *Public Ledger,* March 28, 1917, p. 5; *American Cricketer,* May 1916, p. 132; *Philadelphia Inquirer,* April 11, 1916, p. 12; May 5, 1916, p. 15; *Public Ledger,* June 11, 1917, p. 11.

61. Lester, *A Century of Philadelphia Cricket,* p. 91.

62. *Public Ledger,* April 20, 1918, p. 17; *William Penn Charter Record,* 1905, p. 97; *Cricket,* April 20, 1899, p. 71.

63. *American Cricketer,* July 15, 1915, p. 156; March 1920, p. 739; *Public Ledger,* April 28, 1922, p. 25; *William Penn Charter Record,* 1923, p. 78.

64. *Philadelphia Inquirer,* April 16, 1916, p. 8; Lester, *A Century of Philadelphia Cricket,* p. 250; *American Cricketer,* Oct. 1913, p, 252.

65. *Cricket,* Oct. 25, 1906, p. 447; *American Cricketer,* Oct. 1913, p. 255; *Public Ledger,* Oct. 20, 1919, p. 16; Lester, *A Century of Philadelphia Cricket,* p. 252.

66. *American Cricketer,* June 15, 1915, pp. 125, 126; Sept. 1915, p. 209; *Philadelphia Inquirer,* March 16, 1915, p. 10.

67. Lester, *A Century of Philadelphia*

Cricket, p. 252; *Sporting Life*, May 20, 1916, p. 26; *American Cricketer*, March 1921, p. 32.
    68. *American Cricketer*, Sept. 1913, p. 223; *Philadelphia Inquirer*, Jan. 26, 1921, p. 11; *American Cricketer*, Dec. 1919, pp, 662–663; Marder, *The International Series*, p. 89. Other prominent early Philadelphia cricketers who died during this decade included Spencer Meade (1912) and A. Charles Barclay (1919) (*American Cricketer*, Oct. 1912, p. 244; *Philadelphia Inquirer*, June 8, 1919, p. 78).
    69. *American Cricketer*, Sept. 1915, p. 207; July 1916, p. 205.
    70. *Public Ledger*, Sept. 13, 1920, p. 15; *American Cricketer*, Dec. 1918, p. 335; Dec. 1924, p. 268.
    71. *Public Ledger*, Sept. 6, 1920, p. 15; Lester, *A Century of Philadelphia Cricket*, p. 259; Harte, *A History of Australian Cricket*, p. 347. The "Bodyline" incident occurred in the England-Australia cricket series of 1932/33, the English bowlers, in an attempt to restrict the Australian batters, bowling at their leg stump ("tight inside"), resulting in a number of Australian batters being hit (Birley, *A Social History of English Cricket*, pp. 236–238). Though Lester was well aware that Jardine had been on the Incogniti when the team visited Philadelphia in 1920, he makes no mention of the Englishman's involvement with the "Bodyline" episode.
    72. *American Cricketer*, Sept. 1921, pp. 199, 208; Lester, *A Century of Philadelphia Cricket*, p. 344; *Philadelphia Inquirer*, Sept. 6, 1920, p. 9.
    73. *Philadelphia Inquirer*, Sept. 6, 1920, p. 8.
    74. Graham, *Cricket at the University of Pennsylvania*, p. 149; *Daily Pennsylvanian*, March 4, 1920, p. 1; *Philadelphia Inquirer*, April 25, 1922, p. 19; *Daily Pennsylvanian*, April 12, 1924, p. 1; Graham, *Cricket at the University of Pennsylvania*, p. 149; *Daily Pennsylvanian*, May 9, 1924, p. 6; Graham, *Cricket at the University of Pennsylvania*, p. 5.
    75. *Haverford News*, Jan. 11, 1926, p. 3; *Philadelphia Inquirer*, Dec. 24, 1921, p. 13.
    76. *Haverford News*, Sept. 25, 1925, pp. 1, 4.
    77. Ibid., May 13, 1929, p. 3; May 13, 1941, p. 6.
    78. *Philadelphia Inquirer*, Dec. 24, 1921, p. 13.
    79. Lester, *A Century of Philadelphia Cricket*, p. 218; *American Cricketer*, July 1927, p. 162; *Philadelphia Inquirer*, Sept. 18, 1921, p 21.
    80. *American Cricketer*, Oct. 1928, p. 28; *Philadelphia Inquirer*, May 23, 1921, p. 12.
    81. *American Cricketer*, April 1929, p. 99; *Public Ledger*, May 26, 1922, p. 20.

Epilogue

    1. *Spirit of the Times*, Oct. 26, 1839, p. 397.
    2. *Clipper*, Sept. 7, 1861, p. 164.
    3. Harry Palmer, ed., *Athletic Sports in America, England, and Australia* (Philadelphia: Thubbard, 1889), p. 683.
    4. Robert Minton, *One Hundred Years of Longwood* (Lynn: Zimman, 1971), p. 3.
    5. Valarie Brooks, "It Is So Cricket," *Philadelphia Magazine*, July 1983, p. 85.
    6. G.W.F. Hegel, quoted in Rolf Saltzer, ed., *German Essays in History* (New York: Continuum, 1991), p. 68; Henry Pleasants, "When Philadelphia Played Cricket," *Philadelphia Forum*, May 1947, p. 14; George Wharton Pepper, *Philadelphia Lawyer* (Philadelphia: J.B. Lippincott, 1944), p. 27; Lester, *A Century of Philadelphia Cricket*, p. 208. Sadly, the cricket world let pass the 150th anniversary of this important cricket event in 2009 without any commemoration.
    7. Henry Sayen, *A Yankee Looks at Cricket* (London: Putnam, 1956), p. 2.
    8. *Kent Messenger*, July 19, 1957.
    9. Burckhardt, *Reflections on History*, p. 314; www.theguardian.com/sport/2000/aug/09/cricket6.
    10. *Cricketer*, Nov. 1965, p. 31; "Obituary: John Barton King," *Cricket Quarterly*, vol. IV (1966), p. 61.
    11. *American Cricketer*, March 23, 1923, p. 27.

Appendix

    1. Belfield was one of the stronger non-Halifax cricket clubs, admitted to that competition for a single season in 1898 (Lester, *A Century of Philadelphia Cricket*, p. 365).
    2. "Woodie," i.e., Arthur Wood, the captain of King's Belmont club.

3. Hugh Trumble, standout Australian bowler of the late 19th century.

4. Probably a reference to either R.C.N. Palairet's innings of 66 in Somerset's match against the Philadelphians in 1897 or his more famous brother Lionel's second innings 46 against the Philadelphians in 1903.

5. One of India's princely states, today the state of Jamnagar.

6. In cricket there's no penalty if the bowler hits the batter with the ball.

Bibliographic Essay

Anyone approaching the subject of Philadelphia cricket or, for that matter, the history of American cricket in general must begin with, and owes a deep sense of gratitude to, John Lester's *A Century of Philadelphia Cricket* (University of Pennsylvania Press, 1951). Written by an individual intimately involved with Philadelphia cricket at the height of its popularity as player, observer and critic, the work stands not only as a thorough and detailed record of cricket's rise, growth and decline in the city but also a deeply personal testimony to the depth of loyalty the game inspired among its most conscientious followers. For close to seventy years, the work stood as the sole and solitary monograph on the subject, without which this unique chapter in American sports would have been effectively effaced from history.

For all the popularity cricket enjoyed in its city, the Philadelphia cricket community left surprisingly few in-depth personal accounts of its game, which only augments the value of Lester's work with its inclusion of a number of personal reminiscences from some of the most influential figures in Philadelphia cricket, such as King, Percy Clark and C.C. Morris.

These firsthand accounts are complemented by W. Henry Sayen's work, published a few years after Lester, *A Yankee Looks at Cricket* (Putnam, 1956). Narrated by a teammate of Lester's on the Gentlemen of Philadelphia team that toured England in 1908, the work provides a personal glimpse into the world of Philadelphia cricket in the early 20th century.

For his information on early Philadelphia cricket, Lester, like every student of the subject since, relied heavily upon W.R. Wister's *Some Reminiscences of Cricket in Philadelphia Before 1861* (Allen, Lane & Scott, 1904). Though relating incidents half a century after the fact, the work provides the most detailed account of Philadelphia cricket during its formative antebellum years.

Invaluable as all three of these sources are, it should always be remembered that the voice of proper, strictly Halifax Cup, Philadelphia society is speaking here. It was a segment of the Philadelphia cricket community that operated, for all its strength and weaknesses, as a strictly defined social world that's thoroughly examined by E. Digby Baltzell in his *The Philadelphia Gentlemen: The Making of a National Upper Class* (Quadrangle Books, 1971).

By far the most significant single source for information on Philadelphia cricket and cricket in the United States in general after the 1870s is the *American Cricketer* magazine. In this now rare and hard-to-find serial (the C.C. Morris

Cricket Library and the Pennsylvania Historical Society are the only public institutions known to hold a complete run of the periodical) is to be found, over its 52-year existence, the most complete record of the games, clubs, teams, people and opinions that made up the world of Philadelphia cricket.

Supplementing this American publication is England's leading cricket periodical of the era, *Cricket: A Weekly Record of the Game*. Founded and edited by C.W. Alcock, himself a lifelong supporter and well-wisher of Philadelphia cricket, the periodical carried frequent and, at times, extensive reports on American cricket up to its demise in 1914.

No less significant than these periodicals for insight into Philadelphia cricket were the city's daily newspapers of the period (*Philadelphia Inquirer, Philadelphia Times, Public Ledger*) that provided extensive, in-depth coverage of the sport, coverage that for a period in the early 1890s was comparable to, and even surpassed, the *American Cricketer*.

The story of cricket at the University of Pennsylvania has been well served both with Archibald Graham's standalone work, *Cricket at the University of Pennsylvania* (privately printed, 1930), and in the more comprehensive histories of the university's athletics (Edward Bushnell, ed., *A History of Athletics at Pennsylvania, 1873–1908* [Philadelphia, 1909]).

Surprisingly, there exists no standalone work on the history of Haverford College cricket, though the subject receives extensive attention in the general histories of the college: Philip C. Garrett, ed., *History of Haverford College for the First Sixty Years of Its Existence* (Porter & Coates, 1892) and Rufus Jones, *Haverford College: A History and Interpretation* (Macmillan, 1933).

The history of cricket not only in Philadelphia but America in general has always been, and probably always will be, something of a neglected stepchild in the eyes of sports historians, a subject of limited interest from American scholars because it's cricket, of limited interest to foreign scholars because it's American.

Despite this, a flurry of publications in the late 1980s and early 1990s prominently brought this subject to the attention of the scholarly and lay communities, principally through the ground-breaking publication of Melvin Adelman, *A Sporting Time: New York and the Rise of Modern Athletics, 1820–1870* (University of Illinois Press, 1986) and George B. Kirsch, *Baseball and Cricket: The Creation of American Team Sports, 1838–72* (University of Illinois Press, 1989). These were augmented by a number of scholarly articles by J. Thomas Jable specifically analyzing the social composition of the Philadelphia cricket community.

This void in interest from the scholarly community has been partially filled by popular-oriented works by non-academics such as Tom Melville, *The Tented Field: A History of Cricket in America* (Popular Press, 1998), P. David Sentance, *Cricket in America 1710–2000* (McFarland, 2006) and Jayesh Patel, *Flannels on the Sward: History of Cricket in the Americas* (privately printed, 2014). Authored, for the most part, because of personal subject interest, these works, however, vary greatly in originality and analytic rigor.

Under much the same circumstances the subject of American cricket has also attracted the attention of other non-academic authors such as Scott Reeves, *The Champion Band: The First England Cricket Tour* (Chequered Flag, 2014), David Beaumont, *From Third Man to Third Base; Richard Daft's Tour to Canada and USA in 1879* (Russell, 2015) and Stephen Musk and Roger Mann's *Bart King of Philadelphia* (Matador, 2022). Largely narrative rather than analytic in their treatment, with an emphasis on statistics and playing technique, all these works, nonetheless, provide useful information and insight into what still remains a yet to be fully appreciated area of American sports history.

Index

Abel, Bobby 99
Adams, "Doc" 204n5
Adelman, Melvin 199n4
Afro-Americans, and cricket 179
Alcock, C.W. 232
All-American Cricket Team (1890) 68–69
All-England cricket team, 1859 23, 24, 28, 29, 33, 74, 181
Altemus family 24
Altham, Harry 130
Altoona, PA 166
amateurism 79
American Cricket Club 228n44
American Cricketer 50, 68, 69, 137, 187
"American Plan" 176, 177
Amherst College 24
Americans vs. English 25–26, 27, 55
Anderson, Bobby 180, 185
Anson, Cap 68
Aris, Francis 169
Ashland Cricket Club 35
Associated Cricket Clubs 35
Astoria, OR 138
Athletics Baseball Club 34, 36, 56
Atlantic Cricket Club 35, 36, 102
Australia 126; 1878 team 62, 76; 1882 team 53, 77; 1893 team 105–109, 217n8; 1896 team 108–109; 1912 team 156–157, 225n30; 1913 team 94, 157–159, 225n37
"Average System" 176, 177, 228n40

Bachelor Cricket Club 36
Bailey, Henry 70
Bainbridge, H.W. 113
Baker, Daniel 137
Baker, F.W. 129
ball playing, early American 16
Baltimore 9, 19, 88, 100, 170
Baltzel, E.D. 121
Band of Brothers 185
Barclay, A. Charles 23

Bardsley, Warren 157
Barnes, Syd 99
baseball 2, 10, 14, 34, 36, 132, 169, 175
Bates, Fred 93, 114, 215n49
Belfield Cricket Club 84, 119
Belmont Cricket Club 24, 54, 59, 84, 118, 120, 163, 166, 170–171
Benjamin, R.B. 157, 158, 180
Bennett, R.A. 97
Bermuda 100, 155
Biddle, Lynford 114
Blackham, John 76, 106
Blackheath 156
"bodyline" series 184, 229n71
Bohlen, Frank 40, 51, 70, 90–91, 105, 108, 139, 161, 214n35
Bosanquet, Bernard 96, 140, 145
Boston commons 24
Boston Cricket Club 14
Boston Red Stockings 40
Bowen, Roland 83
Bradshaw, William 20, 26
Braithwaite, Charles 53
Braund, Len 145, 180
Brewster, Frank 121
Bromhead, George 53, 55
Brown, Hazen 76
Brown, Henry 95
Brown, Reynolds 51, 70, 161
Bryn Mawr College 180, 228n54
Burckhardt, Jacob 43
Burnup, C.J. 96

California 165, 166
Camac Woods 29, 36
Cambridge University 112, 142
Camden Baseball Club 35
Camden Cricket Club 35
Campbell, G.C. 130
Canfield, Lionel 145
Cardew, A.E. 130

235

236 Index

Carncross Theatre 103
Carvill, William 130
Cassett, A.J. 121
C.C. Morris Library 190
Central High School (Philadelphia) 94, 124, 219n27, 220n34
Central Manuel Training School 125
Chadwick, Henry 30, 31, 32, 176
Charleston 9
Charterhouse school 129
Chestnut Hill 87, 180
Chicago 69, 166
Childs Cup 55, 101
Chinnery, H.B. 116
Chippewa Cricket Club 35
Civil War, and cricket 205n15
Clark, Edward 109, 116
Clark, H.L. 114
Clark, Percy 51, 70, 101–102, 109, 157, 158, 187
Clay, Richard 24
Cleveland 99, 138, 166
Climenson, Silas 94
Club Record Cup 55, 120
Cobb, M.R. 69
Colahan, John 51
Collis, C.N. 35, 121
Columbia University 128
Conway, John 76, 212n21
Conyers, Gregg 163
Conyers, Reggie 163, 164
Cope, Henry 134
Cornell University 128, 168
Cornish, H.H. 156
Cregar, Eddie 94, 144, 183
Creighton, James 30, 92
Crowhurst, Ernest 68
Cuppitt, R.C. 65

Daft, Richard 52, 53, 74, 78, 106
Dale, Tom 65
Darling, Joe 97, 108
Dartmouth University 12
Davis, J. 26
Davis, J.C. 69
Delancey School 125
Delphian Cricket Club 21, 23
Derbyshire CCC 98, 140, 153
Detroit 65, 139, 166
Dickinson, Emily 12
Doesticks 40
double plays (baseball) 175
Douglas, J.W. 97
Doyle, A.C. 135
Drexel Institute 126
Duce, F.N. 112

Duckworth-Lewis method 228n40
Dudson, Sam 11, 13, 25
Duhring, Warren 93
Duluth, MN 138
Dupont, William 166
Durham CCC 152, 153

Eakins, Thomas 51
Edmonton 158
Eisenbray, N.W. 138
elites 37, 120–122, 219n14
Ellis, Rudolph 121
Elysian Fields (Hoboken) 19
Empire Cricket Club 23
Enterprise Cricket Club 35
Episcopal Academy (Philadelphia) 124, 125
Essex CCC 156
Etting, Newbold 161
Ewing, Maskell 59, 121
Excelsior Cricket Club 24
Eyre, C.H. 97

Facon, Thomas 20, 32
Faire's Classical School 124
Fairservice, Bill 192
Federal Baseball League 170
Fitzgerald, Robert 42, 56, 93
Fordham 12
Foulkrod, William 51, 163
Frankford Cricket Club 51, 166, 170
Frankford High School 125, 182
Franklin Field 128
Free Academy (New York) 18, 26, 30, 32
Free Foresters 156
French, John 26, 92, 137
Friends Select School 125
Frye, C.B. 99
Furness, Harold 192, 170

Gentlemen of Philadelphia 121; 1884 team 66, 73, 79–80; 1889 team 66, 82, 164; 1897 team 73, 110–115; 1903 team 223n33; 1908 team 55, 91, 149–150, 224n6; name adopted 54
Germantown Academy 124, 125, 126
Germantown Cricket Club 21, 23, 27, 36, 58, 60, 68, 84, 119, 126; 1911 tour 155, 159, 178
Germantown High School 125
Gibbsboro Cricket Club 119
Giffen, George 98, 109
Gilbert, F.M. 96
Girard Cricket Club 60, 64, 209n8
Glamorganshire CCC 144, 145
Gloucestershire CCC 80, 112, 144

Godfrey, Lincoln 121
golf 119, 171
Goodall, Herbert 181
googlie bowling 129, 145
Gordon, John 163, 164
Grace, W.G. 56, 62, 68, 80, 91, 110, 112, 140, 153, 156
Graffen, S.M. 23
Graham, Charles 129
Grand Rapids, MI 138
Graves, Nelson 141, 142, 145
Green, Frank 149, 159
Green, John P. 24, 51, 59, 105, 121, 138, 172, 183
Gregory, David 76
Gregory, Syd 99
Griscom, C.A. 121
Groom, A.G. 181
Gunn, William 99, 113

Haddonfield Cricket Club 119, 135
Haigh, Scofield 113, 153
Haileybury school 186
Haines, Harold 139, 143
Halifax Cup 22, 54, 84, 119, 120, 123, 162, 187
Hamden, NY 199n6
Hammond, William 21, 51, 55
Hampshire CCC 100, 153
Hargreaves family 60, 64, 65, 173, 209n9, 210n28, 210n30, 212n30
Harrington, Eliott 24
Harris, Lord 52, 72, 73, 75, 78, 81, 153, 160, 185
Harrisburg, PA 166
Harrison, Charles 121, 130
Harrow school 129
Harvard University 12, 127, 168
Haverford College 91, 126, 130–135, 166, 169–170, 172, 186
Haverford Grammar School 124
Hawke, Lord 102, 106, 111, 216n85
Hayward, Tom 146
Helliwell, J. 13
Higginson, T.W. 12
Hinchman, Walter 214n35
Hirst, George 96, 113
Hirst Cup 120
Holder, John 25
Hordern, Herbert 97, 99, 129, 130, 149, 164, 216n66
Hornby, A.N. 113
Houston, Henry 87, 121, 180
Howitt, R.H. 97
Huntington Manor Cricket Club 138

Imperial Cricket Conference 224n20
Incogniti (cricket team) 102, 183
India 116, 224n18
Interacademic Athletic Association 124
Intercollegiate Cricket Association 128, 168
Interscholastic Athletic Association 125, 182
Interstate League 162, 183, 225n54
Irish cricketers 153; 1879 team 54, 79; 1888 team 66, 81; 1892 team 105; 1909 team 154
Irving, F.C. 93

Jable, J. Thomas 20, 121
Jackson, F. Stanley 99, 111
Jackson, H.L. 153
Jackson, Isaac 26, 137
Jackson Cricket Club 23
Jamaica 155, 164
James, C.L.R. 206n26, 209n9
James, Henry 136
Jardine, Douglas 184, 229n71
Jarvis, William 19, 202n8
Jenkintown Cricket Club 119
Jephson, W.V. 97, 113
Jessop, Gilbert 93, 98, 112, 116
Johns, W.P. 24
Jones, Ernest 109
Jump, George 94

Kansas City 138
Kelleway, Charles 97
Kensington (Philadelphia) 10, 50, 179
Kensington Cricket Club 19
Kent CCC 100, 112, 144, 148, 153, 163, 192
Kephardt, Sylvanus 21, 24, 36, 203n35
Keyes, J.J. 138
Keystone Cricket Club 22, 23, 35
K.I.B.A. 99, 119
Kimball, F.J. 121
King, John B. 70, 93, 94–101, 110, 114, 116, 150–153, 154, 157, 161, 183, 192, 215n55, 215n58, 215n61; bowling to empty field 216n81
Kingston, Henry H. 121
Kirsch, George 228n47
Knickerbocker Baseball Club 34, 41, 206n29
Kortlang, Bernie 163, 164

Lacy, F.E. 113
Ladd, William 200n10
Lancashire CCC 99, 113, 144–145, 224n2
Landis, Henry 121
lbw law (cricket) 174

238　　　　　　　　　　　　　Index

Leach, Eddie 163
Leavenworth, KS 139
Leicestershire CCC 91, 144, 145
Lester, John 51, 67, 91–92, 112, 126, 134, 144, 182, 199n7, 203n30
Lillywhite, Fred 28
Lillywhite Cricket Club 60
Linden Cricket Club 119, 209n8
Longwood Cricket Club 88
Louisville 9
Lowry, William 81, 161
Lycett, E.H. 138
Lyons, James G. 130

Magnolia Cricket Club 35
Malcolm, Dominic 201n30
Mallinckrodt, Kelsey 93
Manhattan Cricket Club 99
Marriott, H.H. 116
Marsham, C.H. 97
Martins school 33
Marylebone Cricket Club [MCC] (England) 80, 91, 99, 112, 134, 144, 153, 173, 191, 214n35; 1872 tour 56, 63, 64, 75; 1905 tour 149; 1907 tour 149, 156
Marylebone Cricket Club (Philadelphia) 22, 24
Mason, John 138
"Mason Plan" 177
Mathews, T.J. 97
Mayne, Edgar 157
McBride, Dick 29, 35, 56, 205n11
McBride, Frank 35
McCarthy, Michael 136
McCartney, Charles 157
McDonald, Robert 128
McDonogh, J.J. 163, 164
McIntyre, Martin 53
McKean, Henry 121
McKean, Thomas 21, 121
McKim, Charles 121
McLaren, Archie 98, 145
McNutt, Howard 51
Meade, George 58, 93
Meade, Spencer 58, 93
Media cricket club 131
Mellor, Edward 121
Melrose Cricket Club 119, 210n30
Melville, Ralph 162
Merion Cricket Club 54, 58, 85–86, 120; 1914 tour 155
Merion Cup 125
Middlesex CCC 113
Milwaukee 18
Mitcham Green 156
Mitchell, Frank 22, 90, 107, 109, 217n22

Mitchell, S. Weir 13
Mitchell, J.K. 12, 15
modernization (sports) 2, 37
Montgomery, William 59
Montrose Cricket Club 123
Moon, L.J. 97
Moore, D.W. 36
Moorestown Cricket Club 119, 170
Morgan, W.C. 23, 183
Morley, Christopher 135, 193
Morris, C.C. 135, 143, 185
Morris, Edwin 136
Morton, Cope 95
Mote (England) 156
Multnomah Athletic Club 138
Murdoch, W.L. 97, 110

Nassau Cricket Club (Princeton University) 127, 128
Natchez MS 9
Nauright, John 223n34
New York 7, 26, 158, 163, 183
New York Clipper 17
New York Cricket Cub 29
New Zealand 82, 117, 148
Newark Cricket Club 20, 26
Newcomb, Charles 46, 211n38
Newhall, C.S. 138
Newhall, Charles 51, 62, 80, 95
Newhall, Daniel 62–63, 76, 136, 176
Newhall, George 62, 66, 76, 118, 172, 182, 184, 202n45
Newhall, Robert 62
Newhall, Thomas 22
Newhall, Walter 21, 25, 31
Newhall, William 159
newspapers 136–137
Nicetown 58, 65, 84
Noble, William 95, 106
Norfolk, VA 199n6
North End Cricket Club 67, 84, 119, 123
Northeast Manual Training School 125, 126, 182
Nottinghamshire CCC 111, 143, 153, 224n2

Olympia Cricket Club 21, 23, 36, 58
Olympics (1904) 166, 226n71
Onassis, Jackie Kennedy 222n97
O'Neil, William 159, 185
Oriental Cricket Club 24
Osceola Cricket Club 24, 58
Oxford Cricket Club 165
Oxford University 99, 108, 144

Palairet, Lionel 99, 112, 142
Palairet, R.C.N. 230n4

Index

Palmer, Charles 93, 95
Panola Cricket Club 24
Patterson, C. Stuart 127
Patterson, George 51, 56, 70, 89–90, 103, 109, 111, 147, 176, 178, 208n33, 215n56
Pearce, Henry 94, 180
Pearson, Job 52
Peatfield, A. 97
Pennsylvania Cricket Club 127
Pennsylvania Railroad Cricket Club 84, 88, 119
Pepper, G.W. 51, 191, 222n91
Petersburg, VA 199n6
Philadelphia Cricket Club 20–21, 26, 27, 49, 52, 58, 86–88, 164, 183; 1912 tour 155, 164
Philadelphia Pilgrims 184
Phillips, Barnett 43
Pittsburgh 17, 158, 165
Pleasants, Henry 191
Poole, J. Lawrence 93, 215n44
Portland, OR 166
Potter, William 121
Pottsville Cricket Club 21, 166
Powelton Fairgrounds 24, 203n39
Pratt, Tom 29, 35
Princeton University 186
professionalism 53–55
Provost, John 24, 93
Putnam Cricket Club 24

Quaife, Walter 97
Quaife, Willie 97, 113
Quaker City Cricket League 84
Quaker State League 120, 123

Racine College 131
Radliff, A.E. 65
Radnor Cricket Club 123, 170
Radnor Cup 120
Radnor High School 125
Ralston, Frank 70
Ranjitsinhji, Prince 92, 98, 99, 110, 116
Rastall, Joseph 65
Reed, H. 121
Repton school 130
Richardson, Tom 113, 145, 146
Richmond Cricket Club 7
Roanoke, VA 89
Rockefeller, Nelson 51
Roller, W.E. 62, 66
Roosevelt, Theodore 138, 222n95
Rose, J. 69
rounders 7
Royal Artillery 150
Rylott, Arnold 54

St. Davids Cricket Club 119
St. George Cricket Club (New York) 8, 11, 14, 19, 26, 29–30, 49, 60, 75, 209n13
St. George Cricket Club (Philadelphia) 28
St. George League 162, 225n54
St. Louis 62, 138
St. Louis Browns Baseball Club 23
St. Pauls School 90, 93, 128, 131
St. Timothy Cricket Club 60
Sale, R. 130
San Antonio, TX 139
Sanders, E.J. 81
Savage, J. Howard 126, 159
Sayen, Henry 94, 191
Scattergood, J. Henry 51
Schenectady, NY 158
schools, cricket in 124–126
Scotland 146
Scott, J. Allison 51
Seabright Lawn Tennis and Cricket Club 74, 180, 212n12, 215n44
Seattle 166
Senior, Tom 20, 26, 52
Sergeant, J. Dickerson 20
Sharp, A.T. 130
Sharp, Henry 31
Sharp, John 145
Sharpless, Fred 141, 143
Sharpless, Isaac 51, 132
Shaw, Alfred 53, 62, 78, 113
Shibe family 35
Shiffert, John 205n11
shortstop, (baseball) 205n4
Shrewsbury, Arthur 113
Shrewsbury school 129
Singh, Amar 192
soccer 119
Somerset CCC 112, 142
South Africa 82, 91, 140, 146, 217n23, 223n34
South Wales 150, 152
Southwark Cricket Club 27
Spalding, Albert 72
Sprague, Edward 92
Star Cricket Club 19, 26
Staten Island Cricket Club 65, 88, 180
Stevens, Richard 27
Stocks, F.M. 116
Stoever, David 127
Stoke Poges 156
Super Bowl 192
Surrey CCC 80, 82, 112, 146
Sussex CCC 98, 100, 110
Sutcliff, Fred 67

Taft, William 166
tennis 119, 171

Thayer, John 70, 128, 176, 183
Thomas, Frank 121
Ticknor, John 15
Tioga Cricket Club 70, 84, 94, 124
Toledo, OH 138
Tonbridge school 130
Toronto Cricket Club 139
townball 7, 34
Trafford, C.E. de 97
Trenton Cricket Club 89, 216n81
Trinidad 155
Trinity College (Hartford, CT) 128
Trumble, Hugh 230n3
Trumper, Victor 92
Turner, R.H. 97
Tyers, Henry 53
Tyldesley, J.T. 145

Ulster 150
Union Cricket Club 11, 12, 15, 16
United Cricket Club 23
United States Cricket Association 31–32, 74, 122, 137, 154, 165, 176
United States vs. Canada 8–9, 11, 13, 17, 25, 29, 31, 73, 154, 183
University of Pennsylvania 12, 107, 124, 126–130, 169, 185–186, 221n53; 1907 tour 129–130
Ursinus College 186

Vernou, Charles 24, 31, 139, 183
veterans' cricket 219n7
Villanova University 179
Virginia 89

Wakefield 10, 60
Wakefield Cricket Club 60
Walker, W.H. 163
Waller, Robert 11, 15, 28, 30, 204n55
Warner, Pelham 94, 98, 99, 115, 142
Warwickshire CCC 110, 144
Washington Cricket Club 19, 22
West, Benjamin 7
West Indies 66, 81, 146, 148, 155, 223n34
West Philadelphia High School 125

West Point 30
Western XI (1882) 66
Westtown school 125, 126
Weygandt, Cornelius 213n7
Wheaton, William 200n10
Whigham, H.J. 49–50
White, Frank 149, 150
wicket (game) 7
William Penn Charter School 125, 182
Williamson Training School 125
Wilshire, Edgar 23, 52, 64, 75, 208n27
Wilson, E.R. 65, 96
Winchester school 129
Winter, Charles 129, 192
Winnipeg 89
Wister, John 13
Wister, Jones 15, 21, 25, 64, 121, 138, 183
Wister, Sally 136
Wister, William 21
Wister, William, Jr. 22
Wister, William Rotch 12–13, 15, 19, 25, 64, 183, 201n15, 203n30
women (and cricket) 118, 179–180
Wood, Arthur 53, 67, 89, 91–92, 111, 150, 161, 163, 177, 229n2
Woodcock, Arthur 55, 133
Woods, Sammy 112
Woolley, Frank 98
Worcestershire CCC 142, 144, 152
Work, Milton 51, 114, 127
Wright, George 40, 42, 62, 68, 176, 212n30
Wright, Harry 104, 212n30, 217n2
Wright, L.G. 97
Wright, William R. 121
Wynyard, E.G. 113
Wyoming Cricket Club 35

Yeadon 119
Yonkers 18
Yorkshire CCC 111
Young, Sidney 168
Young America Cricket Club 22, 24, 27, 35, 52, 53, 54, 58, 60–63, 85, 209n13

Zouaves 35

www.ingramcontent.com/pod-product-compliance
Lightning Source LLC
Chambersburg PA
CBHW032038300426
44117CB00009B/1101